TERROR

Suddenly they a[re]
least 10 or 20 of the[m]
pletely. Each one is
ver rod. One's got
He's got his hands, [fi]ngers wrapped
around the back of my neck. Another
one's pushing me on the left shoulder.
He's pulling me up. They are picking me
up.

The creatures tilt me back and lift me.
Their hands are rough, like a snake skin.
I cannot remember falling down, but I
am lying in the sand. I have to think.
What to do?

I begin to spin around and around while
lashing out with my fists and kicking in
an effort to defend myself.

A voice warns me to "stop" and calls me
"Zehaas."

They hit me with a white flash.

My muscles freeze.

I can't move . . .

UFO ABDUCTIONS IN GULF BREEZE

ED WALTERS AND FRANCES WALTERS

AVON BOOKS ◆ NEW YORK

UFO ABDUCTIONS IN GULF BREEZE is an original publication of Avon Books. This work has never before appeared in book form.

AVON BOOKS
A division of
The Hearst Corporation
1350 Avenue of the Americas
New York, New York 10019

First Avon Books Printing: January 1994

AVON TRADEMARK REG. U.S. PAT. OFF. AND IN OTHER COUNTRIES, MARCA REGISTRADA, HECHO EN CANADA

Printed in Canada

UNV 10 9 8 7 6 5 4 3

In memory of Dr. Dan C. Overlade.
His advice was foremost in my decision to
write this book.

ACKNOWLEDGMENTS

The sixteen dedicated members of the Gulf Breeze Research Team deserve full credit for the professional ongoing documentation of the Gulf Breeze UFO. Under the leadership of Walt Andrews and chief investigators Gary Watson and Bland Pugh, nightly they carry on with the scientific research necessary to solve the UFO mystery.

CONTENTS

FOREWORD

I am a clinical psychologist practicing in Pensacola, Florida. I received a Ph.D. in psychology from Purdue University in 1954. I am a past president of the Florida Psychological Association and a past president of the Florida State Board of Examiners of Psychology.

I hold diplomas in clinical psychology and forensic psychology of the American Board of Professional Psychology and a diploma in clinical hypnosis of the American Board of Psychological Hypnosis. I am a fellow of the American College of Forensic Psychology.

I have concluded that the regressive hypnosis episodes presented in this book are not shams nor hoaxes and that they represent the truth and accuracy to the best of Edward Walters's knowledge and belief.

—Dr. Dan C. Overlade

INTRODUCTION

by Robert E. Reid

Colonel Robert E. Reid retired in July 1987 after twenty-six years in the U.S. Air Force. During his career he logged six thousand flying hours as a navigator in aircraft including the C-124, C-130, and C-141. In Southeast Asia he flew O-2s and OV-10s, directing air strikes against military targets. He has also made over 250 parachute jumps as a Combat Controller. He was a Deputy Commander at NATO's newly formed cruise missile base in Comiso, Sicily. He was decorated with the Legion of Merit, three Distinguished Flying Crosses, three Meritorious Service Medals, and eleven Air Medals.

For five and a half months Ed Walters and his family were involved in the most astounding UFO events that I have ever studied. As you will soon discover, Ed's UFO encounters were only the most recent and most spectacular segment in a progression of experiences that date back to his childhood. The thirty-nine photos he took of UFOs from November 11, 1987, to May 1, 1988, have proved the reality of his long-term involvement with an alien intelligence and technology. It's an incredible but true story that challenges the imaginative limits of the human mind.

Gulf Breeze is a thirty-five mile drive from my home in Fort Walton, Florida. In the course of my investigation of the Gulf Breeze sightings I was soon making the round trip regularly, sometimes twice a day. Along that stretch of U.S. 98 many sightings have been reported, including some at very close range, that confirm details of Ed's photos not known to the media at the time. I have talked at length with many of the adjunct witnesses and found a solid consistency in their sincerity, their conviction that what they saw was not "normal," and their unanimous desire to know what it was and what it meant. Scores of people in the surrounding area were seeing anomalous aerial craft on an almost regular basis in late 1987 through 1992. (And I might add, they're still seeing them today.)

My first meeting with Ed Walters was a bit awkward; too many people and a highly charged and nervous atmosphere. By mid-January it was already obvious to the Walters family that the phenomenon was focused at least partly on themselves. But no one knew how much physical danger might be present. Ed's demeanor belied his serious concern, both for his family and for himself. He did not at that time have conscious recollection of the fantastic details that have since come to light, details that are the substance of this book. But in retrospect I believe he did have an impression through dreams and vague recollections that his UFO experience was deeper than his photographs, and more enduring.

Ed and I spent many hours together, mostly with Ed talking and me listening. He shared many events from his past, some to do with his pioneering experiences on a coffee farm in Costa Rica, others with the youth parties he and Frances organized for the local teens. The most interesting stories he shared were about recurrent dreams and those strange little vignettes from the far past that didn't seem like much on the surface, but that obviously meant much to Ed. The "black dog" that followed him home, the "dark fog" that overtook and engulfed his car, the case of the "heat prostration" in the canoe. They seemed to give him almost cathartic relief just in the telling.

These oddly incomplete stories were classic signals to me. I am certain that Ed had no knowledge of the "UFO abduction phenomenon" in January 1988. I suspected that given his involvement with strange craft, blue beams, and small alien beings, the experiences he was describing were but the conscious remnants of a bizarre truth his subconscious had long repressed. Dr. Dan Overlade's careful probing of Ed's psyche through hypnotic regression has now laid bare the provocative details of these suppressed memories. That's what this book is all about.

It's been many years since I first met Ed Walters in 1987 and what began as a guarded professional interface has developed into a close friendship and a sense of understanding. I have watched Ed wrestle with the question of whether or not to go public with his experiences. From the start he's been torn between a concern to protect his family from the clamor that can attend any publicity and an imperative to tell the world the truth about his almost life-long interaction with something so utterly alien.

PROLOGUE

The Gulf Breeze UFO sightings have been an astounding and profound catalyst. Their reality is much more than unexplained lights in the sky or flying disks that hover and then suddenly disappear. These sightings and attendant activities have shown that the phenomenon has a presence and the presence has a motive.

During the years since I first saw and photographed the UFO in Gulf Breeze, I have been reluctant to deal with the extraordinary story behind the sightings. Documenting the reality of UFOs was as far as I wanted to go. I was satisfied to accept UFOs as just being there—for reasons unknown. In short, I was in denial.

I cringed when media reporters asked what I had to say about "alien contact." The word "abduction" made me choke and I tried to avoid any discussion about the four-foot-tall gray alien beings that my wife and I had seen. I rationalized that admitting I had seen UFOs made my credibility questionable enough. Add to that alien contact and abduction, and my solid reputation as a general contractor might not survive.

With the passing years and the many national media shows have come thousands of letters from UFO witnesses and others, like myself, who have experienced "alien contact." I no longer fear the word "abduction." I accept the ongoing UFO sightings and bizarre alien encounters as a part of life, a part that I would change if I could. But, since I don't have that option, I am left to consider the possibilities.

In this book I present reports and photographs from UFO witnesses which are examples of the continuing UFO phenomena in Gulf Breeze. Included are details of unexplained spirals of flattened grass, and reports of repeated atmospheric tremors in the Gulf Breeze area. But my primary focus is on the sessions of clinical hypnosis which I had with Dr. Dan Overlade, and my search to understand the results, the conscious recall, and the "sleep memory" recall.

Some facets of the UFO phenomena may be difficult to accept for those who have not seen a UFO and experienced an incident. Reasonable skepticism is a prerequisite for any reader in judging what seem to be unbelievable reports, even though they come from very reputable people. With claims of blue beams flashing, UFOs winking in and out, and alien close encounters, it would be very easy to dismiss all these reports as fantasy, but these outrageous events are supported by hundreds of witnesses, video film, and photographs taken by scores of people.

Consider the stereo photographs that I took on May 1, 1988 (see photo 38R). For the first time in history, UFOs have been photographed with stereo cameras capable of determining the size and distance of the object from the camera. The analysis is conclusive. In photo 38R, the unidentified object is over twenty feet in diameter and is approximately 475 feet distant. (For technical scientific details, see Appendix 3, F.U.F.O.R.)

Can you accept the fact that our technology doesn't have the capability displayed by the UFOs? If so, then problems you have with accepting the other events might begin to make sense.

Certainly, given the nature of the advanced flight which was witnessed and videotaped, the UFOs may very well have other equally bizarre abilities. Is it impossible to believe that a technology which supports a soundless craft of immense speed might not also display a blue beam of "energy" capable of immobilizing and lifting an object? Dozens of eyewitnesses report this "blue beam," which has also been photographed. Consider the group UFO sightings that resulted in multiple photographs and included Gulf Breeze police officers, City Council officials, and scores of local residents. What about the unexplained atmospheric tremors which shook Gulf Breeze and have come to be called "sky quakes"?

Mysterious flat spiral circles of grass have been discovered in Gulf Breeze Shoreline Park. Is it only a coincidence that the timing of the "sky quakes" coincides with the discovery of these perfectly flattened and swirled circles of grass in a park where so often UFOs are sighted? If our military truly knows nothing about UFOs, as they say, then why the repeated influx of special low-level radar blimps patrolling over Gulf Breeze? How can we explain away the deployment of portable 150-foot radar towers being set up in local parking lots? What brought the NASA research ship to our port at the same time that the United States Joint Chiefs of Staff held secret meetings at the nearby Pensacola Naval Air Station?

The sheer volume of Gulf Breeze UFO witnesses is overwhelming. Study the evidence and the eyewitness reports and then consider the possibilities.

CHAPTER 1

BEFORE THE ABDUCTION—
THE UFO SIGHTINGS

The events that my wife and I describe in this book are the
direct result of UFO encounters and experiences we had
between November 11, 1987, and May 1, 1988. A full description of those experiences is recorded in a book we
wrote in 1990 entitled *The Gulf Breeze Sightings*. But in
order to understand the abduction experience and the magnitude of those close encounters, I here provide a short re-
cap of that information.

November 11, 1987, is a day that will forever remain an
ethereal shadow following me and my family as a reminder that we were given a glimpse of a secret not often
shared so openly. It was a secret so fascinating and profound that our minds were shocked into a new reality, the
reality of UFOs.

Just before dark on that November day I saw a UFO
glide at treetop level over my suburban neighborhood. The
five photographs I took before the craft flashed away reinforced my description of what I saw. The UFO became a
frequent visitor to our town and dozens of my neighbors
stepped forward during the following weeks to report seeing the unusual craft.

The UFO intruded into our town and my life. With each
passing week more sightings and events occurred, giving
me the opportunity to take more photographs, all prompting questions as to why.

After five and a half months I had taken thirty-nine
photos with five different cameras. This was proof of the
reality of UFOs and alien encounters. But many of the

questions that the encounters raised were left unanswered. Why did the UFOs show themselves to so many residents of Gulf Breeze, and why did they repeatedly seem to taunt my family? What happened to me during the hour and fifteen minutes of missing time during my UFO sighting on May 1, 1988? What was the meaning behind the strange word "Tamacuari" that haunted me in recurring dreams?

These and other questions have been asked of me many times by reporters who assumed that I had gained insight into the meaning of it all. I have no quick answers and those that I do propose have been arrived at by tying together clues from my conscious memory, and the hypnotic memory regression supervised by Dr. Dan Overlade.

A twilight UFO sighting and physical encounter on November 11, 1987, began the series of events which finally led me to a lonely park on May 1, 1988. Armed only with a special stereo camera, I confronted the staggering force which seemed intent on a single purpose—abduction.

The jarring realization that we are not alone in the universe has had an effect on every decision I've made since. But from the first commitment to show the UFO photographs to Duane Cook, the *Sentinel* newspaper editor, to the daily defense of my family from the unknown, I was stunned by the reality of the repeated sightings and encounters.

Media reports of the UFO events and sightings created a storm of investigation which disrupted my home and threatened my reputation. When the UFO showed itself the second time, tormenting me with an aggravating hum, I drew strength from my wife and children's unwavering support. The UFO seemed motivated and was deliberately returning, over and over again.

On December 2, 1987, through the French doors of our bedroom, I came face to face with a shielded creature (see drawing B). The creature fled and the resulting photograph of the UFO flashing a blue beam down to the ground (see photo 11) created a terror mixed with the need to share this awesome reality.

The dilemma was clear—step forward and tell all, or live with the experiences in secret to protect my wife and two children from the possible public ridicule frequently associated with UFO sightings. The price of revelation seemed too great, so I delayed the inevitable by withholding my identity.

I intentionally crowded my workday and activities with other people. By night I became a prisoner in my own house. The UFO would frequently entice me with outrageous aerial demonstrations only to wink out after commanding that I "Step forward," or declaring, "We are here for you."

My repulsion from, and intrigue with, the UFO filled me with contradictory emotions, but soon I had detailed photographs to support my experience. The UFOs I photographed seemed to be of different sizes and configurations and the color varied from bright white to blue-gray to golden orange and brilliant red.

Reports from other witnesses continued to mount, which added even more credibility to this unbelievable situation. Gulf Breeze was in an uproar as witness after witness reported sightings that attracted nationwide media coverage. In January of 1988, and about a month after my first sighting, the volume of UFO sightings was high. I decided to seek out the Florida MUFON (Mutual UFO Network) director for help. Assured that my identity would be held in confidence, I detailed my UFO encounters for the investigator.

I expected that the MUFON investigators would bring me relief. Relief in understanding the UFO phenomena— and thus relief from the continued UFO presence. Naively I hoped that if I cooperated with the investigators, the UFO would no longer intrude in my life. How wrong I was.

Nightly surveillance by investigators with walkie-talkie linkups chronicled only suspicious unidentified helicopters that circled my house. Multiple government radar devices were deployed in the area. In mid-August 1988 the military Joint Chiefs of Staff met at the local navy base but the military continued to deny any knowledge of the UFOs.

Photo experts, from top optical physicists to local professionals, were drawn into the investigation to reenact the events and, of course, to study the possibility of a hoax. The evidence and the numerous witnesses were so compelling that even the most skeptical investigators were shocked by the scope of the sightings.

As with any UFO event of this magnitude I soon learned that there were skeptics, critics, and debunkers with whom to contend. I could understand the average skeptic because I, too, might have been skeptical if I had not been a witness. Some of the critics had their own personal reasons for rejecting the existence of UFOs, but the debunkers were a different story. I was advised by the investigators that the debunkers would try to discredit the evidence, but I was unprepared for their fabricated personal attacks against my family. This strain, added to by the continued harassment from the UFO, increased the tension in our household, especially since there seemed to be little we could do to resolve either problem.

After several more photographic sightings, I was given a special four-lens stereo camera by the MUFON investigators and asked to use it. The camera was loaded and sealed, and control shots had already been taken to prevent tampering. At a local park with my wife one evening, I shot ten photographs with the camera (see photo 25). I immediately turned the camera over to MUFON for them to remove the film and have it developed.

The photo analysis established the existence of a "probe" craft which would show up with larger UFOs in later photographs (see photo 38R).

The increasing numbers of local witnesses and my photographs, as well as those taken by others, added to the mounting evidence—but none of it answered the why here? why now? and why me? questions. Those questions never left me, occupying my waking hours and my dreams.

One recurring dream seemed to be related to the UFO and in a meeting with Budd Hopkins, an expert on the "abduction phenomenon," I learned about the possibility of abduction.

The MUFON investigators felt that certain memories from my past needed to be explored and suggested that I undergo regressive hypnosis. My initial response was a flat "no." I insisted it would be a waste of time, that there was nothing to uncover, but as time went by, I had to reconsider.

Often, as I awoke in the morning, my subconscious released bursts of memory which made very little sense. Although I always wrote down these insights, I only showed them to a few researchers. They quickly connected these memories to what seemed to be a telepathic message I'd received while driving to the site of a dramatic UFO encounter on January 24, 1988. The message was, "In sleep you know."

The researchers felt that regressive hypnosis was the only way to unravel the mysteries connected with the UFO and my life. In an effort to answer "why?" I finally agreed. If there was something more to all of this than just the sightings, I decided I wanted to know.

This book discloses each "in sleep you know" memory and details the many hours of regressive hypnosis. Each session was videotaped and is transcribed herein, with my intermittent descriptions and comments.

Based on those "in sleep you know" memories and the hypnosis, I have suggested certain answers. Much of what has happened might be interpreted differently, and you may choose to do so. But no matter how one speculates, it is clear to me that I have experienced contact with an "alien" life-form.

CHAPTER 2

ENCOUNTER IN THE PARK

MAY 1, 1988

By the end of April 1988 I had not seen the UFO for over a month. At the request of Dr. Maccabee, an optical physicist, I remounted the large stereo camera (the SRS camera) in a way meant to improve its ability to measure distances. Although I hoped the UFO was out of my life, I was also a bit eager to use the improved SRS camera at least once. I wanted to look for the UFO. Frances agreed, and we began a modest form of surveillance on Tuesday, April 26.

Frances and I also hoped we might have the chance to settle a long-running debate between the two of us about the distance to, and size of, the object we had seen and photographed with the NIMSLO stereo camera in South Shoreline Park. A second sighting of the object one night while we were out walking, without a camera, had left the question unanswered.

Dr. Maccabee advised us to take along the video camera for Frances to use, and a radio which would validate the time. He also asked that additional measuring posts be placed in a circle around the SRS camera. Each post was white and placed ten feet from the camera lens.

For several nights during the last week of April, around 11:00 P.M. after the children were in bed asleep, we would set up the SRS camera in Shoreline Park and patiently wait for at least two hours, hoping some craft would appear. On Wednesday, the twenty-seventh, the mosquitoes were so bad, we stayed only an hour or so. I was always disappointed when nothing happened, but a halfhearted promise given to Frances made it even harder to call it quits that night and go home.

She was leaving Friday morning on a four-day trip and didn't want me to go to the park until she returned. Since she was to leave so early on Friday, we would be at the park on Thursday night for only a short time, if at all.

At four o'clock Friday morning Frances set off on the Friday-through-Monday trip and all day I debated setting up the SRS in the park while she was gone. I didn't have the video camera because Frances had taken it with her. On Friday I gave in to the temptation but that night was another disappointment at the park, with only lack of sleep to show for it.

Because Laura was a bit later than usual going to bed on Saturday night, I didn't arrive at the park until 11:30 P.M. There were several couples parked overlooking the Sound, plus a few boat trailers awaiting the return of the fishermen after their fishing trips.

I set up the SRS camera near the same picnic table we had used so many times before. Secluded by the woods on three sides and overlooking the water to the south, the location was perfect because I was inconspicuous. The UFO case investigation was a high profile in the newspapers, but for the good of my family I did not want our name to be associated with the UFO.

The tripod-mounted SRS was capable of swinging 360 degrees and elevating in the event the UFO showed above the tree line in any direction. There was a very slight sprinkle of rain but I continued to set up the perimeter of measuring poles at a ten-foot radius from the lenses. I used a flashlight and tape measure to insure that the poles were the exact required distance from the camera. Finished, I sat down to wait. The concrete picnic bench got harder the longer I waited.

At 12:30 A.M., I took a break and went to the van to relax in the adjustable captain's chairs. Because I was less than fifty feet from the setup and there was nobody walking around, I wasn't worried about the cameras. While I relaxed, I tried to picture the UFO in my head and at that moment I heard a humming sound.

I sat up and looked over the park into the darkness that surrounded me. My heart began to race as I got out of the van. The other cars I had seen earlier were no longer there. Only a single boat trailer, sitting at the other end of the park near one of the few streetlights, was visible to me.

A shiver came over me and I suddenly thought about Laura, alone in the house. I had to resist the urge to grab the camera and quickly get away from the presence that was someplace in the darkness. The breeze off the Sound felt cool on my face. I noticed that I was flushed and the beads of sweat touched by the breeze caused me to shudder with a chill.

I whispered encouragement to myself, "Calm down, they haven't hurt you lately." Then I said aloud, "Hey, here I am. You call me Zehaas. Here I am."

I looked at my watch; it was 1:10 A.M., May 1. I started along the path back to the SRS camera. The tree branches were close by and I either heard or imagined that I heard sounds in the bushes. I spoke again, this time louder.

"You call me Zehaas. I want this to be over. I want you out of my life."

When I reached the picnic table I sat at the edge of the bench with my hand on the tripod handle. I heard faint sounds coming from the bushes that surrounded my small clearing. My veins throbbed as my heart beat with rapid-fire pounding.

"I know you're here," I yelled. "Just do whatever you have to do to get this over!"

My attention was mostly directed toward the right, to the area in the southwest where the UFO had winked in on March 17, but as I turned my head to the left, there it was south of me, way out over the water of Santa Rosa Sound. The glow from the bottom was intense and the small top light was again clear. The midsection was much darker but I could still see several small lights around the middle. This familiar, yet incredible, sight caused a tingle down my neck and across my temples.

I took a quick breath to steady myself and swung the tripod around to aim the SRS camera toward the UFO. Through the right camera viewfinder I could clearly see it rocking gently back and forth. The bottom glow would almost disappear and then return. I fired the shutter buttons at the same time and took photos 38L and 38R.

When I looked up again the craft was still there, but off to the right and a little bit higher was another array of lights. It looked very similar to the object I had photographed with the NIMSLO camera. This second UFO was moving to the right, so I lowered my eye to the viewfinder again but saw nothing, not even the bright glow of the first UFO.

My instinct was to quickly adjust the tripod, so I looked up to see where to aim the camera. In a fraction of a second my eyes caught the glow of the first UFO about thirty-five feet above me. I flinched and my right hand squeezed the shutter button. Then, with the UFO just above a small oak tree, my field of vision went completely white, just as if a flashcube had gone off in my brain. I could not tell if the whiteness was also around me, like a floodlight, or just within my head. Instantly I felt nothing, no sensations from my body, only a vague sense of falling.

The next instant I was lifting my face and chest up off the sand at the edge of the water. My head pounded and, as I tried to stand, I stumbled in dizziness. Disoriented, I crawled up the beach twenty feet to the bench and sat there with my head in my hands.

A smell from my hands was making me nauseated. Then it dawned on me. How could I fall to the ground while standing at the SRS camera and get up a second later twenty feet away? I checked my watch and couldn't believe the time. It was 2:25 A.M. What had happened to the hour and fifteen minutes between taking the photographs and finding myself on the beach?

I shivered and sat and shook my head. I had a massive headache, but finally managed to stand. I yelled obscenities into the night sky, then started to cry. I wasn't crying from pain. I was aware that my sobbing was caused by something of great significance, but I didn't know what. As I collapsed the SRS camera, tears ran down my face. I needed to see Frances, but she was far away.

Laura! Laura was alone. I had to get home and check on

Laura. I quickly loaded the equipment back in the van, leaving some of the measuring posts in my rush to get home. When I arrived at the house I saw Laura was resting peacefully. Protectively, I sat up outside her door the rest of the night, frightened that "they" might return.

At daybreak I was exhausted and collapsed into bed. My right hand smelled so bad, even after washing it, that I had to wrap it in several towels to block the odor. At noon I awoke suddenly and cried out for Frances. She could help me talk about what had happened, but at the moment she was where I couldn't reach her. I got up, but made no mention of the incident to Laura.

In the bathroom, I ran a comb through my hair and felt a bump at the back of my head very close to the center of my neck. It felt bruised and I went to the mirror to try to see what I could feel. When I looked in the mirror I couldn't see the lump, but as I turned around I immediately saw more than I expected to.

A large bruise, with a red dot in the center, was prominent between my eyes right at the bridge of my nose. Two more similar red marks were centered on my temples, each surrounded by a bruise (see photo D). I was shocked. What the hell had they done to me?

When Laura saw the marks, I told her I was fine and dismissed the bruises as an accident. I just had to talk to somebody but I couldn't tell Laura the truth without frightening her. The MUFON investigators were the logical choice, but the inevitable hours of questioning wasn't something I wanted to face right then.

A few hours later I decided to call Dr. Maccabee, just to give the facts to someone, but as I detailed the event I was swept away and began reliving the moment-by-moment feelings. Dr. Maccabee, a concerned and patient gentleman, listened and recorded the details.

I complained several times about the stench from my hand and during the course of that phone conversation discovered the odor was coming from tiny bits of black material beneath my fingernails. Dr. Maccabee asked me to save the black material and put it in the freezer so it could be analyzed later if the necessary sophisticated equipment could be located.

Talking with Dr. Maccabee helped, but it also reinforced what I had already suspected. Very obviously something strange had happened to me during that missing time. It left me feeling anxious and empty. The shadowy memories in my consciousness aggravated the situation, increasing my desire to know what had happened. I felt "they" had taken me but, as hard as I tried, I could not remember what happened.

Don Ware, MUFON state director, and Mark Curtis, WEAR ABC reporter, suggested that I make an appointment with Dr. Dan C. Overlade, a clinical psychologist specializing in therapeutic hypnosis. Dr. Overlade agreed to see me at the request of Charles Flannigan, the MUFON state section director, and scheduled an appointment for June 6, 1988.

My initial resistance to undergoing hypnosis had yielded to my own inner pressure. I was haunted by what I could not recall. I had to remember. Regressive hypnosis would give me the chance to at least know what had happened even if I could do nothing about it.

Frances's Account

In the almost six months since Ed's first sighting, the UFO had become a part of our lives. We had reached a point of resigned acceptance since there seemed to be little we could do to alter events. But we didn't allow the UFO to dominate our lives. We still hosted frequent parties for Dannie's friends and it was a rare weekend when Laura didn't have at least one girlfriend spending the night.

Life went on in an amazingly normal way. Laura worked on constructing a papier-mâché model of Stonehenge for art class, leaving Styrofoam blocks and strips of newspaper scattered over one end of the breakfast bar. Dannie fretted over which college he should attend, reading and rereading the more than half a dozen acceptance letters he had received.

As mid-April approached, we had gone almost a month

without a personal sighting and I hoped that, for us, it was over. Ed had even disassembled the self-referencing stereo (SRS) camera, as if that might somehow affect the visits by the UFO. Then Dr. Maccabee decided *one* more stereo camera photograph would be a tremendous help in his photo analysis.

After talking it over with me, Ed reassembled the SRS camera. Near the end of the month we began new, late-night watches in South Shoreline Park. Once again I found myself hoping the UFO would allow us one more photograph.

Three nights in a row we kept our vigil in the park, battling mosquitoes, boredom, and the feeling I should be home, resting up for my trip to Nashville chaperoning the high school band. No UFO appeared to make those long hours worthwhile. When the alarm went off at 3:00 A.M. Friday morning, I wished I had spent most of that time in bed. The last thing I did before Dannie and I left for the school was elicit Ed's promise that he wouldn't go UFO watching alone while I was gone.

The trip with the band was wonderful, and hectic. Our students won best in their division, and best overall band. What a way for Dannie to end his high school band experience. Their triumph translated into greater than usual exuberance and by the time we chaperones had the students in their rooms and settled for the night, it was too late for me to call Ed. The situation was the same each night we were gone.

I tried not to worry. Ed had promised. But I knew how disappointed and frustrated he'd been that we hadn't seen anything those last nights in the park and I wasn't sure he would resist the temptation to go without me.

Ed was waiting at the high school when our buses pulled up around six o'clock in the evening, May 2. As soon as I was close enough to really see him, I knew something was wrong. He had attempted to cover the bruises and red marks on his face, but my liquid foundation he'd used was too light and sheer to hide the marks.

"Are you all right?" I hoped my question sounded ordinary and innocent to anyone who might overhear.

"I'm fine. I'll tell you all about it later."

Once we reached home, he still couldn't tell me. Laura had to bring me up to date on all that she had done while I was gone and Dannie insisted on giving his father a detailed, animated account of the contest and our visit to Opryland. Finally, with the kids in bed, Ed told me about his trips to the park.

"You promised me you wouldn't go." My relief that he didn't seem to be truly hurt couldn't hide the fact that I was upset he had broken his word.

"I know I did. But I couldn't seem to keep from going."

Most of my anger was directed at the entities. They had done something to Ed, for a reason only they understood. Maybe whatever happened that night was what they had wanted all along. Maybe it really was over now. If we never saw the UFO again, if Ed never had any more strange dreams or early morning "memories," I wouldn't miss them. For months I had wanted our life to return to normal, to what it had been like before November 11. Maybe now it would.

I touched the marks on Ed's face, clearer now that he'd showered. His insistence that they didn't hurt only partially reassured me.

"You should go see a doctor."

"And tell him what? That I was zapped by a UFO's white light and woke up an hour later with these bruises? I don't think so. I'm fine. I don't feel sick, or anything, so I think the best thing to do is just keep this to ourselves."

"Does that include not telling Dannie and Laura?"

Ed told me he'd explained away the marks to Laura as being the result of an accident. Dannie had been so keyed up about being home he had only mentioned them in passing. Both Ed and I felt certain the question would come up again and keeping the truth from them didn't seem right, or fair. But how much should we tell them? Especially when we didn't really know the answers ourselves. And those answers were something we both wanted, yet dreaded, to know.

CHAPTER 3

SCHEDULED HYPNOSIS

by Dr. Dan C. Overlade

I am a clinical psychologist specializing in forensic psychology and clinical hypnosis. In mid-May of 1988 I received a telephone call from Charles Flannigan, asking me if I had seen the UFO photos which had been published in the *Gulf Breeze Sentinel* over the past six months. Charles, who is MUFON state section director for Escambia and Santa Rosa Counties, sounded out my attitudes about UFO sightings. I told him I had not seen the *Sentinel* publications, although I had watched the television airing of those pictures by Mark Curtis over local television channel WEAR.

I told Charles that more than two decades earlier I had read the *Keyhoe Report* and portions of the *Blue Book,* but that I was not a serious student of the UFO phenomenon. I was able to tell him that my mind was not made up, that I was neither convinced nor skeptical. I pointed out that I had lived in Gulf Breeze for thirty-three years without ever having a sighting—there or anywhere else.

The photographer, whom Charles did not identify, was said to have delivered the photographs to Duane Cook, the *Sentinel*'s editor, pretending to be only the courier for a Gulf Breeze businessman, "Mr. Ed," who wished to remain anonymous. Subsequent to the publication of the photos, the "courier" acknowledged to MUFON investigators that he was, in fact, the photographer and now he was interested in seeing whether hypnotic regression would provide additional information to fill the gaps in his memory of experiences which seemed to include visualization of humanoid beings and some unknown type of physical contact made with the craft.

I told Charles that hypnotic regressions were a regular part of my clinical practice and that I had conducted hundreds of such regressions to identify memories repressed as a result of traumatic emotional experiences—although until now, no regressions pertaining to possible UFO experiences. I wanted some time to think it over. I wanted to give consideration to the possible ramifications to my quite successful practice if the controversy became more heated and further public disclosures were made.

Soon, both Charles Flannigan and Donald Ware, MUFON's Florida state director (and now also Eastern regional director) were providing me with information that was to pique my curiosity further and ultimately draw me into the MUFON organization. I learned that the man I was to meet had in February "passed" two extensive polygraph examinations which found no evidence of deceit. (I was soon to receive a copy of the polygrapher's report.)

I contacted Charles Flannigan, and told him that I would be willing to proceed if the man (still not identified to me) would be willing to subject himself to an extensive battery of psychological tests. My reasoning was simple: the man was either psychologically and emotionally stable, or he was not; and his condition would need to be known before I could proceed with a hypnotic regression. If he were psychotic, hypnotic regression could easily enhance a delusional thought system. If he were an hysteric personality, the encounter of traumatic and seemingly repressed memories could precipitate personality decompensation and, possibly, physical disorders. If he were a dyssocial psychopath, his entire story might be a sham.

I was told the man was agreeable to examination and I soon received a telephone call. He made an appointment for his initial visit and when he came in on June 6, he identified himself as Ed Walters.

At that initial visit, as is customary, I sought to learn something about his personal history. The younger of two brothers, he had grown up in Jacksonville, Florida. As a high school senior he had been a successful local rock and roll musician and he studied architecture for two years at Jacksonville University before leaving there in 1966. He had developed a building business that employed two hundred hourly wage earners and was on his way to becoming highly successful when the bottom fell out of the building industry in 1974. He and his wife and two children then moved to Costa Rica, where he owned a coffee plantation for almost five years before coming back to the United States in the interest of the children's cultural development. They lived in Corpus Christi before moving to the Florida panhandle in 1980.

Ed regarded his general health history as "perfect." He said he was rarely sick and couldn't remember the last time he had had a cold. Six months prior to our meeting he had passed a physical examination for an insurance application; that was prior to his UFO sightings, which began on November 11, 1987. He disclaimed any history of surgery, convulsions, significant head trauma, gastrointestinal complaints, treatment for any nervous, mental, or emotional problem, and suicidal ruminations. Leisure time activities focus on his own kids and other youths who congregate at the Walters home in the summer and on weekends. He had been married one time (now for nineteen years); he and his wife, Frances, have a son eighteen and a daughter fourteen.

As do others, I found Ed pleasant and congenial. He is witty and has a ready laugh to relieve tension. We both quickly became comfortable with our dialogue and were to spend about eight hours engaged in the administration of the standard psychological measurements which had been selected: the Rorschach (the progressive personality assessment technique popularly designated "the inkblot test"), the Thematic Apperception Test (another projective personality assessment technique in which the subject constructs stories to a set of standard pictures), the Wechsler Adult Intelligence Scale (Revised), and the Draw-A-Person Test.

As a result of my examination, I developed the opinion that Ed was emotionally and mentally stable and a somewhat conventional and nonassertive man. There was a good balance between introversive and extroversive factors: he is neither excessively gregarious nor withdrawn. He meets and talks with other people with relative ease and is not likely to be anxious in social gatherings. There were no indications of any bizarre ideation, hysteria, or other neurotic pattern nor any sociopathic personality. In short, no psychological condition was identified which would suggest that his report represented an aberration of thought or deliberate deceit—and nothing to contraindicate the utilization of hypnotic regression.

Ed spent about six hours through a number of extended sessions familiarizing me with vague memories of several peculiar experiences over a span of four decades. It was important that we ultimately be able to distinguish between memories available before regression and those that might be retrieved during a regression or might surface after a regression as a consequence of a reduction in covert apprehension about recollection. Even before a repressed memory is able to "percolate" up into conscious recollection, it is typical for the traumatic experience to be identified below consciousness with the associated anxiety prompting an expectation that the still repressed memory, if recalled, would be accompanied by a somehow devastating abreaction, revivification, or reliving. The skilled hypnotherapist has techniques for minimizing the abreacted emotion—despite the unconscious expectation. I regularly apply such techniques in my practice.

It was my plan first to teach Ed a technique for entering hypnosis—in preparation for ultimate regressive sessions which were to be video-recorded. This planned recording had two purposes: to make a permanent record of any memories that might be retrieved in order to assist investigation and to permit careful review and critique of the procedure by other hypnotherapists in order to assess the possibility of my having used any leading questions, intonations, or inflections which might have unintentionally and unwittingly influenced his responses.

A trance was easily induced and within seventeen minutes Ed had produced four discrete muscle fasciculations (twitches) not ordinarily subject to conscious and voli-

tional control, an accomplishment that serves to ratify the
trance for the hypnotized subject and make it clear that he
has access to unconscious controls as well as (perhaps) unconscious memories. These muscle movements typically
involve contraction of a small bundle of muscle cells
within a larger muscle (much as one might experience in
an eyelid when reading late at night) and, in the procedure
employed, the location of the muscle responses is determined first by his own unconscious choice, then twice at
locations chosen by the hypnotist, and finally at a location
consciously selected by Ed.

During the course of the trance, which lasted approximately forty-five minutes, Ed not only accomplished the
muscle fasciculations, but also displayed a great many
choreiform movements of the trunk, head, and limbs—
apparently involuntary and irregular jerking movements of
skeletal muscles. These seemed to occur somewhat more
frequently to the right side of his body—as if he had been
struck in the right jaw or at the right thigh—but occurring
in these locations and elsewhere at least two dozen times
during the trance.

Such jerking movements can generally be supposed to
represent some form of "body memory" residual to some
past experience. Such unconscious memories are responsible, for example, for the selection of that part of the body
that might involuntarily jerk as one falls asleep. Typically,
that part of the body has at some time in life been physically traumatized or threatened and thereafter carries a su-
perfluous tension which may be suddenly discharged when
one falls asleep or enters the hypnotic trance. It is not uncommon for such unexpected movements to produce a
startle response and a momentary elevation of anxiety—
briefly interrupting the depth of sleep or the depth of
trance.

While similar to those familiar body memory movements, Ed's differed in their intensity and in the fact that
the movements were sustained and repetitive rather than
only momentary. The writhing of his body and the changes
in his countenance easily suggested that he was—at some
level of consciousness—engaged in a physical struggle.

And yet, despite the facial grimacing and tears, he made no attempt to open his eyes nor to get out of the reclining chair in which he had entered the trance. Clearly, his unconscious expectation had for a long time associated hypnosis with regression and, finding himself in the hypnotic trance, a regression had spontaneously begun.

It was possible to calm him and bring him out of the trance. He had full recollection of the writhing, convulsion-like movements of his body but neither in the trance nor posthypnotically was there any associated memory. I explained to him the concept that body memories produced involuntary muscle movements in the trance and asked if he had ever noted similar movements when he was falling asleep. He said he had not, and later was to tell me that, when asked, Frances said she had never noticed any such vigorous skeletal muscle responses when he was sleeping.

The intensity of his physical responses made it seem to me imperative that we postpone deliberate regression until after I had an opportunity to teach him some techniques that would lessen the intensity of any physical or emotional abreaction. I intended to employ an ideomotor response technique which would make possible the repeated unconscious review of any traumatic experience and permit a covert desensitization, thus making any conscious recollection less stressful emotionally.

I also intended to employ some double dissociative techniques—such as having him imagine that, from a theater projection booth, he is watching himself down in the theater viewing the experience on the movie screen. This technique often permits the individual, thus twice-removed from the emotional experience, to tolerate without undue distress the retrieval of memory which might otherwise be quite traumatic or even not be tolerated in consciousness. Moreover, from the projection booth he would be able to stop the projector or freeze the action if his apprehension were building more rapidly than he wanted to tolerate.

Before Ed left my office I gave him a hypnosis practice tape and told him that at his next visit I would introduce some additional techniques. In the meantime, it would be a good idea for him simply to rehearse the basic induction technique he had just learned—entering the trance, prompting the discrete muscle responses, contemplating any constructive changes he might desire in himself, and coming out of the trance. He assured me he would devote part of the weekend to such practice.

CHAPTER 4

VISIONS OR VISITATIONS?

During my first visit with Dr. Overlade I was impressed with his calm, understanding, yet intense demeanor. Our one-hour session had turned into two hours before we realized it. At the end of that session he scheduled another appointment to administer some standard psychological tests.

I wanted to be tested, not to prove anything to myself, but to quiet the critics. I found the debunkers' innuendos which implied that I was "crazy" and a "pathological liar" intolerable, particularly after passing two lie detector tests. So patiently I went through the testing process for the Wechsler Adult Intelligence Scale, the Minnesota Multiphasic Personality Inventory, the Thematic Apperception Test, etc. I completed the enormous number of tests, which were prerequisite to the regressive hypnosis, in four sessions over more than eight hours.

On June 17, the long-awaited hypnotic training began. Dr. Overlade explained the technique that he would use to induce a trance and we proceeded with the hypnotic session. No attempt was made to regress my memory.

Although the trance was peaceful, I could feel the throbbing of memories trying to burst into my consciousness. My body reacted to events I could not recall, jerking in protest during the entire session.

Dr. Overlade informed me that during a trance I would always understand that I was safe and could, at any time, discontinue the hypnosis by counting from five to one. Before I left his office he gave me an audiotape and told me to practice at home the techniques that he had taught me.

This practice would in the future allow me to reach hypnotic states quickly and fully.

That evening, after dinner, I lay down in our bedroom. In the kitchen, Frances explained to Dan and Laura that I should not be disturbed. I could hear them question her about the hypnosis practice tape. Dan suggested a plan to Laura. Dan's whispered voice carried down the hallway.

"Hey, Laura, once Dad's hypnotized, we can tell him our allowance is fifty dollars a week."

"Yeah," Laura answered, "and let's tell him to buy me a new stereo, and a—"

Frances interrupted their plot and shortly the house fell silent.

Our bedroom was dark, with only the soft glow of my bedside table lamp focused on the cassette tape recorder. I turned on the tape and took a deep breath, still smiling to myself about the kids' plot. Dr. Overlade's voice guided me into a peaceful trance. For a half hour the tape directed me deeper and deeper into a hypnotic state of mind. As in Dr. Overlade's office, I could again feel the pulsing of memories trying to invade my consciousness.

In what seemed to me only minutes, Dr. Overlade's voice prompted me to count backward from five to one and awaken.

I slowly turned my head in the direction of the lamp and began to open my eyes. The room seemed unusually dark above me and I blinked several times to clear my vision. For a split second the hazy image of a face with huge almond-shaped eyes looked into my face. I jerked my head deeper into the pillow and flinched to the side. With a quick shake of my head I looked again. Nothing.

Frances's Account

The first half of June had been hectic. First there was Dannie's commencement and Project Graduation. As we had the year before, Ed and I helped organize and chaperone the all-night party for the newly graduated senior class. Then there had been a whirlwind three-day trip up to Vanderbilt for freshman orientation. Last, but far from least in my mind and concern, were Ed's psychological testing sessions with Dr. Overlade.

Now, with the tests behind him, he and the doctor were ready to go on to the hypnosis. I had agreed with Ed that regression was the way to get the answers we both so desperately wanted. But seeing him holding a tape, listening to him tell me he would use it to practice going in and out of the trance state, I found my enthusiasm waning. What if the regressions left us with more questions instead of answering the ones we had?

Still, I knew Ed felt compelled to know what had happened during that missing time. The process would be easier for him if he had my support, so I kept my worries to myself. After dinner, when Ed went to our bedroom to work with the tape, I explained to Dannie and Laura what their father would be doing.

"Will he be like those people on TV who've been hypnotized? You know, could we tell him to do something crazy and he would?" Laura looked up at me, her face shining with impish delight.

"I don't know."

"Coolness. This could be good." Dannie grinned at his sister and laid out his allowance increase scheme.

"Forget it, guys. This is serious. Daddy needs quiet."

Having foiled their plans, I went with Laura to her room. Dannie stayed behind in the kitchen to study the course catalog and other information he had received from Vanderbilt. Some time later I heard the telephone ring, followed immediately by Dannie's shout that he'd get it. I continued sorting clothes, fighting another round in my never-ending battle to maintain some semblance of order in Laura's room.

"Mom!" Dannie's yell shot through me. There was near panic in his voice. Before I could get up, he dashed into his sister's bedroom. "Mom. You gotta come see this!"

"Is it your father?" I stood and started toward him.

"No."

The word was hardly out of his mouth when the hall bathroom door slammed shut. Dannie spun around and looked into the tiny hallway that separated Laura's bedroom from his. "Who did that?"

"I'm sure it's just your father." Wanting to prove that to myself and the kids, I walked past Dannie and knocked on the bathroom door. "Ed, honey, are you in there?"

No answer.

By now, Dannie and Laura were crowded right behind me. I knocked again. Still no answer. My hand unsteady, I pushed down the door handle and shoved the door. It swung inward. Suddenly the sound of running water filled the silence. All three of us looked into the room. Steam rose from the hot water streaming into the sink. The bathroom appeared empty. Gathering my courage, I stepped into the room and looked into the curtained shower stall. There was no one there.

I paused only long enough to turn off the water before I left the bathroom. "Dannie, did you somehow do this to scare your sister?" Even as I asked, I knew he couldn't have. We would have heard the water running and, with the window closed, there was no way the door would have slammed shut.

"No. Just like I didn't stack my books."

"What?"

"It's what I came to tell you."

The three of us headed toward the kitchen, Laura asking questions I couldn't answer, Dannie trying to drown out his sister's babble with an explanation I couldn't hear. We arrived in the kitchen about the same time Ed did.

"The weirdest thing just happened." Ed looked at us, his face pale.

"Make that three weird things," Dannie said and pointed at a stack of books and pamphlets on the countertop. "When I got up to answer the phone, these were scattered, open, all over the place where I'd been reading them. When I turned back around, they were like this."

We all looked at the neat pile, then at one another. I quickly told Ed about the bathroom incident. He related his own experience as he was coming out of hypnosis.

"I don't know if what I saw was actually there. Or if it

was some sort of memory that came out under hypnosis and I just somehow remembered it when I first woke up."

"Why is all this happening?" Laura stepped over to her father and put her arms around his waist. "I don't like it."

"Neither do I, baby. But I think we'll only get answers if we keep digging into this." Ed hugged her and looked at me. "I think I should try using the tape again and see what happens this time."

I agreed, but only if he did it with me there. Dannie and Laura both immediately said they wanted to watch. After some discussion, I agreed with Ed they could stay. He went to our bedroom and came back with the tape recorder.

Dannie and Laura sat on the sofa. Ed lay back in the recliner. I sat on the floor at his feet and pushed the "play" button.

CHAPTER 5

ENCOUNTER IN THE PARK— THE HYPNOSIS

I could not explain away the image of the gray being that I saw standing over me when I awoke from the practice hypnosis. Was it a vision, a flash of memory, or was something really there in the room? Nor could I make any sense of the "moving books" and "self-operating hot water" that the family had experienced.

I had managed to induce the trance and recover from it using Dr. Overlade's instructions and my curiosity was now at a peak. It was too much to resist. I decided to try again. Frances, Dan, and Laura sat with me in the living room. With another microcassette recorder, Frances would tape-record anything that I might say. Once again, I sat and concentrated on the instructions that soon eased me into a deep hypnotic trance.

The hypnotic images were so vivid that I began to hear the night sounds and see the dirt path I had followed through the woods on May 1. My memory was open and my senses were sharp. As if time had been turned back, the damp night air touched me again and I heard the quiet swish of the tide pushing the edge of the water across the white sand beach.

The darkness seemed thick and in the shadows of the brush along each side of the path I heard the rustling of what I thought to be nocturnal creatures. My heart was pounding and the cold concrete bench on which I sat and waited added to the chill.

My recall jumped past seeing the UFO and using the

special SRS camera and I was suddenly reliving the exact moment when the creatures were over me.

ED: Okay, okay. I can see them over me. They are standing over me. They're standing over me. I heard them in the bushes. The sons of bitches were in the bushes. They are in the bushes. He's looking right down at me. They are all around me. Those gray things are all around me. One's got ... one's got a hold of my neck. He's got his hand on the back of my neck. He's got his hands, his fingers, wrapped around the back of my neck. Another one's pushing me on the left shoulder. He's pushing me on the left shoulder. He's pulling me up. They are picking me up. Picking me up.

I could not remember falling down, but I was next to the picnic table, lying in the sand. The creatures were all around me. They moved in bursts of speed that seemed like the movements of small jumping spiders.

At least ten or twenty of them surrounded me completely. Each one was equipped with a silver rod and covered with the box-type suits that I first saw on December 2, when one creature was on my back porch and which I described in *The Gulf Breeze Sightings* (see drawing B).

ED: I can't move. I can't move by myself. They are standing me up. Okay. I'm standing up. Oh. Oh, geez. I can't move. I can't move. Oh, gee. I hear Zehaas. "Zehaas, twelve wait. Zehaas, twelve wait." There's a voice, it said "twelve wait." Said, "Zehaas, twelve wait."
      (groan)

The terror of having no control over my movements, combined with the throbbing voice that spoke as if every word was an order, made my mind swirl with anger and confusion. The command, "Zehaas, twelve wait," was familiar to me. Those words were a direct connection to the memory I had recalled from my sleep on April 5, 1988 (detailed in Chapter 14). The memory had described twelve "news" to learn at forty-one. I was forty-one years old and now I was being told that "twelve wait."

ED: I want to scream. Ah! (distress, followed by a groan) I want to scream! I can't scream. I can't scream. (loud sigh, loud groan) I want out. (loud groan, another groan with pain, sighs) I want out! (groan) I can't do this. (crying) Okay, (groan) I bit my tongue. Something went down my back. I can move. I can move. (sigh) I'm pretending not to move.

The creatures were moving me. They tilted me back, keeping my head higher than my feet, and lifted me. Several of them held my legs and even more pressed their dry, smooth hands around my shoulders and waist. I also noticed that, when felt from the opposite direction, their hands were rough, like snakeskin.

How I bit my tongue is unclear. A burning spiral of pain twisted down my spine like an electric shock. Suddenly I could move. My muscles were freed from the visegrip of control inflicted by the white flash and the creatures dropped me to the ground.

My pulse was pounding. I had to protect myself. Adrenaline rushed through me as I lay on the sand, unmoving, playing 'possum. It was all happening so fast, I had to think. What to do? Don't move. Maybe they don't know I can move.

ED: (Excited) They know! They moved. They ran! They scattered around me. They scattered around me. There's a voice (loud groan) There's a voice. (groan) They know I can move. They know I can move. (sounds breathless) It says, "Zehaas, twelve wait.

Zehaas, twelve wait." (excited breathing) Get away from me! (screamed loudly, then sounds as if struggling) I'm not an animal. There is a voice. There's a voice. "Stop, Zehaas, stop. You are not that strong." He says, "Zehaas, stop. You are not that strong." (hard breathing) "We know," he says, "we know your passion." He says, "We know, your passion we know. Your passion we know." No! (loud yell) Go away! (shouted) Get away. Get away. I will fight you. (strained, as if struggling) I will fight you. (strangled yell followed by heavy breathing)

I rolled over in the sand and grabbed for the nearest alien. I missed. While rising to my feet I scooped up a double handful of sand, threw it at the creatures in front of me, and rushed forward.

As if the creatures were tied together they instantly formed another circle around me. I began to spin around and around while lashing out with my fists and kicking in an effort to defend myself. The voice warned me to "stop" and called me "Zehaas." My panicky thoughts told me to charge into them. The voice seemed to know my plan and answered, "You are not that strong." Before I could charge, the creatures flashed forward in one swift motion and I was hit on the shoulder with a silver rod, causing the white flash.

ED: They hit me with another white flash. (soft) They hit me with another white flash. (repeated, softer) It's in my head. (sigh) Oh, Jesus. Oh, Jesus. (heavy breathing, sigh) My muscles froze. (soft sigh) I can't move. I can't move again. I can't say anything. I want to scream. I can't talk now. I can't talk now. They are surrounding me. They are moving me. They're moving me to the water. They're moving me. (soft sigh, pause followed by loud scream, then another scream even louder)

> I want . . . (anger) Stop it! (heavy breathing, and sounds as if struggling)
> I won't allow this. (sounds distorted) Move! (command) Move! (telling self to move) My body is mine. (sounds distorted, as if struggling) I will move.
> I *will move.* I will move. (softer) I will move. (louder) I can move. (yelled, groan)

This battle was very physical and I was losing, but my spirit could not tolerate this violation. I forced my body to react. My tongue was bleeding from where I had first bitten it and I again locked my teeth down on the edge of my tongue. I choked on my own blood and winced, my eyes watering in pain. A strange "static shock" vibrated down my legs. I was free again.

ED: They dropped me. (voice weak, groan) Get away from me. Get away from me. There's a voice. "Zehaas, your passion is strong. Twelve wait. You must come."
Fuck you, bastard! You can't touch me! Says, "You are Zehaas. Remember the thirty-five." (painful sigh)

Backing up, I felt a low-growing bush drag across the back of my leg. There was a creature behind me. With an out-of-control spin I tripped and fell backward into the brush. Somehow my right arm ended up around the creature's feather-light body and we crumpled into the dense underbrush together.

I was on my back, looking at the semicircle of creatures standing motionless less than five feet from me. The creature, locked in the grip of my right arm, had its back against my chest. In the darkness, I almost didn't realize what I held. If the creature's helmet hadn't also protected its neck, my arm would have been around its throat.

Sand on my sweaty arm gritted against the smooth,

glassy surface of the creature's chest plate. The creature began to struggle and a sour smell, like mildew, filled my nostrils. Its helmet rubbed on my shoulder, the angle exposing the clear faceplate to my view. Only a few inches from my eyes, my tormentor seemed frail. Its eyes met mine and showed nothing but my reflection.

Tightening my grip, I pulled the two of us backward farther into the brush with my left hand. The creature still grasped the silver rod and began to thrash in panic, striking blow after blow toward my head and left shoulder. The bushes deflected the rod, which I'm sure was some sort of stun weapon.

I wrapped my legs around its legs and finally managed to grab the rod-swinging arm. At that moment my eyes became blurry. Only a few seconds passed before I saw my daughter, as clear an image as possible. She was crying out for me and choking. I yelled.

ED: Laura! Laura, Laura! I see Laura. I can see Laura. (crying) I can see Laura. I can see Laura in my head. (crying, sigh) She's in a room. I see Laura in a room. I see her through a window. Oh, God. Laura! (struggling) Laura, oh, Laura. She's yelling. She's yelling. I can't hear her. (soft) I can't hear her. (louder) I can see her yelling. Laura! She's calling. She needs me. Laura, Laura . . . She's choking. Laura. (crying)

At the time I believed completely that Laura was there, in that room. This mental vision of her, which seemed so real, was most likely a diversion. I had one of the creatures around my neck, so what more effective distraction than the image of my daughter choking. It worked.

ED: Get your goddamn hands off me. You bastards. (crying, yell) I'll get you. I'll get you. (struggle, then

sigh) I don't want to do this. (referring to the hypno-
tism) I've got to stop this.

The struggle had ended and I had been unconscious.
How long, I don't know, but when I awoke I was no
longer on the beach.

ED: They hit me with the light. I'm on a floor. I'm on a
       floor somewhere. I don't see anything. They are not
       around me. I'm on my hands and knees. I'm crawl-
       ing around. I'm alone. I'm alone. It's small in here.
       I'm standing up. I'm standing up, but I'm kind of
       stooped over. Oh, my head. Oh, my head. Oh, my
       head is hurting. (clear throat) My throat is hurting.
       Laura? Laura? Laura must be here. I saw her. Laura?
       (confused) I'm alone. Nobody is here. It's just a
       room. It's hazy, kind of a round, hazy room. (sigh)
       I want out of here. I've got to stop. I want to stop.
       He said count from five and I can stop. Said count
       from five. I can stop. (softer, sigh)

Dr. Overlade's instructions and hypnotic suggestion that
I could always escape the hypnosis by counting from five
worked. I could even hear Dr. Overlade's voice counting
with me. I came out of the hypnosis. Dannie was shaking
my shoulder and Frances was staring at me with a stunned
look that quickly turned to horror. Laura was crying and
jerked backward when I yelled her name.

What had happened to Laura that night?

When I awoke on the beach, after the struggle and the
hour and fifteen minutes of missing time, I felt compelled
to abandon the area quickly and get back home. My subconscious had been controlling my actions and for reasons
hidden to me at the time, I had felt the need to sit up all
night and "defend" Laura from an unknown aggressor.

I hadn't understood why before. Now, through hypnosis,
it was clear why I had been so overwhelmed with fear for

my daughter. But had the unthinkable happened? Had Laura also been taken?

Frances's Account

Dannie, Laura, and I sat transfixed as Dr. Overlade's voice led Ed into a hypnotic state. As soon as Ed seemed "under" I switched off the practice tape and sat quietly on the floor, the microrecorder in my hand. At Ed's first word, I pressed the record button.

Within minutes I felt certain Ed was describing what had happened to him on May 1. That he was, in fact, reliving it. Agitated, his voice strained, he twitched and jerked. He was mentally locked in the physical struggle, living again the terror he'd experienced that night.

My instinct was to speak to him, touch him, comfort and reassure him. But I was afraid to. Would he know it was me? Or would he think my touch was the aliens'? I wished I knew more about hypnosis. My heart pounding, I felt panic rising in me. This had been a bad idea. We weren't ready for this.

Ed screamed Laura's name and I looked at her. Knees drawn up, she pressed into a corner of the sofa. She stared at her father, her eyes wide and full of fear. Dannie was standing, a look of confusion and helplessness on his face. Ed continued to call for Laura. It was time to end it. I dropped the microrecorder on the arm of the recliner and grabbed the other tape player.

"Dad, it's okay. Snap out of it."

Dannie's tense voice interrupted my frantic efforts to locate the right part of the tape. I looked up to see him shaking his father.

"Dannie, don't do that! It could make things worse." Near panic now, I ordered him away from Ed. I returned to my search, fast-forwarding the tape, then pausing to listen. Finally I heard Dr. Overlade's reassuring voice. Calm and quiet, he directed Ed out of the world of subconscious memory.

Ed relaxed and fell silent, then opened his eyes. He looked at Dannie and me, leaning over him, then turned to

Laura. He called her name and she shrank farther into the sofa cushions. After a moment she jumped up, ran across the room, and threw herself into her father's arms.

Tears streaming down her face, she stared up at him. "Daddy, what happened to me?"

"Nothing, baby. It was just a hallucination." He hugged her close and stroked her hair, then looked up at me. I knew from the terrorized expression on his face, he wasn't sure that he was telling Laura the truth.

For once Dannie didn't tease his sister. He did his best to reassure her, although it was obvious to me that he was confused and worried. So was I. An hour of talking, listening to Ed explain in greater detail what he had reexperienced, helped. But it didn't answer the one question Ed and I both avoided. What was Laura's involvement?

I felt sure the answer was in Ed's subconscious. But I had no intention of trying to retrieve it with Dannie and Laura around. I finally got Laura to bed with the promise that I'd be back to sleep with her. Then, asking Dannie to keep an eye on his sister until I could get back, I returned to my bedroom. Ed was there, listening again to the tape recording of what he'd said under hypnosis.

"I want to try it again." He switched off the recorder and looked at me.

"No." Shaking my head, I turned back the bedspread and picked up my pillow. "We shouldn't have done what we already have."

Angry at the entities, angry at the fear this had created in my children, I insisted that Ed shouldn't try hypnosis again. I knew I didn't want Dannie and Laura to witness another regression. At that point I wasn't even sure I wanted Ed to undergo that ordeal again, even with Dr. Overlade there to help him.

"I have to. I can't stand not knowing what really happened with Laura." He paused and then looked me, a determined set to his jaw. "I'm going to do it again. I'd rather have you with me."

I was defeated and knew it. There was no way I could stop Ed from doing what he wanted. And there was no way I could let him go through that experience without me.

"I need to tell Laura I'll be there in a little while. I'll be right back."

Ed's Account

We had to know and, therefore, I had to go back. Back into the trance. Back into that small room.

Once again following Dr. Overlade's instructions for getting into a hypnotic trance, within a few minutes I again succeeded in setting my subconscious free. Heavy breathing accompanied the vivid reliving of the experiences within that small room where I called out to find my daughter.

ED: Laura, Laura? Laura? (louder) Laura? There's nobody in the room. (loud) Laura! Laura! Laura! She is not in this room. I think I saw her—I know I saw her. Ah! (surprise) There's a door behind me. It opened up. There's a creature coming through.
He's smaller than me. Where is Laura? Where is . . . no, no, there's three. There is one and here are three more. They are behind him. He has got white hair. He's got white hair.
Hey! Hey! What have you done with Laura? They, they have rods. They have rods. He's staring at me.

The small room was bare and seemed dirty. The walls were smooth, like glazed china, and I could see no cracks to indicate a door or passage. The creatures that entered behind me were shielded except for the central figure, cloaked in a gray hood (see drawing C). Wisps of white hair outlined the edge of his massive head where the hood pulled tight, as if it had elastic in it. He remained slightly behind the shielded escort.

ED: I am not afraid of you. I *am not* afraid of you. They're moving closer. Ah, the hell with this. I'll go to you. Yeah, come on. Come on, come on. All right.

Yeah. There is a voice. There is a voice in my head—says, "Calm down." Says, "Calm down. You are so angered."
You have my daughter. You got my daughter and you want me to be calm. Yeah, yeah. I'll give you calm.

I was afraid, but I yelled out defiantly. They eased closer toward me. I also took a step toward them, my mind set on a diving tackle. The image of my hands around the skinny neck of my tormentor was clear in my head.

ED: There is another voice, says, "She's fine." Says, "She's fine. See, see. Remember. See." I see her. I see her in my head. I see her. She's in her room. She's in her bed. I see her in her bed. It's in my mind.

The command "Calm down," distracted me as I demanded Laura. During the exchange I could suddenly see Laura clearly. A picture in my mind showed her resting peacefully in her bed. The alien's mouth did not move and, as before, the voice groaned in my head.

ED: There's another voice. This guy's talking to me. This white-haired guy is talking to me. He's just looking at me and all of a sudden I hear him. He says, "Zehaas." He says, "Zehaas. You are always like this. Try to remember." He said, "You are always like this. Try to remember." (sigh, then agitated)
Yeah. Always like this. Well you remember, you remember. Yeah, you didn't ask me to come up here. You didn't ask me to come to this stupid place. I want you out of here; I want my daughter. Oh, Laura's all right, unless that's a trick. Are you tricking me?

The white-haired figure was talking to me as if he knew me. He had his hands crossed over his chest. His fingers were thin, the tips very pointed, and with a "nervous" motion he opened and closed his fingers, wrapping them around his arm.

This squeezing motion caught my attention. So did the solid, motionless posture of the three shielded beings, apparently standing guard. They were exactly like the creatures I had seen before. Five months earlier in the road incident, which resulted in photo 19, there had been five. And there was the single creature I encountered on my back porch, the creature I believed had been lifted back into the UFO by the blue beam in photo 11.

The hooded alien used the same name for me, Zehaas, that I heard so often during sightings. The implication that he had seen me before was obvious when he said, "You are always like this. Try to remember."

ED: There's another voice. Another voice says, "Remember." Well, I don't want to remember. I want out of here. I can leave too. (referring to the hypnosis) All I've got to do is count from five. I can leave. They are backed up around. They are not coming towards me. He says, "Remember."

The next memories were very confused. I knew I was safe in my living room with Frances, but I was also reliving the face-to-face event with the white-haired alien and suddenly a powerful vision swelled into my brain.

ED: I can see something in my head. I can see . . . I see a light shining through a window. In my head. Oh! (shock) I'm in my . . . in my head I can see my old bedroom. I can see my old bedroom. Something coming through the window. There's a light coming through the window. I'm running out of the house.

I'm running out across the yard. Across the yard and I'm yelling for help. Yelling for help.

I was reliving unknown experiences in my past. The events were happening in the actual bedroom and house where I grew up. There was no mistaking the setting and the incident involved my brother being carried away as I ran out of the house and across the yard to escape. Escape I did, but only briefly before I went charging back to grab my brother. Then I found myself being lifted by the creatures.

ED: Yeah. Oh. (confused) There is a white flash. There is a white flash. What is this? What is this? I'm in this room someplace, but I'm remembering this. Oh, I don't know. This is crazy. I know I'm in my house. I'm in my house. I'm in my house. I'm okay. I'm in my house. The doctor said I could say, I'm okay. I'm not in my old house. I'm sitting in my own house. I'm sitting in my chair. (trying to reassure myself that this was only memories) I'm okay. I'm not in my old room. I'm not there. Okay. Okay. Okay. I'm running across the yard. They've got my brother. They've got my brother. I'm going back. Those bastards can't do that. They can't do that. I'm going back.

This memory began to fill in the speculation prompted by the "sleep memory" of March 31, 1988 (also to be detailed later in Chapter 14). I recalled a "contact" at age eleven when I had fled terrorized out of the house then rushed to help my brother. The "sleep memory" had clarified this incident and now I was even more confident of the reality of those revelations.

I could not control my arms or legs and was helpless as I was taken to a small room where my head was clamped in a device. One by one, five smaller creatures were also clamped in an opposite device. The device is also detailed later.

ED: They can't do that! Okay. Okay. I'm back in the room. He said, "Remember. You remember now." Oh, God. Oh. This little creep. I'd like to get my hands around his neck. He can't do this to me. (sigh) The three around him have got shields. And they've got those rods and every time I step forward toward him the rods start to glow.

He says, "You remember now." Yeah, I remember. You take people like me, and you take them and do what you want. He says, "It's necessary." He says, "It's necessary." He says, "We must renew. The news must learn. The news must learn."

This little guy with the thing over his head. Kind of partly over his head. He's got a little white-looking hair coming out from under it. He said, "The news must learn."

The overwhelming confusion of reliving an abduction experienced as a child of eleven while reliving a regressive memory of the abduction on May 1 was almost too much to comprehend. The realization of what was said did not register fully until I listened to the tape recording several days later.

"We must renew" and "The news must learn" are graphic. I would soon understand that these phrases cut to the absolute meaning of the alien abduction motive.

ED: (sigh) I want out. I'm going to count. I'm going to count. Laura's okay. It was just a trick. That little bastard tricked me. I'm going to count. (pause) I'm going to be in my chair. I'm going to count from five. They can't hurt me.

(distressed) I'll fight you. I'll fight you. (loud) I'll fight you. Get away from me! I'm counting. Get away from me. I'm counting. I'm counting. (silence, sigh) Okay. I'm okay. I'm here. That little creep. Okay.

The small beings began to edge closer to me and I pushed backward along the smooth wall. Frantic to escape, I evaded them by disappearing into the hypnotic corridor leading back to Frances sitting across from me and the safety of the present.

The vision of Laura suffocating was false, only a trick used by the beings to distract me. My mind swirled with questions. I needed help and Frances was there for me. We talked for hours into the night. We struggled with possible answers but none of it made sense. Finally we decided that there would be time to uncover the rest of this encounter, but not now, and not without the help of Dr. Overlade.

CHAPTER 6

COMMENTARY ON MAY 1 HYPNOSIS

by Dr. Dan C. Overlade

I had last seen Ed on Friday. I was not prepared for what he told me on Monday. His impelling need to fill in the gaps and his desperation to have an understanding of what had transpired (typical of the vast majority of persons suspecting they have had alien contact) had combined with his impatience at the delay occasioned by the long hours of testing and introductory instruction. He had started without me! I felt a rush of anxiety, realizing that an unguided abreaction of a severe trauma is itself not only traumatic but capable of prompting an extreme emotional upset.

It was two days since Ed's undirected regression and his mood was still quite intense. He wanted to play the cassette recording of the regression in order to have my help in integrating the apparent memories. Because his agenda was totally unexpected, I was not prepared to make a fully adequate recording of his comments and asides as together we listened to the cassette of his spontaneous regression. I was only able to turn on another cassette recorder.

An accurate transcript of our session together was obviated in part by the fact that he was in my office often talking at the same time that his recorded voice was speaking, partly because the standard audiocassette tape he had brought with him was a copy of his original, which had been made during the regression on a minirecorder. There was a great amount of hissing distortion. Even so, the intensity of his feelings two days after the fact was very strong and he was obviously frightened by having relived the May 1 encounter. The following is based on what I recorded.

I chided him gently for having sought the independent regression, explaining that the techniques I had intended to teach him would likely have reduced the intensity of his emotional experience. I asked him if he were in a big hurry.

"No, I'm in no hurry—it's just that this popped out!"

I sensed what had happened. Just as his long association of hypnosis and regression had on Friday prompted a motor regression without ideational content, that same association and strong desire for regression and understanding had combined to produce a regression that added mental imagery to the muscular body memories.

Listening to the tape, I mentioned that it seemed implicit in some of his comments that the aliens were capable of projecting into his mind that either Laura, his daughter, was home safe or Laura was in danger, and that he was unable to know which of those projections was accurate. He agreed and went on to explain how these beings picked him up. He fought back but was struck again and found himself awakening on the floor of a small room.

"I can see it just like I'm sitting there right now."

Ed described a bowllike device, the size of half a soccer ball, located in the center of the ceiling, an extremely bright room with no apparent light source, and the entrance of four small beings, in detail. I encouraged him to draw what he was able to visualize the first opportunity he had and acknowledged to him that I had not heard everything that had been said. I observed that he seemed to distinguish one of the beings as dominant or senior and the others in some sense of underlings. I asked what was the difference between the one that seemed to be in charge and the others.

He told me that the ones grabbing him on the beach were just like others with the shields he had seen before—the one on the back porch on December 2, and the five coming down the road on January 12. As in the other incidents, they had the rods. He felt that there were at least ten of these shielded creatures on the beach, but he wasn't certain because they moved around, at one point forming a big circle.

Ed answered affirmatively when I asked if they were also represented in the room. I repeated his statement that three of these shielded ones surrounded one other, the one with white hair, and attempted to clarify the matter of who was doing what. Ed told me the white-haired one was being protected by the other three and was also the one doing the communicating.

I asked my next question hesitantly. "Was there only—I'm risking contaminating because I'm not sure—in the room, as we'll call it—did you at any time hear a different voice or was that at another experience?"

"The voice has always been like this; it's been a voice that *sounded* the same: 'biddle-liddle lip.' But sometimes I think my brain interprets that 'biddle-liddle, lip'—I think sometimes—for instance, early on there were two occasions when the Spanish part of my brain intentionally or unintentionally engaged and I heard it in Spanish. That makes some sense and there were times when my brain interpreted it to be a female voice ... because I couldn't—it didn't seem that important to me, but it almost sounded like what was being said—if I didn't know my mother was six hundred miles away, I'd think that's my mother. You know, it had that kind of quality of a female voice, like, 'Johnny, come wash your hands.' Like, you know, when a mother gives orders to a child or something."

I steered his thoughts back to the room and asked what was the apparent intent of the beings. What were they up to besides keeping him confined or restricted?

"When he walked into the room, I was ... there was this thing over his head ... fancy-looking clothes and they closed in around him and the rods glowed immediately and then he proceeded to try to tell me that I am always so angry, to calm down, try to remember. His emphasis was more on remembering something. Then they put this image in my head about being back at my old, old house thirty years ago and my room and light coming through my bedroom window—and me running out, yelling for help and all that. That was the image he put into my head and then after the image was over, he said, 'You remember now, you remember now' like, don't you remember now? I didn't respond too well to that."

I questioned Ed further about this regression into his past. "I think I understood you to say—as we were listening to the recording—that being in the room with the apparent leader felt like a very real memory, but the thing back in your childhood seemed more dreamlike. In the—let's call it 'dreamlike' sequence of your youth—what age would you guess?"

Ed answered, "Eleven."

After we discussed this spontaneous regression a little more, I asked Ed how he wanted to proceed. "Is your present intention—and I'll let you reserve the right to change your mind—is your present intention to stop the quest for regression to the other scenes until after you get back (from the MUFON conference in Nebraska)?"

"Whatever you want me to do. My intention was not to *relive* what I remember. I don't want this, in my house, in this chair, or anywhere, to cry and scream. I don't want to do that." While he was willing to learn more, he was quite adamant about what he didn't want.

"My suggestion is that you put off any more solo work. You know that you can interrupt it: if you were to simply practice your hypnotic relaxation and then start spontaneously to regress, all you need to do is count backward from five to one. There are less painful ways for you to retrieve these memories and I don't want you going through a lot of unnecessary stress. I've always acknowledged to you that I think the fact that you have had some recollection is probably going to make it possible for you to remember some other information without so much tension. But there are techniques we can employ that will make hypnotic regression less stressful."

We discussed the probability that his strong desire to remember had prompted the spontaneous regression when he had attempted to follow my earlier instructions for simply getting into hypnosis. We also talked some about the techniques that we would employ together that would avoid revivification. I told him that if he had called me and asked me if he should attempt a regression, I would have said, "Not yet—and not alone." He certainly didn't want another emotional experience such as accompanied his impromptu regression and agreed that further attempts to retrieve memories could wait for his return from the 1988 MUFON International UFO Symposium in Lincoln.

CHAPTER 7

"WHAT'S A DEBUNKER?"

From the time of my first UFO sighting on November 11, 1987, I withheld my name from the media while working patiently with UFO researchers and MUFON investigators. But locally, seven months into the investigation, it was no real secret that I was a witness and most of the community knew that I had taken photographs of the UFO. I merely withheld my name from the media as a way of shielding my family and protecting my business reputation. General contractors rely one hundred percent on their reputations and most of the people I build homes for come to Gulf Breeze from out of town. It was my thought that being known as the "builder who saw UFOs" would not be good for business.

The community accepted my decision. Those who had also seen the UFO understood completely while others seemed to keep an open mind. I have learned that the normal reaction to hearing or reading about a UFO sighting is curiosity. Most people are either interested or not, but simply don't have the time to study the details of a UFO sighting case. Before I saw the Gulf Breeze UFO on November 11, 1987, I was a good example of an average person with no time for UFO stories.

What I thought I knew about UFOs I had learned from Hollywood movies and from the tabloid headlines at the supermarket checkout. I had never heard of MUFON or UFO investigators. Nor had I heard of the hard-core critics, the anti-UFO people, also known as "debunkers."

Skeptical study is the cornerstone of science. The average person who is skeptical about UFO reports should not be criticized. Often a good rule is: "if it sounds impossible, then it most likely is." UFOs certainly sound impossible but in this case the "show-me" rule from Missouri is correct: "seeing is believing." An open-minded skeptic isn't the same as a debunker.

So what is a debunker? Who are these people? "Bunk" is described as "empty talk" spoken only for the purpose of distraction. The UFO cover-up is full of debunkers who spread bunk.

Intentionally, I won't name these debunkers. I believe that these people want to be named to gain media attention, a primary motive for their actions. The campaigns of disinformation cannot be easily explained. The two most likely reasons for their actions are 1) a radical personal rejection of UFOs and/or 2) involvement in an official cover-up. As the years have passed, I have steadily grown to accept the official cover-up theory.

Who and what debunkers are only became important to me when I was unexpectedly confronted with manipulated libel and "dirty tricks" designed to ridicule my family and discredit the Gulf Breeze UFO sightings. My phone rang early on a Sunday morning, the one day my construction business takes a rest. It was a friend of many years, Bob Haines, and after a hearty "Good Morning" he began to read parts of a "flyer" that had been stuck in his mailbox. The "flyer" was printed anonymously and labeled me a nut, a Satan worshiper, and a drunkard.

The organized extent to which debunkers go exceeds anything within the boundaries of a rational personal opinion. Would a personal rejection of UFOs motivate someone to distribute UFO ridicule flyers from mailbox to mailbox in the dead of night? I think not, but that is what happened. Hundreds of flyers were circulated, an act requiring a dozen or more people to accomplish, anonymously under the cover of night. This was clearly an orchestrated effort to ridicule me and put an end to other UFO witnesses' coming forward. Here are excerpts from the flyer that was spread throughout Gulf Breeze:

DO YOU KNOW EDWARD WALTERS?

We are proud to disclose that he is the nut that would have the fine people of Gulf Breeze believe that the Martians have landed!

THIS IS HIS PHONE NUMBER . . . 932-3056

Call this idiot and let him know what you have discovered about him. Let him know that we all know he is a liar and nobody believes him. (Don't be deceived by the other reports that you read about—The Sentinel newspaper is making up the stories to sell papers.)

Many of our sources report how often this UFO nut can be seen drunk at the local bars and we are now investigating his DEVIL Worship meetings that include other UFO witnesses. Do you want this type of element in town? Let us all speak up against Ed Walters and tell him and anybody else who supports him to STUFF IT.

Those responsible for distributing these flyers were from out of town. We know this to be true because of an error within the flyer. There are no "local bars" in Gulf Breeze, a fact apparently unknown to them. Gulf Breeze is in Santa Rosa County, a dry county without a single bar or tavern.

Of particular importance in this flyer is the first mention of "Devil Worship," a theme that would later be promoted by the debunkers, distorting ghost stories told at teen parties into "ritual séances."

I believe that the accusation of "Devil Worship," "Cult," etc., is a standard tactic used as a first effort to distract public attention. (The tactic was also used against six

U.S. Army soldiers who, for unknown reasons, fled their secret clearance electronic listening post in Germany and came to Gulf Breeze. They were arrested and labeled members of a cult. The details follow in Chapter 23.)

The official UFO cover-up is a tangled web of shadowy figures intent on distracting public attention. Consistently, when the average man-in-the-street reports seeing something unexplainable in the sky, he is met with denial at the official level.

Usually a simple "weather balloon" comment from local military representatives is sufficient to dismiss a UFO sighting as long as there are no photographs. Consistently, little or no attention is given to the hundreds of Gulf Breeze residents who report seeing the UFO but have no photos to support what they saw. Only those witnesses with photographs draw the wrath of the cover-up; when the photographs show the structure of an unidentified object, the official cover-up invokes the debunkers.

Very little is known about this small group of motivated critics, but these are the people who demand personal background checks of witnesses who have photographed the UFO. This is done in the hope of finding anything that can be used by the debunker to discredit the UFO witness. On the other hand, we know very little about these debunkers. Who are they? How do they earn a living? I decided to do some checking on the most vocal of the lot. I'll call him Mr. Jones.

Mr. Jones is listed in the book *Who's Who in Ufology* and claims to have a Ph.D. in physics and a Masters in astronomy from the University of Michigan. A letter to the registrar's office uncovered no record of his receiving a Ph.D. in physics nor a Masters in astronomy.

Mr. Jones also promoted himself in the *American Men and Women of Science* as being the head of the department of physics and astronomy at the University of Valencia, Spain. A letter from the University of Valencia and a personal conversation with the director of the department of physics verifies that the University of Valencia has no record of Mr. Jones.

Effectively, Mr. Jones created the story that he had a

Ph.D. in physics and did so in the early 1980s, seven years before the Gulf Breeze sightings. It would appear that Mr. Jones is a setup in the official cover-up. In the spy business he would be called a "mole." Digging himself deeply into the private UFO research community, he would be a source of information to aid in the official UFO cover-up. Under his fake academic credentials and cover as a private UFO researcher, he could be called upon to debunk high-profile UFO sightings which involve photographs.

The Gulf Breeze UFO sightings were his prime target, an assignment that he bungled at every step. Mr. Jones faced the difficult task of debunking a UFO case in which the UFO would not cooperate. The UFO kept appearing. Witnesses continued to see and photograph the UFO while the official debunkers insisted everybody was hallucinating, and those with photographs were perpetrating a hoax.

Frances's Account

Ed and I dismissed the "flyer" which had been spread around town, even though it had also been placed in newspaper racks and on a table in the foyer of the local library. We felt certain that our friends and neighbors knew us and would see the "flyer" for what it was—trash.

We were right. No one we spoke to took the allegations in the "flyer" seriously. Neither Dannie nor Laura experienced any ridicule or negative comments because of it. For that reason, and on advice from the MUFON investigators, we let it go without rebuttal from us.

Later, the attacks became more vicious. When an inaccurate and scurrilous "report" was mailed to the media, I decided the time to just "sit and take it" was past. Other UFO witnesses, nonwitnesses whose only "crime" was being our friends, and especially Ed, were accused of everything from helping perpetrate a hoax to conjuring up demons at a séance. I wrote a letter refuting the details in the "report." That seemed to take the debunkers by surprise. Apparently witnesses didn't generally fight back with the facts.

We weren't the only ones "fighting back" on our behalf.

Dr. Maccabee wrote a letter to the editor of the *Pensacola News-Journal* after the paper had quoted one debunker as saying there was only a one-in-a-jillion chance that our sightings were not a hoax. In his letter, Dr. Maccabee pointed out that this man had never talked with any of the witnesses or done any on-site investigation. At the time, Dr. Maccabee had already invested more than a hundred (unpaid) hours of his own time on investigating the sightings, interviewing witnesses, and analyzing the photographs.

Dr. Maccabee compiled his information on the Gulf Breeze sightings case in a ninety-page report which he planned to present to the international MUFON symposium in Nebraska in late June. In addition to his technical analysis of the photographs, and witness interviews, he included in his report responses to the theories and accusations of critics and debunkers explaining why they were incorrect.

Irritating as the debunkers were, Ed and I refused to allow them to become a bigger part of our lives. We pointed out the errors, at times outright lies, in their attacks and went on with everyday life as well as we could, all things considered.

Our greatest hope was that once Ed completed his hypnosis sessions with Doctor Overlade we could put this all behind us. The sightings, whatever had happened during the missing time, the debunkers—would all become just another part of our lives, lives which would truly return to normal.

CHAPTER 8

IN SEARCH OF ANSWERS

During a discussion with Duane Cook, the *Sentinel* newspaper publisher, and Dari Holston, the topic of "why me" was the focus. We engaged in a great deal of speculation. Many ideas were considered and discarded. At one point I described, briefly, how sometimes as I awoke from sleep, strange memories of unknown places, words, and things would surface. These memories were more than remnants of dreams. They were vivid and exact. Duane and Dari suggested that perhaps I could solve the whole UFO affair and exhorted me to concentrate on a UFO-related question before going to sleep.

I reluctantly agreed and tried. When I awoke the next morning the vision of a tropical forest and a strange sounding word kept flashing through my head. "Tamacuari." Somehow I knew this was the name of a mountain in Venezuela, South America, a granite mountain, 7670 feet high.

In my mind's eye, as if flying hundreds of feet in the air, I see miles of savanna with more than a dozen huge vertical plateaus rising thousands of feet above the grasslands and distant jungle. The panorama of the savanna disappears and, still several hundred feet above the treetops, I clearly see the lush green forest below. Scores of huge rocky mounds jut above the thick treetop canopy as I approach a distant mountain (Tamacuari?). Suddenly I plunge toward the earth and wake up, startled and sweating. What does it mean? Was it real? Did this mountain exist or was it just a dream?

I was hesitant to share this name or my thoughts with Duane or Dari but their enthusiasm was impossible to resist. After I told them about this sleep memory, Dari promptly placed a telephone call to the library research department trying to verify such a mountain. Encyclopedias and atlases were checked but to no avail.

Several weeks passed with no solution to the existence of Tamacuari when Duane received a phone call in answer to the earlier question at the library research department. The mountain had been found. It was in Venezuela. The library researcher reported it to be a granite mountain 2340 meters high. A quick conversion from metric matched my description of approximately 7670 feet.

Did this prove or disprove anything? Maybe, but it was much easier to rationalize away as a coincidence. I convinced myself that for some reason this bit of information must have been stored in my memory from an earlier exposure, perhaps when I lived in Costa Rica. What, if anything, it had to do with the UFO, I didn't know. So it answered no question that I knew of and only confirmed my ability to recall subconscious memories during my sleep.

The question that I had fallen asleep with that night was, "Where did the UFO come from?" It did not seem reasonable to conclude that the answer was, "From a mountain named Tamacuari." A week later the same "dream" startled me from my sleep and continued to recur, sometimes twice a week. Tamacuari was now at the top of my list of many haunting questions.

I wanted to learn more about the UFO phenomenon but I had promised Dr. Overlade that I would not read any books that might influence my memory and the scheduled hypnosis. Though books were off-limits, there were other educational forums available which the investigators agreed would be useful. One of these was the 1988 MUFON Symposium to be held in Lincoln, Nebraska, that June.

Frances and I debated attending the symposium. We were both concerned about leaving Dannie and Laura alone for the first time. Frances was especially worried because of my hypnosis memories of seeing Laura suffocating. Finally we decided to go to the symposium—under assumed names—hoping to learn as much as we could about the amazing events that had overtaken us. The references by investigators to many other sightings across the country and the world had intensified our desire to know more. If we could understand the motive for this information, perhaps we might know better what to do, how to respond.

The possibility of finding answers at the MUFON Symposium heightened our anticipation of Wednesday, June 23. We drove to Lincoln, expecting to be on the road for two days. Frances had plotted our route through St. Louis and Kansas City.

On the second day we drove steadily for ten hours, past mile after mile of farmland. As we crossed the "Show-me" state of Missouri, I wondered how often UFOs had been sighted and how many of the witnesses had ever filed reports. Imagine how surprised I was to learn that each year St. Louis holds a "Show-Me" conference featuring local and national UFO reports. We arrived at the Lincoln Center late in the afternoon.

At the opening reception the next day, Frances and I faded into the crowd and listened to people discuss us. One woman said she knew us personally, as in "close friends." We were standing right next to her. I looked at Frances to see her response to the woman's remark. Humor filled Frances's eyes but somehow we both managed to keep straight faces.

Excusing ourselves from that group, Frances and I strolled through the crowd, listening to snatches of conversation. More and more people continued to surround the display of our photographs prominently occupying the center of the lobby. The discussions about our photographs by strangers who could hardly believe their eyes ran from other UFO witnesses to skeptical researchers interested in further study. But all the debates ended in anticipation of the presentation of an extensive photo analysis by Dr. Maccabee, scheduled for the next night.

During his lecture, the only questions Dr. Maccabee didn't answer fully were those pertaining to the one minute and thirty-eight second videotape I had shot of the UFO on

December 28, 1987. That study and analysis, initiated by Bob Oechsler, a former NASA systems specialist, was only in the preliminary stage at the time. (For a complete analysis see Appendix 3—Where to Write: F.U.F.O.R.)

Oechsler, working with Ed Weibe at NASA Goddard Space Center, had begun to examine the revolution rate of what appeared to be the power source at the bottom of the craft and the pulsing rate of the beacon light. He later reported at a news conference:

An extensive analysis of the two-part video was started in March, 1988. Various enhancement techniques were performed at NASA Goddard Space Flight Center. Among those tests, a variable speed element was employed to make tapes for viewing the entire tape at one-tenth speed. A Sony Video Editor model BVU820 was used with a digital time base corrector to supply a direct signal to the Video Hard Copy Unit made by Tektronix, model 4632. The thermal printer generated photo images of both phases of each frame. A ten-second portion of the videotape requires 600 single copy prints. Each print is measured to define altitude, flight path, rotation characteristics, frequency of beacon lights, power ring aberrations, attitude in flight, airspeed/velocity, acceleration/deceleration and an analysis of direction reversals. A preliminary analysis of the audio track indicated that no sound could be identified with the object. A preliminary analysis concludes that the object observed in the videotape closely resembles objects photographed with the Polaroid cameras. The power ring at the bottom has a clockwise or left-to-right rotation. The dome or beacon light blinks on and off at no consistent rate or pattern and displays a variable luminosity with each cycle. The object loses altitude moving to the left of the camera just prior to blinking out. A ghost image appears in the first phase of the next frame, approximately two object widths to the right, that may be related but is apparently not visible through the transmission medium. There are certain restrictions in the evaluation of the videotape. Due to the horizontal resolution lines, we are viewing the object through what is analogous to jail bars turned sideways. Nonetheless it appears conclusive that the bottom or power source light has a variable luminosity characteristic which is not synchronic with the beacon light on the top of the object.

As an experienced robotics technician I've built many remote-controlled devices in the past ten years. As a prototype designer I am well versed in exotic techniques used to operate various sizes of apparatus from very small to very large using sometimes inexpensive semiautomated frequency-controlled equipment. The specifications detailed in this case, most notably the absence of audible sound from the UFO craft in the 8-mm video and the rotational characteristic of the "power ring," create enormous difficulty when an attempt is made to recreate what is observed by constructing a model to examine the technology. It is quite clear to this investigator that we are examining a truly anomalous technology.

Several months before Bob Oechsler had begun the videotape analysis, I had been asked to try to remember any technical information that might be helpful to the scientific study. While discussing this request with him one evening, I hinted at those strange memories that sometimes surface in the mornings.

He seemed very intrigued and pressed me to talk about it. I made light of the whole idea but he asked if I would concentrate on a question for him. I said I'd try, but not to expect much. His question involved the research he was doing on the vibration frequency of UFOs. Oechsler's exact question was, "What is the vibration rate of the UFO?" I thought to myself, what a crazy question, how would anybody know that?

Several days later I did make an effort, one night, to think about his question before going to sleep. The next morning a small number kept rushing through my mind—seven point five (7.5) cycles per second.

Certainly the vibration rate of a UFO would be some huge number or complicated formula. I wrote the 7.5 figure down and dismissed it.

About a week later Bob Oechsler called and asked if I had learned anything. I apologized and told him that all I got was a small number of 7.5 cycles per second. He seemed intrigued and asked for more details. He did not explain his interest nor did I have any idea of the significance of this number.

Although I suspected he was disappointed when I had no further details to offer, he assured me he would continue his study of the videotape. He had been using a NASA computer with frame-by-frame capability that could reveal what went unseen to the naked eye. About thirty days after my subconscious had released the 7.5 number the NASA computer confirmed the same data. The data printouts showed that on the 8-mm camera I had there are thirty scanning frames per second. The glowing power ring at the bottom of the UFO revolved once in every four scanning frames. So what is the frequency of the revolution rate per second? Seven point five! (One revolution in four frames, divided into the thirty frame per second equals a frequency cycle of 7.5.)

A very powerful connection between the rotation rate of the power ring and my memory recall had been uncovered. By understanding Bob Oechsler's discovery I knew that I could accept that the sleep memories were significant. I could not accept that I was recalling actual events. A real memory and not a dream was the only way to explain the 7.5 cycles per second recall. What lay behind the other sleep memories I'd had? What about the Tamacuari dreams that continued to intrude into my sleep?

Maybe the answers were locked in my subconscious. I hoped hypnosis was the key.

CHAPTER 9

TAKEN IN THE NIGHT—AGE 17

I repeated the words hypnotic regression over and over as I drove toward my appointment with Dr. Overlade. I no longer had an uneasy feeling about letting go and sliding into the peaceful trance. My uneasiness was from not understanding, from not wanting to know but needing to know.

After greetings were exchanged, Dr. Overlade began setting up the video camera and recorder. His explanations of what would happen instilled a mood of confidence in me. During my first experience with a regressive trance, I had raced pell-mell into actually reliving the moment-by-moment confrontation. Those vivid images were not easy to disregard and I was concerned that I would have to reexperience the stress of other memories. But now Dr. Overlade explained a technique by which he could desensitize the emotional recall, which gave me confidence that I could always count backward from five and come out of the hypnosis. I lay back in the recliner and focused on Dr. Overlade's voice.

The doctor had decided to concentrate on a suspected missing-time incident. During an earlier session I had described to him what I remembered of an event which happened when I was seventeen years old. The following is my conscious recall of that experience.

My older brother, Bert, and I lived in a small "mother-in-law" apartment connected to our house. It was about 3:00 P.M. and my mother asked me to go to the local grocery store for a loaf of bread. I raced off on my bicycle with little notice of the large, black dog sitting at the corner of our yard near the road.

As I pedaled along the flat pavement, I felt uneasy and looked back. The black dog was behind me. I mean right behind me. I jerked to the left when I saw it and ran off the road into the ditch.

I looked up from my uncontrolled stop. The dog was nowhere in sight. It was gone. Chills raced down my spine. I righted my bike and took off as fast as I could, trying to get to the store and to people.

There were another five blocks to go when I felt that same eerie sensation again. I knew if I looked around, the dog would be there. I didn't look. Instead, I pedaled faster and leaned forward to get all my weight into my speed. When I hit the curb at the grocery I glanced back. I saw only the vacant road.

I walked slowly through the aisles to the bread section and took my time getting to the checkout counter. I wanted to give that strange black dog a lot of time to get someplace else. Finally I left the store and rounded the corner to get my bike. There sat the black dog, with its head next to, and taller than, the handlebars.

Frozen in my tracks, I stared at the dog. It didn't flinch. It just looked at me. I eased over to the opposite side of the bicycle and slowly wheeled it away. As soon as I dared, I jumped on the bike and took off.

I had never pushed a bike so hard—must have been a speed record—but the black dog followed. It should have been impossible for it to keep up with me. But calm and unwavering, it just looked straight at me, keeping up that steady gait.

I rode into the yard, jumped off the bike, and let it fall as I ran for the front door of our apartment. I slammed the door behind me and yanked the shade over its glass window. My heart was pounding. I doubled over, pulling a mad rush of air into my lungs.

Something was very wrong with that dog. It was much too deliberate. I leaned against the doorframe and peeked out the window. The dog slowly turned its head and met my eyes with a vacant glare. I let the shade drop back in place. After a few minutes I took another peek.

The dog sat there on the small entry porch, as if it were in a trance. Unmoving, barely five feet away, it was as if it were a guardian. Had there been another one on the opposite side of the porch, they would have resembled a pair of sinister statues. I waited and kept checking during the next half hour until the dog was gone.

Later that night, as my brother and I prepared for bed, things were normal. Mom had turned on the yard sprinkler as she did every night during the summer. Around ten-thirty I put the cat out, locked the door, and turned off the light on my way to bed.

Sometime later, I felt a force press down on the outside edge of my bed close to my feet. My mind registered that it was the cat jumping up on the bed. Again the bed pressed down, and my knees dipped and rose as the mattress absorbed the pressure.

Suddenly my mind whirled and adrenaline rushed through me. I had put the cat out! What the hell was creeping along the edge of my bed? I wanted to jump up and scream, but I was too afraid. I lay there and listened.

The silence was thick and I could only hear the sound of my breathing. Then the sprinkler splashed water against the front windows. My head was aching and I felt a knot in my stomach that turned to nausea. Fear paralyzed me, but I had to do something.

I was lying on my side, my left eye covered by the pillow. Ever so slowly, I cracked my right eyelid to peek through my lashes. The room was dark, my vision fuzzy. I could see shadowy gray forms move back and forth as I tried to focus my eye.

At that moment, straining to see, it happened again. The bed pushed down, this time harder. My chest moved sharply with the direction of the mattress. I was just short of panic. The thing was moving closer and closer to my head.

I closed my eye tightly and pretended to toss in my sleep so I could curl up into a ball. There must be some madman in the house was all I could think of.

Again the pillow went down, this time within inches of my head. The pillow tugged downward and my head bobbed down, then up. A sour scent wafted across my nostrils. I wanted to jump up and scream. But what if the "madman" had a knife?

Once more I edged my eyelid open just enough to see. My muscles locked in rigid fear. A slight gleam of light from a crack in the curtains reflected off a bald head just six inches from my face. Large blackened sockets, with no outline of brows or normal features, filled my view.

Eye-to-eye with this thing, terror seized me. I squeezed my eyes closed and screamed in my head. *I'm asleep . . . Please go away.* I lay ever so still for a few minutes, conscious of every sound, every feeling. I noticed how wet the pillow was beneath my head. I was sweating, but not enough to have soaked it. The sprinkler pattered against the window, the sound muffled by the blood pounding in my ears.

Panicky, I couldn't stand it anymore. In one motion I grabbed my pillow to the front of my chest—hoping for some protection—and leaped for the bedside lamp. At the same time I started yelling.

"Bert! Bert! Wake up! There's somebody in the house!"

Bert answered with a grumpy, "What do you want?" as I turned on the light.

Nothing! I could see nothing in my room. I squatted on the floor next to my bed with my back against the bedside table. I called to Bert that there was something on my bed. He reacted in a sleepy voice.

"Yeah, it was the cat. It was on my bed too."

I quickly said, "Turn on your light. Somebody's in here. I put the cat out."

His light snapped on and I saw Bert coming toward me. I jumped up and ran toward him. We met in the small hallway and whispered a plan to check the closets and bathroom.

We whipped open each closet door, ready to run, only to see nothing but hanging clothes. When we started to check the bathroom, Bert noticed that the hallway and bedroom floors were wet.

Strange, wet footprints led from the locked front door, down the side of my bed, and to Bert's bedside. The small tracks showed the paths of several comings and goings. Most of them turned into my room. Shaped like flat-bottomed slippers, the tracks covered much of the floor with wet prints.

Then Bert noticed that I was wet, as if I'd been outside. I told him that I hadn't been anywhere. But I couldn't explain why I was wet or what I had seen.

Dr. Overlade found the event to be very suggestive and had decided to pursue it during this hypnosis session. His voice was calm and, as the hypnotic state replaced consciousness, Dr. Overlade began to establish a subconscious motor reflex communication with my body. By hypnotic suggestion my body would answer with the twitch of a different finger to answer, "yes," "no," or "I don't want to answer." This technique would enable him to address my fear, possibly my avoidance of recall, directly with my subconscious. More instructions were given to encourage me to diminish the many muscle spasms, which had spontaneously developed.

The doctor explained that with this technique he could have a meaningful conversation with my subconscious even if I fell sound asleep. Having established my index finger movement to be "yes," the thumb movement to be "no," and the little finger to be, "I don't want to answer," Dr. Overlade began.

DR. O: My first question is, would it be all right if we (referring to my subconscious) have a conversation in his (referring to me) interest.

ED: (The videotape shows a quick flick of the index finger indicating "yes.")

DR. O: I ask that you go back to the day of the black dog and, below consciousness, review the events of that afternoon. Signal your entrance into that review by movement of the "yes" digit, and the conclusion of that replay by movement of the "no" digit.

ED: (Camera shows a "yes" and "no" movement.)

DR. O: Thank you; begun and concluded. As you see, unconscious review can be very, very accelerated. Now kindly review the events of going to the store, leaving the store, getting home, and the dog being on the porch. Again, subconsciously, use the "yes" and "no" digits to indicate the beginning and conclusion. Yet again, please review the same events.

ED: (The videotape shows quick finger movements indicating response to the subconscious review.) (Brief pause)

DR. O: Now, is there any other unconscious information, additional information, that he (referring to me in the third person) has not already retrieved concerning this event?

ED: (The reflex quickly indicated positive with the "yes" digit movement.)

DR. O: Does the information concern something in addition to the dog? Was there some other kind of organism or creature? Your head is nodding, tell me what you see. You don't have to relive it, just tell me what you see. Put it up on a screen. Sit in a theater and watch from up in the projection booth.

ED: (Negative head shaking)

DR. O: You don't want to tell me? (Noticing increased stress) You can cut it off. Freeze the action any time you want to. You are safe, you are here, you are here in 1988. Tell me what you see.

ED: (The camera shows an "I don't want to answer" digit signal.)

DR. O: You don't want to answer. Okay. Can you tell me something of how you are feeling? Verbally, can you tell me that?

ED: (More negative head movement with agitated breathing)

DR. O: You realize this is August, 1988. Whatever it

was, was quite remote. You are in control. If you want to diminish the picture, you can open your eyes briefly. Move your hands deliberately if you want. Are you reluctant to talk about it because it is a scene that is too upsetting?

ED: (Camera records a positive finger movement answering "yes.")

DR. O: Would it be all right for him to freeze the action and see part of the scene in full frame? Would that make it possible for him to tolerate?

ED: (Camera shows a "yes" movement.)

DR. O: Freeze it. A still slide projected on a screen with you up in the projection booth watching Ed down in the theater.

ED: (This technique finally prevailed and I began to describe the memory.) The dog is at the edge of the porch with its body facing away but with its head twisted almost backwards. (The words were soft and uneasy.)

The hypnotic regression had taken me back to that exact moment where I could see the black, shorthaired dog, stoically sitting at the edge of the porch like a statue. I could feel the same sense of fear, taste the salty sweat drops that ran down my face into the corners of my lips. I was reliving the pounding of my heart and the shaking of my legs from the strain of pedaling the bicycle to its limits.

ED: Almost so its neck would have to be broken to look at me. As I was looking through the window the dog was staring back. The eyes are not normal.

DR. O: Do you want to advance it a couple of frames now? No. Okay, take another look at the same picture and see what else you notice.

ED: The dog doesn't have any teeth.

DR. O: What other thoughts do you have about the dog?

ED: It's not normal; it's not a normal dog.

DR. O: Is it similar to any particular breed of dog?

ED: No, I don't know about dog breeds.

DR. O: Okay.

ED: It's big, really big.

DR. O: Now, ultimately the dog goes away. Disappears. Is that correct? Please advance to that point when the dog is no longer there.

ED: (With a slow negative turn of the head, the subconscious resistance continued.)

DR. O: Okay, maybe just a few frames at a time, just move a couple of seconds.

ED: I was hiding and peeking out the window and when I looked again it was gone.

DR. O: Feel the relief that this unusual dog has gone. Now I have a question for your unconscious to answer by your finger movement. Has any harm been done to Ed during the course of the dog's presence?

ED: (The camera records a quick negative movement.)

DR. O: Now below consciousness, would you be willing to review the events of that night, without Ed consciously perusing it?

ED: (The camera records a positive movement.)

DR. O: Okay. As before, kindly signal the beginning of your review by a movement of the "yes" digit and the conclusion by movement of your "no" digit. Begun (noticing a "yes" movement). He does not have to relive this. Thank you, concluded (noticing a "no" movement). Same thing, begun; (pause) concluded. (Dr. Overlade was trying to have my subconscious desensitize the event without conscious memory by repeated, rapid, below consciousness review.) Again, please. (The camera shows a rapid begin and end signal from my hand.) Yet again, please. Begun; (pause) concluded. Excellent. Review it yet again please—paying close attention to the identification of any person or persons or beings significantly a part of that scene besides Ed himself. Begun and, (pause) concluded. And begin again please, attending to any words significantly a part of the scene, spoken or unspoken. (Pause) This question is for your unconscious mind. Am I correct in assuming that this scene begins with him sensing something bumping the bed? Is that where the scene begins?

ED: (The camera shows a negative response by the quick movement of the thumb.)

DR. O: No. Does it begin earlier than that?

ED: ("Yes," the camera records a positive.)

DR. O: Does it begin five minutes earlier?

ED: ("No," indicated with a negative movement.)

DR. O: Ten minutes? (visual "no") Twenty minutes? (visual "no") More than an hour? (visual "yes") More than two hours? (visual "no") Can we say it was about an hour and a half? (visual "yes") Was there anything done to Ed physically during that hour and half? Head is saying "no" and finger movement is saying "yes."

My conscious mind was beginning to recall and reject the memories while my unconscious answered a positive "yes."

DR. O: Shoulder is talking as well. (Referring to shoulder muscle movements) Let your body be at ease; we will review this below consciousness. You do not have to reexperience it. You have safely made it here to 1988. This is a quite remote experience, back when you are about seventeen. (Pause) Was something done physically in that scene?

ED: (The camera records a burst of skeletal muscle movement from my legs along with the positive signal from the hand.)

DR. O: What does it feel like your legs are doing, Ed?

ED: It's not my legs. (Spoken softly with distress)

DR. O: Genitals?

ED: Yes.

DR. O: Unconscious, would it be all right for Ed to have a conscious recollection of that scene that you have been reviewing below conscious?

ED: (The camera shows a firm negative movement.)

DR. O: He does not have to experience it; he can see it up on the screen. Under that circumstance would it be okay to have a conscious recollection?

ED: (The camera shows a slight positive response.)

DR. O: Okay, there is the scene, with Ed in the projection booth, tell me what you see. You don't have to reexperience it, just tell me what you see.

ED: (The camera shows massive body movements, both flexing and extending.)

DR. O: Allow your body to be at ease. Then was then, and now is now; you are safe and comfortable. What is on the screen?

ED: I'm naked. (Whispered with intense agitation)

DR. O: Explain to me what you mean.

ED: They took my clothes.

DR. O: They?

ED: (More strong movement caused the leg support on the recliner to collapse.)

DR. O: Remember that you can interrupt the trance if you need to. In the meantime, just let a little bit come to consciousness at a time. As much as you can tolerate. Clearly, you are here in 1988, that was this chair that collapsed and not anything back there at age seventeen. How many of them were there?

ED: Five. (Spoken softly)

DR. O: Five, and they took your clothes. And then what happened?

ED: They put something on me. (Very heavy breathing and agitation)

The memories were confusing and somehow disconnected. Pieces of the recall were shooting through my head. Many, many shadowy figures were around me and I could not seem to move.

Dr. O: What was the nature of that something?

Ed: A disk, bowl, a device.

Dr. O: They put this on you, where?

Ed: Between my legs. (Whispered with a grimace)

Dr. O: Okay, and what was the effect of that? Freeze the action.

The videotape shows a heavy muscle reaction as I was flooded with terror and did not want to answer or even remember. My head began to shake in a negative reaction.

Dr. O: Is the "no" for then or for now? You keep shaking your head "no."

Ed: For now.

Dr. O: You don't want to talk about it?

Ed: No.

Dr. O: Do you want to be able to remember it after you come out of the trance?

Ed: No.

Dr. O: Do you want to be able to remember it some other day?

Ed: No.

Dr. O: Okay, accept that decision for now; you may want to revise it at a later date. That's up to you. (Pause) Do you want to go on beyond that and finish this scene up? Get back into the bed?

The videotape shows a rapid body reaction and head shaking in the negative but within the confines of my mind I began to see the small gray figures closing in around me. Dr. Overlade's voice broke into the darkness that disguised the creatures that were tormenting me.

Dr. O: You want to interrupt it now?

Ed: I want to go.

Dr. O: Below consciousness I want to ask your hand

some questions. Hand, in the course of that encounter, did he ever leave his bed?

Ed: (Positive index finger response, "yes")

Dr. O: Was he removed from his house?

Ed: (Another "yes" response)

Dr. O: Was this bowl-shaped device placed on him in the house?

Ed: (A rapid "no" response)

Dr. O: Was it in some kind of structure?

Ed: (The index finger movement indicated "yes.")

Dr. O: Would it be all right for him to remember the things he could see there?

Ed: (An animated negative response)

Dr. O: Without reliving the experiences, would it be all right for him to remember what he could see?

Ed: (The little finger jumped with a reaction that Dr. Overlade recognized as the "I don't want to answer" response.)

My mind had shut down all recall and was rejecting Dr. Overlade's efforts to push open a door that would expose its disturbing secrets.

Dr. O: Would it be all right then to see this being projected on a screen, without anything happening to him?

Dr. Overlade continued to address my hand in an effort to break down the barriers preventing the recall. The videotape shows a reflex of "I don't want to answer."

Dr. O: You said aloud a moment ago, "I want to go," but you never said where you wanted to go. Would you repeat that for me?

Ed: I want to see that room. (Very softly spoken)

Dr. O: Please say again.

Ed: I want to see what happened in that room.

Unknown to Dr. Overlade, my mind had leaped from the events when I was seventeen to the small room in which I had been held captive only months ago on May 1, 1988. But there was no indication of this time change for Dr. Overlade to follow.

ED: I feel my body as if it were ... Oh my ... the light.
DR. O: Tell me about the light.

The video shows my body racked in a twisted rejection of an unseen flash of white light bursting into my head. The detailed recall of the light flash was not revealed to Dr. Overlade, as he only witnessed the repeated collapse of the footrest on the recliner where I twisted in reaction to this mental "whiteout." So strong was my physical reaction that he immediately tried to reassure me.

DR. O: Open your eyes, Ed. It's 1988. You are all right. It's okay.
ED: Okay. (Stuttering in a whisper. The video shows my face was pale and drawn tight with stress.)

I looked at Dr. Overlade and understood where I was. Still partly in the trance, I listened to his assurance that all was well.

DR. O: Okay, go back when you are ready. I just want you to see that you are in charge. You are in control and not somebody else. (Pause, as I once again rested.) What is your impression of the light? What does it do?

Dr. Overlade recognized that I had again fully slipped back into the hypnotic trance, back into a small angular room. Into a room where I was suddenly hit with a pain that shot through my nose. I was reexperiencing, reliving, feeling everything around me. A rod was being probed into my nose. I was semiconscious and lying on the floor; I could see the beings move around me.

DR. O: See if you can tell me what you are experiencing. What are you experiencing?

ED: Something is going into my nose. It hurts. Going into my nose, it hurts.

DR. O: You're sensing that something was put into your nose. What was it?

ED: Something was put in my nose.

DR. O: And left in?

ED: Some kind of rod was stuck in my nose. They are coming at me. Coming at me.

DR. O: Was this in order to put the rod in your nose?

Dr. Overlade was still unaware that the time frame in my mind had leaped forward to the May 1 event and I was once again lying on the floor in that small room. The floor felt like that of an old movie theater, with years of use leaving a sticky residue.

I was reliving the exact moment and pushing myself up against the slick wall. I could feel its vibrating hum against my back when, suddenly, I was no longer alone. I slid back toward the corner and braced myself for the unknown.

My head still pounded and I could taste the blood that ran from the bite in my tongue. I was reliving what had happened following the confrontation on that lonely beach.

ED: They are coming towards me.

I was backing up along a wall directly opposite four beings. Three of them were clad in the box-type shields and stood around another one, who was cloaked in a gray hood and pale pink bodysuit. I recoiled from the creature.

This recall was so salient that the video camera shows a frantic gasp for air while I pressed myself back into Dr. Overlade's recliner. The doctor tried to calm me.

DR. O: You don't have to reexperience it. Watch it on a screen.

ED: I'm moving around the side of a wall and they came in.

DR. O: Describe them.

ED: They are smaller than I am. The ones in front have silver sticks.

DR. O: What is the impact of the silver sticks? What does that do?

ED: They can hit you with it.

DR. O: With what result?

ED: It makes you "white out." I'm going around the wall. Around the wall. They are close, very close. There is an opening behind me. I'm going through the opening.

DR. O: Is that what they want you to do?

ED: I don't know. I'm going. I look behind me.

The videotape shows an active attempt of turning my head to see behind me while my eyes were closed and I was impatiently tossing back and forth, seeing objects only in my mind. The brightly lighted room into which I went was dominated by a narrow table cantilevered from the wall.

ED: I look back around, they are gone. They're gone. They're gone. There's no opening.

DR. O: There had been an opening but it is no longer there? Am I understanding you correctly?

ED: I went through a door or something as they were coming at me. It's not there. It's gone. I'm in a room. It's bigger. It's a bigger room. It's bigger than

the other room. There is a table over here. I'm looking at a table. It's shiny.

I continued to breathe heavily as I reexperienced my
efforts to pull the thick, warm air into my lungs. I felt le-
thargic and plodding, somehow unable to react without
delay.

ED: The light is hurting my eyes.
DR. O: Turn the brilliance down like it was a TV set.
(Pause) Is it less bright now?
ED: Yes. There is the table. There is another thing in the
ceiling. It's silver. The table is silver. There are some
bumps. There's bumps on it. Looks like a serial
number. (The video camera records that I began to
trace the symbols in the air as I looked at them in
my mind.) Looks like a serial number.
DR. O: Is there more?

Again I outlined the symbols with my finger and described them in detail. Dr. Overlade asked me to remember
the symbols so that I could draw them at a later time. The
symbols or "letters" have since been studied by Budd
Hopkins and he found them to be identical in style to symbols described by other UFO witnesses who also experienced similar alien contact. The release of these symbols
has been withheld so they can continue to be used as a
control. Obviously abductees who report seeing the same
conditions in a small pie-shaped room should be taken seriously; but if they also report the same symbols, then
there is no doubt that we witnessed the same abductors.

ED: The guy with the white hair came in.
DR. O: Was he there before?
ED: No.

The video shows my breathing rate and anxiety level increased as I focused on the being that was now with me in the small room. He was no longer accompanied by the three shielded creatures.

DR. O: Does he speak?
ED: (The recliner's footrest collapsed under a sudden muscle reflex that contorted my legs.) I was hit.
DR. O: Say again.
ED: I was hit! (Showing great distress) Oh shit!
DR. O: How were you hit?
ED: From the ceiling. He was by himself. I can get him . . .

Here the audio recording of the videotape recorded very soft mumbling as I was recounting the moments just prior to being hit by a blue beam that froze my movement. This was the same sensation, smell, and helplessness I had encountered on November 11, 1987, when I took the first photographs of the UFO and was lifted off the street by the blue beam.

My intentions were to rush over and grab the being but as that idea came to me, the instant before I could react, I was struck by the blue beam.

ED: I ran, I ran . . . no I tried to run. I didn't make it. I tried to grab him but as I tried to leap, I was hit. I don't know what happened, all of a sudden I was sitting on the table. The beam was coming from the ceiling.

I had been stopped by the beam and somehow moved to the table and could clearly see the beam shooting from the half globe at the center of the ceiling. I could feel my arms and legs but I could not move them against the force of the blue light. My panicky reflexes were cause for Dr. Overlade to again reassure me.

DR. O: Open your eyes, it's 1988. You are safe.

In a half-aware twilight, I could hear Dr. Overlade's voice but within seconds I faded back into the trance and back into the small room where I lay helplessly on the side of the table, and the being had control of my body.

ED: It's in my throat.
DR. O: What's in your throat, Ed?
ED: Awful taste, a burning sweet ammonia in the blue beam. They're sticking something on my head. It's hard. It's on my neck. It's hard on my head. The blue is gone but this thing is on my head. (Rapid breathing) I don't want it on my head. (Louder) I don't want it on my head! Get this off of my head. Take it off me! (Louder) Get it off me!

Again, Dr. Overlade tried to help me through the moment that I was experiencing and I heard him.

DR. O: 1988 you are safe. (Pause) What is the nature of this "thing" besides being hard?
ED: Clamped to my head, it's a head thing. There is another one connected about three feet away . . . can't touch it. They got a critter. There's a critter. They're setting him in there. There is something red, something red going up. There's visions in my mind.
DR. O: Can you describe some of the visions?

Dr. Overlade was surely having difficulty following my rapid, nondescriptive utterances when even I could not understand what was happening to me.

A device, much like an audio headset, was clamped over my head and pressed hard onto my temples. Another clamp held me tightly from between my eyes and across the top of my head to the base of my neck.

The blue beam had disappeared and I had struggled to free myself. The more I pulled away the tighter the clamps held, as I watched a single file of nonshielded beings pass before me and stand in a row with their backs to the outer curving wall.

Each being was about four feet tall and wore battleship gray bodysuits that so closely matched the color of their skin as to make it very difficult to tell where the suits stopped and necks and hands began. They stood in uniform stillness, each holding yet another being closely wrapped within its arms so that the smaller being almost disappeared.

There were twelve beings waiting in line and watching me. Their eyes were intense and yet uncaring. The small beings were also untouched by my futile attempts to escape the headgear. They seemed neutral and unaffected by the disturbance I was creating.

As if on cue, one of the small beings was held out and a matching headgear closed over its head. A brilliant red light throbbed from the connecting rod that joined the headgear devices. My mind was suddenly awash with memories, and I began to relive vivid, joyful, and distressing events of my life.

First, I began to laugh. The joy was so real that I could feel the tears of laughter streaming down my cheeks. Every second that I reexperienced was exactly the way it had happened, a memory of myself when I was twenty-nine years old and living in Costa Rica, Central America.

Frances and I had taken a gamble and purchased a coffee plantation several years before. After a lot of hard work, we had succeeded in the coffee business beyond our expectations. While on my hands and knees arranging some orchids to put in Frances's flower garden, our children had surprised me with the "tickle attack." The kids loved this game which was just that, a sneak attack that always resulted in our rolling around in breathless laughter. If I appeared to be escaping, sometimes Frances would join in. The uninhibited tangle of our arms and legs added to the laughter.

I knew that I was actually sitting in Dr. Overlade's office but every sensation caused me ecstatic laughter, enjoying the sparkle in the eyes of my children. Dr. Overlade must have been puzzled to see me laughing, almost out of control. His voice pushed into the memory.

DR. O: Can you describe what is happening?
ED: They are making me remember.
DR. O: What are they making you remember?
ED: Playing with the kids.
DR. O: Is the device still locked on your head?
ED: Yes.
DR. O: How old are you?
ED: Twenty-nine.
DR. O: You seemed to have jumped from seventeen into something else. Did you know that you made a transition?
ED: Yes.

I didn't try to give Dr. Overlade a more thorough answer. Switching from the abduction at seventeen to the one at forty-one, then adding in the memories from other ages that I was recalling, made what was going on in my mind too confusing to try to explain.

DR. O: I missed it. What happened next?
ED: I'm remembering all kinds of things. They're making me remember. And they've got this critter over there and he is staring at me. He's got this thing on his head and there is red stuff going up or coming down, I can't tell.
He's little, really little, tiny, maybe two feet tall. They are carrying him. There is another one. This one is different. This one has lighter skin. The next one is lighter gray. They are making me remember again. Doing the same thing.
DR. O: What is the same thing?
ED: They are making me remember all kinds of things.

Things with my children. Things with my wife. Things with my friends.

DR. O: What age are you now?

ED: Twenty-nine. Sometimes I'm younger. One after another they keep bringing the little critters. They keep making me remember. I remember when my father died.

The visions were rapid and took me on an emotional roller coaster ride. Each small being was, in turn, placed in the headgear and the memories were suddenly replaying. From the joy of my children and the love of my wife to the death of my father, I was forced to reexperience the feelings as each critter was attached and a red surge of light rushed through the connecting rod.

It was impossible to resist. My senses filled me with the reality of a memory with Frances. I was only vaguely aware of sitting in Dr. Overlade's office. I could feel cool mud squeeze between my toes. Cold springwater rushed from the partly completed pipeline I had been building to supply water to our house site in Costa Rica.

For our evening showers we hand-carried water up to the twenty-foot travel trailer we had parked on the edge of a mountain plateau that we called home. The daily five-hundred-foot climb had become an exhausting chore. Finally we decided that hard-earned water would be saved for cooking and the children's baths. So, with soap and towels in hand, Frances and I made our way to the spring.

Standing naked on the side of the mountain, under the cold splash of the springwater, we took our showers. Frances was modest, so I reminded her that the only ones that could see her were the birds and me, but she didn't have to worry about the birds. She splashed a handful of water in my face and jumped behind a big-leafed tropical plant. The long, dark hair covering her shoulders accented her taunting pose.

I watched her movements behind the leaves and slowly moved closer to her. She laughed and playfully pushed my arms when I reached for her. My feet slipped on the slick ground and down I went into the muddy ditch carved out by the spring. Frances laughed and started to climb up the mountainside, knowing that I was surely going to chase her.

She wasn't very fast in her escape. The mud on my body soon covered us both as we shared a moment of passion. This loving memory with Frances was followed by vivid recall of two other events that also evoked strong feelings in me.

In the flick of an instant the images changed to that of my dying stepfather. His death wasn't sudden, but rather an inescapable result of his battle with emphysema. My family had watched this six-foot-two-inch, barrel-chested, happy-go-lucky man wilt before our eyes. It took over five years for the inevitable to happen. This man, James H. Hanson, had literally taken the place of my natural father, who died when I was a baby. He taught me a great deal that was very important. My pride in being his "son" was indescribable and I felt the loss deeply.

For reasons unknown to me, I was being forced to relive experiences in my life which involved intense emotion. Those emotions were relived over and over in exact sequence, including a memory that reached back into my youth.

I was twelve years old and participating in the school science fair, where each student was required to present a project. I had chosen to make a telescope. After working for weeks on mounting the concave mirror in a cardboard tube, painting and building a tripod stand, I felt confident my project would win. Each detail was polished and I beamed with pride as I presented my work to be displayed at the fair.

The admitting judge looked over my project and asked me, "Who built this telescope?"

I smiled with pleasure and said, "I did."

After the judge had a quick meeting with some other teachers, I was disqualified from the fair and told that projects obviously built by an adult were not allowed entry. At first I cried and tried to defend myself but to no avail.

Later, in the still of that night, while lying in bed I began to smile. I had won and I knew it. My pride swelled, even though my accomplishment hadn't been recognized. I learned a lesson that day that has stayed with me to this one: knowing you have done a job well is the only reward that really matters.

I can only speculate on what these events have in common, and in what the beings were interested. Deeply moving memories that were relived by me and repeated in the same order as each small being was placed in the headgear is very suggestive of a study of emotions. But what if it is more than a study? Maybe the small beings were actually experiencing those emotions vicariously. Were they learning from those feelings, perhaps actually absorbing those emotions?

If these small beings are devoid of emotions, for whatever reason, then I suggest that they purposefully prompted the emotional recall of these four events. The emotion of joy and parental contact was clear during the "tickle attack," followed by the depth of my love for Frances. Grief at my father's death and pride in myself were clearly the other obvious emotions.

So, there we have four different feelings perhaps unique to humans, Joy, Love, Grief, and Pride. Much of this speculation seemed to be appropriate, and the regressive hypnosis continued to reveal more and more pieces of the puzzle.

The deep, heavy breathing of the hypnotic trance was pronounced and partly covered my words as I continued.

Ed: Over and over and over. There are twelve of them.
Dr. O: There are twelve of what?
Ed: Little critters.
Dr. O: Twelve little critters.
Ed: The white-haired guy put his head in there. (Referring to the headgear) He's telling me something. No matter what, I will not remember what he is saying. And if I do try to remember what he is saying ...

I grabbed my chest and yelled in pain. A violent vision burst into my head. My heart was exploding from my chest. I could see myself crumple to the floor with blood pouring from a disgusting pulp of flesh and bones protruding from my body. The white-haired being had revealed something to me and then blocked its recall with the threat of this petrifying vision.

The videotape shows Dr. Overlade jumping backward in his chair. He quickly recovered and began to reassure me. My skin tone was pale and I shivered in fear. Dr. Overlade's words calmed me and, still in the trance, I suddenly moved forward to the end of that May 1 experience.

ED: I'm on the beach. My head hurts and I'm on the beach.

The cool beach sand gritted on my face and I filled my lungs with fresh air. I had been returned to the beach just twenty feet from the SRS camera.

Frances's Account

Ed returned from his appointment with Dr. Overlade in a state of near exhaustion. By the time he finished sharing what he had learned under hypnosis, I understood why. The UFO encounters we had experienced so recently had been a strain, both physically and emotionally, for our family. But the greatest effect had been on Ed. Now, with the UFO apparently out of our lives, I had hoped for a return to normalcy, hoped that the hypnosis would allow us, especially Ed, to finally understand what had happened, and why.

Looking at his drawn face, listening to revelations that seemed even more bizarre than anything I could have imagined, I doubted that was how it would be. I also found myself once again questioning the wisdom of our decision to pursue the hypnosis. Instead of helping Ed, this first session seemed to have left him upset and with more questions he couldn't answer.

And there was more to consider here than just Ed. After lengthy discussion, we had agreed that Dannie and Laura would be told as much as they wanted to know about what their father learned during his sessions with Dr. Overlade. It had seemed right at the time. Now I wasn't sure how our children would handle this new information.

Ed continued telling me about his recollections. When he described the creatures' hands, I felt myself go cold. I knew those hands, those fingers. A feeling of helplessness to protect my children overwhelmed me as if the events I suddenly recalled had occurred only minutes, rather than months, before. With no need for hypnosis, my mind jumped back in time.

"Mom, Becca and I are going over to Mirka's." Laura's voice preceded her into the kitchen.

Her close friend, Becca—who so resembled Laura from the back that Dannie had once shoved her into the pool by mistake—followed Laura into the room. Both girls dumped their cups and paper plates into the trash and headed for the door leading to the dining room.

"Just be home before dark. And if you leave Mirka's to go somewhere else, let me know." It was my standard speech and I often wondered if Laura even listened.

"Mom!"

At the sound of Laura's panicked scream, I dropped my sandwich and ran for the dining room. Both girls met me before I reached the doorway. Two pair of arms circled my waist. Gathering the girls in a protective embrace, I looked down at them.

"What's the matter?"

Eyes wide, they glanced over their shoulders, then back up at me.

"There's bony fingers hanging over the edge of the roof."

"Bony fingers?" I asked. Only the genuine fear in Laura's voice kept me from laughing.

"Yes. Four of 'em. We saw 'em through the window." Becca pointed toward the dining room.

"Okay. Let's go see." Not for a minute did I believe the girls had seen fingers, bony or otherwise. But I knew nothing short of a thorough investigation would satisfy these two.

Untangling myself from their grip, I led the way into the dining room. The vertical blinds were drawn back to each side of the window, leaving the four-foot center pane clear and unobstructed. Nothing extended over the edge of the roof past the eave. Seeing that, both girls stepped from behind me and walked over to the window.

"They were right there." Laura pointed to an area roughly at the center of the window.

"Yep." Becca nodded in agreement.

"Well, nothing's there now. It was probably some pine twigs hung up in the gutter. They either fell off or blew onto the roof."

"Let's go check." The words were hardly out of Laura's mouth before both girls dashed for the front door.

I hurried behind them. A quick look up at the roof revealed nothing there. Nor were there any twigs, or anything else the girls could have mistaken for fingers, on the ground. Convinced that whatever they had seen had fallen into the rain gutter, I climbed onto the decorative brick wall to check.

"Well?" they asked as one.

"Nothing here." My answer wiped the curiosity from their faces. Fear returned. Anxious to reassure them, I offered the only explanation I could think of. "I bet it was a big gray heron perched on the gutter with his toes hanging down."

For a moment I feared the girls understood the long-legged bird's anatomy too well to believe me. Then, with an "oh" in unison, they turned and sprinted across the street toward Mirka's house. I stood staring at the eave of my house. No heron had been the source of what the girls saw. The bird would need toes at least a foot long. But I didn't believe they'd seen any "bony fingers" either. Convinced the culprit was pine twigs that had somehow blown away, I put the episode out of my mind and went back inside.

Several days later I sat at the breakfast bar. With the kids still in bed and Ed already gone to a job site, I sipped my coffee and leisurely read the local newspaper. Lifting the right-hand page to see an article better, I caught a glimpse of something through the half-glass in the door three feet from me. Four thin, dark "fingers" protruded over the edge of the eave. I did a double take. There was nothing there. But the image was firmly in my mind.

Suddenly wishing Ed was still home, I eased off the stool and crossed to the door. Now only three feet from the overhanging eave, I saw nothing out of the ordinary. But the "fingers" *had* been there. Part of me wanted to go outside and investigate more closely. Part of me wanted to stay safely behind locked doors. I went outside.

My search of the roof, rain gutter, and pool deck was as fruitless as the day I had looked with Laura and Becca. There were no pine twigs, heron's feet, or anything else which could have been what I saw. Still seeking a logical explanation, I went back inside and sat down where I had been before.

Maybe a few loose strands of my dark hair had somehow fooled me. I tried leaning forward just a bit and glancing out of the corner of my eye. The dark streaks I saw ran the full length of the glass in the door. No way could I have mistaken my hair for four, bony fingers.

The calm, quiet I enjoyed before the kids got up and general chaos invaded the house had been destroyed. I dumped the rest of my coffee in the sink and went to our bedroom to dress. When Ed came home, I'd tell him about it. But I wouldn't tell Laura. She seemed to have forgotten her incident. I wanted to keep it that way.

Later, when Ed got home, I was sitting in the kitchen with Dannie and his friend Hank. Laura was at Becca's and so I started to tell Ed about what I'd seen, reminding him of what the girls had told me only days earlier.

"Whoa, this is spooky. You people have the weirdest things happen to you." Hank, more like another son than a family friend, leaned back in his chair and stared at me.

"Wait'll you hear this." Dannie had gotten up and now stood between his father's stool and mine. "I didn't say anything about this because I thought it would scare Laura. But a week or so before she saw her 'fingers,' I saw them."

"What!" Ed, Hank, and I all spoke at once.

Dannie went on to tell us what had happened. He'd driven his car into the garage one afternoon. As he always did before he punched the garage door closer on his sun visor, he checked behind him to be sure his car had cleared the doorway and there was nothing else in the way.

"I saw these four, dark, skinny fingerlike things hanging down over the eave. Nobody was home, and later I just forgot about it. Then, when you told me about Laura and Becca, I knew I wasn't seeing things. But there didn't seem to be any point in upsetting everybody. So I kept quiet. But, now, with Mom seeing 'em too." He shrugged. "I just don't know."

None of us did. Sometime later I mentioned it to Don Ware. He asked me if I could draw what I'd seen. I managed to sketch the "fingers" well enough to be satisfied with how they looked. But it wasn't until Ed told me about the entity he'd seen under hypnosis that I felt I might have the answer to what I, and the children, had seen. When he drew the entity, one hand resting in the crook of its other arm, I knew.

Somehow, for some reason, four of us had seen those same fingers, but under totally different circumstances than what Ed had experienced. Had an entity perched on my roof on three separate occasions? I doubted it. But I couldn't say it wasn't possible. Was what we saw some sort of telepathic projection we'd all received for some unknown reason? I couldn't rule that out either. All I knew for certain was that this was just one more bizarre event in the series.

CHAPTER 10

THE ROADSIDE INCIDENT—
AGE 25

Before undergoing hypnosis, when various investigators would ask me whether or not I could remember any strange events or odd, unexplainable experiences in past years, I could only answer with rationalizations. The memories were there, but I had always denied they could be anything but dreams, exhaustion, or heatstroke. After my UFO encounter on May 1, I finally had to admit to myself there was more to these incidents.

Dr. Overlade and I discussed several such unusual events, events that are now recognized as missing-time encounters. The following is my conscious recall, prior to hypnosis, of one of those experiences.

When I was twenty-five years old, I had been married for two years, and Frances and I had a one-year-old son. As with most young couples trying to get ahead, we worked hard. I worked as an architectural draftsman, welcoming all the overtime I could get. We had invested our entire savings in an older apartment building near the beach, and renovations were taking every extra penny we could earn.

One day the chief architect asked me to go with him after work to meet a client and take notes on a proposed building design. Not knowing how late I would be, I called Frances to tell her I wouldn't be home for dinner. The meeting went on and on, finally breaking up about eleven o'clock. I was anxious to get home, and since it was only a thirty-minute drive, I left quickly without calling Frances again.

Halfway home I noticed something strange about the darkness behind me. As I passed a streetlight, or a roadside building, I could see it go by, but it didn't show in the rearview mirror. Both the inside and the outside mirrors were black.

I turned my head and glanced back. Again, all I could see was blackness. It was as if a huge black blanket was blocking out the sight of everything behind me. I shook my head, rubbed my eyes, and stepped on the gas. The engine revved, but the car gradually slowed down. I steered to the right, coasting to a stop on the shoulder of the road.

What the hell! I looked down at the gearshift. It was in neutral. How had I done that? I decided I was more tired than I had realized. What I needed was to stretch my legs for a minute, make sure I was awake, then drive home. I stepped out of the car, confident everything would look normal.

I looked to the front first. Everything was as it should have been. Then I looked behind me. The darkness was gone. I shook my head. Some trick of the light had to have made my mirrors seem dark.

Way down the road I could see a single light, like the headlight of a motorcycle, only brighter. Faster and closer it came, then it rose above the road. I jumped into the car, locking the doors as I started the engine. I fishtailed back onto the pavement and looked in the rearview mirror. The light was gone. The darkness was back.

Racing down the road in panic, I could again see the blackness obscure everything I passed. Maybe it *was* a trick of the light. I rolled down the window and stuck my head out for an unobstructed look.

Less than ten feet behind me was a black, rippling wave that blocked all vision. It seemed just to hang there, shimmering, veiling everything. The hair on my left arm stood straight up. The air was heavy with a burning smell.

I turned back around. As I rolled the window up, the car's right front tire went off the road. I slowed and struggled to maintain control, carefully steering back onto the roadway. When I glanced back again, the darkness was gone.

Once more, a single light approached from the rear. It raced toward me, and I feared it would run me down. I pressed harder on the gas pedal, hoping to outrun it. In seconds it grew to the size of an airport spotlight, flooding the interior of the car with light.

Six hours later, sitting behind the wheel of the car on the roadside, I seemed to awaken with no memory of those lost hours.

Dr. Overlade listened intently to my conscious recall of this odd event. His voice calm and deliberate, he asked a few questions.

DR. O: I would invite you to allow your hands to rest separately on the chair arms. (Pause) Recall for me which digit indicates "yes" . . . and "no" . . . and "I don't want to answer." (Pause) You told me about an experience at age twenty-five involving a bright light approaching your car.

ED: Yes, that was when I was going home from work late one night and ended up asleep in my car the next morning.

DR. O: Conscious recollection was interrupted after seeing the light?

ED: Yes, I just remember waking, and sitting behind the steering wheel.

DR. O: As I am understanding then, there is a lapse of several hours. About what time did this happen?

ED: (Pause) About twelve midnight to 5:00 A.M.

DR. O: Midnight to 5:00 A.M.?

ED: Five-ten.

DR. O: Five-ten A.M.?

ED: Yes.

Dr. Overlade encouraged me to relax and under his instruction I entered a deep trance.

Dr. O: I'm going to be addressing your unconscious now by your hand and digital signals. I would like to ask your hand . . . (Dr. Overlade interrupted himself, mentioning a calming instruction to the strong muscle reflexing.) Be aware of those movements. (Pause) I would like to ask your hand to get back into those unconscious archives and to review below consciousness those events that might have filled the time between twelve o'clock and five-ten, signaling your entrance into this review below consciousness by movement of the "yes" digit.

My mind had begun to open and flashes of memory touched my body. A warmth began to pour over me that suddenly turned rancid. An odor rushing into my nostrils made me jerk. Dr. Overlade's voice slammed closed the corridor of memories with his directions.

Dr. O: You don't need to reexperience it. (A direction prompted by my body movement) Simply review it below consciousness, signaling your entrance into that review by movement of the "yes" digit. At the conclusion of that review below consciousness, signal by a movement of the "no" digit. Now this—(Dr. Overlade was interrupted by my "yes" signal.) Thank you. Begun.
This can be a highly accelerated review, you can just kind of zip through those five hours and ten minutes, signaling an end of the review by a movement of the "no" digit.

Mentally, I was resting quietly and I was only vaguely aware of the disquieted movement of my body. I seemed to be reacting to events that my muscles could remember but my intellect could not. The below conscious recall continued.

DR. O: Simply be aware of any feelings, sensations, or
movements that might occur between the two signals, without reliving it. Without actually
reexperiencing it. Okay. (Pause) Begun and . . .
(short pause) . . . concluded. (Dr. Overlade noted
the rapid signals of "yes" and "no" indicating my
subconscious was reviewing the missing time.)
Review it again using the same signals. Begun
and . . . (short pause) . . . concluded; excellent.
Again . . . begun and . . . concluded. Yet again
please. (Pause) And again. When you review
again, attend to the identification of any beings
significantly a part of this scene besides Ed himself.

My rapid muscle twitching signaled a hidden disturbance that concerned Dr. Overlade. He reassured me
again.

DR. O: You are in 1988. You are not in any danger.
Nothing bad is happening to you, or about to
happen. You are safe here in 1988. (Pause)
(Watching my hand for the "yes"—"no," signals,
Dr. Overlade acknowledged.) . . . Begun . . . Concluded. Again please, attending to any words that
are significantly a part of that scene, spoken or
unspoken. Begun . . . (pause) . . . concluded.

Dr. Overlade had managed to reach into my subconscious. My body reacted and my left hand spoke to him
without my conscious awareness of its decision.

DR. O: In the interest, hand, of his insight and edification
about these matters, would it be all right for him
consciously to recall that which you have been
reviewing below consciousness? Not, do you

think it possible, but do you think it will be all right?

ED: (The index finger moved in a "yes" answer.)

DR. O: Yes. (Dr. Overlade acknowledged.) Emphasizing that he does not need to reexperience it but only to recall it, perhaps as if he were sitting in a theater watching the scene on a screen and somehow disassociated from the Ed seated in the theater to an Ed up in the projection booth where he could stop the action if he wanted to. With that twice removed dissociation, tell me what you can see on the screen. (Very long pause) Tell me what you are experiencing. Even if it does not make sense to you just now. What are you feeling, sensing?

ED: (Very labored) I smell something that stinks.

DR. O: Something that stinks?

ED: I'm lying on a floor. The floor stinks.

DR. O: The floor stinks. Can you describe the odor?

ED: It smells like urine.

DR. O: Like urine, and—?

ED: I'm getting up and a light came on.

DR. O: The light . . .

ED: The room is now light . . . a small room . . . rough walls . . . The walls are sand . . . sandy . . . real light.

DR. O: What is the source of the light from your vantage point?

ED: (Slight head movement, appearing to look around) There are no light bulbs.

My head was reeling and I was confused. This small angular room smelled, smelled like a cage, and a muted hollowness echoed back at me as I cried out. There was a thickness to the air that was hard to breathe. I was trapped in what felt like a tomb, a tomb with sandpaper walls that scraped my hands as I frantically felt for a way out. The light seemed to come from nowhere and cast no shadow. I yelled into the wall, "Let me out of here!" I flinched backward and heard Dr. Overlade's voice.

Dr. O: What is that experience, Ed?

Ed: A door opened up. A door . . . a part of the wall just slid open . . . I hear . . .

Dr. O: You hear something?

Ed: I'm in a hallway. There is something behind this wall. I hear kids crying behind this wall. (Motions that seem to indicate great distress)

Dr. O: What are you experiencing now?

Sliding my back along the wall, I eased into the hallway. Shaped like a tunnel with a flat bottom, the hallway's smooth porcelain-like walls curved out of sight. I could have reached up and touched the very top if I had wanted to but my attention was focused on the crying. I moved closer to the sound that came from beyond the wall in front of me.

My head darted back and forth as I tried to watch each direction down the curving hallway. Every beat of my heart throbbed so hard that I could feel my chest move. What the hell was going on? This had to be a dream! I shook my head. "Wake up," I whispered, afraid to speak up.

I sank to the floor and noticed it was rough, like the walls in the angular room. The distant, muted crying continued while I felt for an edge or a crack that might be a sign of a passageway. I scraped with my fingernails and then with a coin from my pocket. Panic almost consumed me but I concentrated on the crying.

Ed: The wall opened. There are two children. They're standing there crying. (Pause) It's okay. (Speaking to the children)

Dr. O: Say again?

Ed: It's okay . . . It's okay . . . It'll be all right. (Again speaking to the children)

Dr. O: What will be all right?

Ed: It's okay.

Dr. O: What is it that's okay, Ed?

ED: The children ... It's all right. (Tears were beginning to roll down my face.)

DR. O: (In a concerned tone) See it on the screen. Watch Ed watching it on the screen. Stop the action when you want to. You are in charge of the projector and you can stop it if you choose. Are the children still present? Can you describe the children?

ED: A boy and a girl ... they are crying.

DR. O: They're crying. And ... ?

ED: They're scared.

They were standing in the center of the small room—an exact replica of the foul-smelling room that I had left moments ago. They held on to each other and leaned back as they saw me and I them. The boy was perhaps eight years old and the girl a year or so younger. I held out my right hand and signaled them to come to me. I wanted them to move out of the room so I would not have to enter, but they didn't and so I had to go into the room with them.

ED: I can help them. (Speaking quietly and tearfully)

DR. O: You can help them. (Dr. Overlade often repeated my soft-spoken words. I was to learn later that he employed this technique to encourage me to continue without asking me potentially "leading" questions.)

ED: They're so scared. (Softly)

DR. O: Say again.

ED: They're so scared. (Tears running down my face)

DR. O: How old does the boy appear to be?

ED: Maybe eight.

DR. O: And the girl?

ED: A little younger, maybe seven.

My physical reactions were recorded on the videotape and show a continued flinching and jerking reaction to the physical events flooding my senses.

* * *

I was kneeling next to the terrified children. Their trembling fingers pressed around my wrist and forearm. The little girl held her face close to my shoulder, her tears running onto the sleeve of my short-sleeved shirt. The boy was nervous and kept looking at the walls around us. I wanted to calm them but my mouth was dry and I was afraid the words would show my fear. I tried to hide my panic by pulling them close to me.

The opening to the hall was still there. I wanted to get out of the room so I nudged them forward and stood up behind them. My head almost touched a small silver bowl that curved from the center of the ceiling. I instinctively knew that this half-a-soccer-ball–size bowl was more than just a decoration. Outside in the tunnel-shaped hall there were more of these odd ceiling-mounted bowls spaced equally, at about every twenty-five feet. We had to follow the tunnel, but in which direction?

I tried to whisper and my voice cracked, "Come on, this way."

Instantly, the hall was awash with a red glow. To our right an opening had appeared in the wall. I couldn't believe my eyes. I yelled, grabbed the kids by the arms and ran.

The videotape shows a violent muscle reaction to which Dr. Overlade quickly responds.

DR. O: What's happening now?
ED: We're in the hall.
DR. O: You and the children?
ED: Yes.
DR. O: Tell me what you are seeing, hearing, feeling, experiencing.
ED: We're running.
DR. O: You and the children are running?
ED: There's three ... lizards! ... Coming out of the room.
DR. O: Three what?

Ed: Lizards!

Dr. O: Say again.

Ed: Three lizards.

Dr. O: (Pause) Are these children known to you? Are they familiar?

Ed: No.

Dr. O: Are you still running?

The little girl could not keep up and I was dragging her by the arm while in a full sprint. I glanced back and could see only the curve of the tunnel disappear into the same bright lighting that was also ahead of us. Without losing stride I released my grip on the boy's arm and snatched the girl up onto my right hip, then reached out for the boy, who was now slightly ahead of me.

Confused thoughts swirled in my mind and I yelled out, "This can't be!" My chest heaved and I struggled to inhale the thick air. It was heavy, as if laden with an invisible additive. I began to slow while the boy ran on farther ahead, so much so that the girl called to him.

"Gary, wait for us."

I let the girl slide down to the floor so she could catch up to Gary, who was apparently her brother. They both looked back at me but I motioned them on. Alone, I listened and watched the curve for any sign that we were being followed. Bracing myself by leaning forward and holding my knees, I waited, gasping for breath. My eyes watered and I squinted to shield them from the brightness.

I had only gotten a quick look at what was coming out of the red glow but I was sure it was lizards. There had been no mistaking the sight of that huge lizard head swaggering into sight from around the wall opening (see drawing G). Lizards, three of the biggest lizards possible. At least ten feet from nose to tail, there was no confusion about it. They were not alligators or crocodiles. They were lizards.

I stared into the light. A slight movement broke the edge of the inside line of the curving walls. Into my view again came a side-to-side rocking movement of the nose, head, and then the torso of a gray-colored throwback to the dinosaurs. It stolidly rounded the curve and dominated the center of the tunnel. Two more swaggering nightmares flanked it on either side, each with its forked tongue licking the air. They moved with a slow but deliberate plodding gait—fast enough to reach me in a minute or so. The children were far out of my sight around the opposite curve.

I had no idea how to stop these creatures, so I began to yell, "Hey, go on! Get!" It was much like trying to shoo away a stray dog.

Their march continued, now only thirty feet or so from me. I wanted to run but my only open direction led them toward the children. If I could dodge past the lizards to one side, maybe they would turn back after me. There was slightly more room to the right between the arching wall and the rear lizard.

I swallowed hard, took a deep breath, then moved quickly a few steps forward and to the left while flailing my arms. Again, I yelled, "Hey you bastards!" Only now I hoped they would move even more to the left and open a wider passage for me to the right.

As the distance closed, with only about ten feet separating me from the first stalking giant, they seemed to be easing to the left. I jerked to the left, planted my foot and bolted to the right. I passed the first lizard, hit the tunnel wall, tripped, and fell next to its tail. At the same time the flanking creature suddenly raised up and stood on its hind legs only a lunge from me.

The leader turned back and I scrambled over its tail. Off I careened, back down the hallway tunnel, in the same direction as the children. I rounded the curve and to my surprise they were standing there, not crying as before, only staring at me in frozen indecision.

With an effort I managed to gasp, "Run . . . don't stop . . . run."

They sped away but I couldn't keep up. My energy spent, I slowed to a stop. I slid my right hand along the wall to help keep me from falling. The children had stopped ahead of me and I could now see why. The tunnel was closed off.

A wall filled the hall completely from side to side. It was the same type of porcelain material and again I could see no seams or openings. Two containers sat before the wall, each with thick sides exposed by the open tops. About three feet high and two feet in diameter, each container and its top looked like a large, heavy-duty version of a kitchen garbage can, the type that has a pop-up lid.

My mind struggled for answers. Where was I? What about these kids? What the hell could I do now? There were only a few moments left before the lizards would be here. The children looked at me in silence from the corner behind the closest container.

Maybe the lizards had stopped. I eased twenty or thirty feet back down the hall and watched for any movement. "Damn, damn! Shit! Damn!" I yelled when I saw the outline of the first lizard break into view. I leaped back to the children and knew we had to use the containers.

Ed: (A panicky whisper) Get in there.
Dr. O: Get in there? Are you saying, "Get in there"?
Ed: Yes.
Dr. O: Are you instructing the children?
Ed: Yes.

I lifted the boy and set him in the round opening of the container. He seemed to understand and no words were spoken. He wedged himself down and pulled down his sister as I wove her legs and small body in on top of her brother. Hurriedly but carefully I pushed the lid down. It wouldn't close! There was no way; her shoulder and back pushed the top ajar.

Ed: (Showing a panicky display, reacting to the extreme stress)
Dr. O: What's happening?

ED: (Voice cracking in panic) They're coming down the hall.

DR. O: The lizards are coming down the hall?

ED: (My voice was full of terror and panic mixed with frenzied confusion and I breathed out . . .) "We're gonna die . . . we're gonna die."

DR. O: (Reassuring and calm) But you did not die. This is 1988 and you survived whatever this was. (For the first time, Dr. Overlade's reassurance had no effect.)

Realization slammed into me. Somebody was going to die. Two containers and three people left no other answer. My heart pounded and my instincts screamed, *No, no, no! This can't be. I don't want to die.* Somebody had to sacrifice. I wanted to hide in the safety of the container. The lizards were now only yards away when I looked back over my shoulder.

The grotesque trio struck terror deep inside me. The horror of being eaten alive by lizards overwhelmed me and I jumped into the empty container. I started to close the lid . . . I couldn't. Only seconds remained. In a blur I was out, dropped the girl in, and slammed the tops down.

ED: (Uncontrolled hyperventilation brought on by wrenching fear)

DR. O: Stop the action for a moment. Stop the projector. You can open your eyes. Interrupt it, then go back when you are ready. Open—see 1988. Dan's office. You are okay. You're okay. Perfectly safe. (Pause) What is the sensation?

(Dr. Overlade's voice calmed me for a moment but my memory raced on.)

* * *

I fell back into the outside corner behind the containers. I was trapped. I stripped off my knit pullover shirt and unbuckled my belt. Yanking it free, I swung it in front of me.

The lead lizard thrust its jaws at me. I was lucky enough to force my shirt over its head, leaving it tossing wildly back and forth, confused and unable to see. Its flanking companions closed the gap. Disregarding the pelting from my belt and buckle, one raised up on its rear legs. It lunged down toward me.

ED: (Deep breathing, pause, holding both arms over upper abdomen)

DR. O: Tell me about your upper abdomen. What is it you are sensing there?

ED: The lizard was about to tear into my stomach.

The lead lizard's teeth inches from my exposed chest, time suddenly stopped. Each lizard was frozen in mid-action. Three transparent blue beams split the air and enveloped the lizards. The split-second flash of an immense power saved me. I was both thankful and angry. My eyes followed the beams back to the ceiling, where they seemed to begin a few inches outside the closest ceiling-mounted "bowl" about fifteen feet away.

ED: The lizards ... they are frozen. They're frozen.

DR. O: All three of the lizards are immobilized?

ED: Yes.

DR. O: What transpires?

ED: (Shakes with a shocking, jolting reaction to Dr. Overlade's question)

DR. O: Watch it on the screen. The lizards are immobilized. You and the children are safe.

ED: It's very cold. I went through where the wall opened.

DR. O: And?

ED: There is a creature. It's different.

DR. O: What are you seeing now?
ED: It's cold.

I had been squeezing my body into the corner of the hall. The wall behind me opened and I fell backward, away from the now rigid jaws and lifeless stare of the lizards' eyes. I stumbled against an icy cold wall.

DR. O: And then what happened?
ED: She said, "Sit down." I asked her what was going on.

A female creature was alone in the room, another angular room with slick walls but occupied by a long narrow table or bench. She did not react to my excitement but I suddenly heard a sound in my head. Calm and easy, the thought "Sit down" was spoken to me. I was anxious and stuttered the question, "What's going on?"

ED: She says she is one . . .
DR. O: She says she is what?
ED: One of the thirteen.
DR. O: Does that have meaning to you?

At the time this reference to thirteen meant nothing, and the last hypnotic memory regression with Dr. Overlade only suggested possibilities. Now, after months of study, it is inescapable for me not to conclude that she is referring to the earlier encounters which involved the head device and the small beings.

DR. O: What else do you learn from her?
ED: She wants me to sit down. She seems to be nice. I can still see the lizards outside the wall.
DR. O: You can see what?

ED: The lizards.

DR. O: The lizards, immobilized still?

ED: They are being moved.

DR. O: Being moved in what manner? What is causing their movement?

ED: The blue beams are moving them. They're moving out of my view. She wants me to sit down. I sat down against the wall.

My anger, resentment, and confusion were tempered and I felt some appreciation that the blue beam had saved me. I wanted to talk, to understand. Her eyes were large and reminded me of those paintings, popular a few years ago, of big-eyed children. I was not threatened by her nor did she seem concerned that I might harm her. We were alone except for the bowl device mounted in the ceiling.

ED: I asked her where the children are. I can't hear them anymore. She said they are safe. She said she was going to put something on my head. The walls feel cold. There's another one coming in the room.

DR. O: Another?

ED: Critter. He's got my shirt. He gives me my shirt. I put my shirt on. She touches my chest. She says, "You will remember . . . You will remember."

DR. O: What is it you are to remember?

ED: No . . . (Slight physical reaction) She put this thing on my head. She said, "Don't struggle. Sit calmly and remember." (Pause) Bringing in little ones. They're bringing in little ones. A whole bunch of little ones.

DR. O: How many would you say?

ED: (Pause) There's ten of them.

I had not resisted the instructions. I was now sitting on the side of the table with a type of clamp pressing firmly on my temples, forehead, and over the back of my head.

A matching headgear hung three feet from me on a connecting rod. It interfered with my view of the line of gray beings filing into the room. Each being carried a small being, possibly an infant. They looked lifeless and still, with each gray being holding an infant wrapped in a tangle of skinny arms and close to its body.

DR. O: The apparent age of the little ones?

ED: Small with big heads, they're small, really skinny necks.

DR. O: You said they are bringing in some little ones. They?

ED: More critters.

DR. O: The one that brought you your shirt and others?

ED: Yes.

DR. O: And how are they bringing the little ones in?

ED: Carrying them.

DR. O: Are ten big ones carrying ten little ones?

ED: Yes, the big ones are different from the little ones.

DR. O: In what respect?

ED: They are dark, their arms are long. The little ones get lighter. (A reference to the line of little ones getting lighter skinned from the beginning of the line to the end)

DR. O: What is their purpose in bringing the little ones in?

ED: They are putting them in the headset. There is a head thing on my head. They put them in and it turns red.

DR. O: What turns red?

ED: The rod.

DR. O: The rod? What rod is that?

ED: Between the headset, there is a rod from out of the ceiling to the rod that goes from here to over there.

DR. O: There is one rod?

ED: There are two rods, one coming down into the second rod like an upside-down T, with a headset at each end of the bottom of the rod. They put the little critter in the headset.

DR. O: So that the whole contrivance accommodates two of the little critters?

ED: One, just me and one critter.

DR. O: And there is a cross-member at the end of the rod and at one end of that there is a headset for the little critter?

ED: Yes.

DR. O: And what's at the other end of the cross-member? You?

ED: Me.

DR. O: Okay, so the vertical part of the "T" goes up to?

ED: I'll draw it for you.

DR. O: You may do that later. You will remember so that you can draw it.

ED: (Physical reaction to a memory being relived)

DR. O: What's that experience Ed? What is the sensation?

ED: I'm with my friends.

DR. O: This is a memory?

ED: Yes. This rod thing is making me remember. One after one they're putting critters in there.

DR. O: And do you have the same memories over and over?

ED: For each critter, yes.

DR. O: You have to replay it each time then?

ED: Yes, I remember laughing with my friends. Laughing so hard . . . so hard . . .

Vivid memories were being awakened in me. So clear were the sensations that I began to cry with laughter as I recalled how my friends and I howled, held our stomachs, and rolled with laughter at the joke just played. I was nineteen and cruising our local drive-in hangout on a Saturday night. Several of my friends and their girls were already there when I arrived. The word was passed that we should all meet back at our secret place.

"Our place" was actually in an off-limits, closed-down duplex housing complex patrolled by the Navy. With abandoned duplex apartment houses as far as you could see, we thought there was no harm in sneaking into one, blacking out the windows, bolting the doors from the inside, and making our own secret entrance through a small hole that was cut into the unit next door. There was no electricity, so we used candles. You had to know exactly where the candles were to find them because it was so dark, so absolutely black, that you could not see your hand in front of your face. And therein lay the joke.

I arrived ten minutes or so ahead of my friends and parked farther across the highway than normal. They wouldn't see my car and suspect that I was already waiting for them. I took the candles and matches and waited in the dark. Then they arrived and, during the half hour that followed, had no idea that I was standing near them in the dark making lunatic sounds that scared them into a frightened huddle.

The funniest part of it all was that they (two guys and two girls) were holding my arms while thinking they were holding each other. When I finally lighted a candle and everyone saw what had happened, the moment exploded in laughter. This was one of the most hilarious thirty minutes of my life.

The visions evoked by this headgear were all events that had actually happened. Events that I rarely thought of but, nonetheless, events that were deeply etched in my memory. The joy of that laughter moved me to tears, followed by another memory that filled me with sadness.

My love and passion for my wife was next as this roller coaster of emotions washed through me, then a feeling of pride. Finally a replay of the lizards struck terror in my heart as I prepared to sacrifice my life for the children. Over and over these emotions surged through me while the small infantlike critters were, one at a time, clamped in the opposite headgear.

DR. O: And as you are in this fashion connected to the critters, can you tell of any response in them?

ED: No.

DR. O: No noticeable response?

ED: They stare at you.

DR. O: Now I would like to ask you to fast-forward this experience a little bit, to learn how it is that you leave that situation and return to your car.

With Dr. Overlade's instruction to move forward, the brightly lighted room faded away. I had no recall of being returned to my car but I could feel myself resting against the inside edge of the driver's door.

DR. O: After you are disconnected from the headset, what's happening? (Long pause) Tell me what you see. What's taking place now?

ED: I am sleeping.

DR. O: Are you back in your car?

ED: Yes.

DR. O: I want you to assume that it is approaching 5:10 A.M. You are going to be able to remember after you awaken this time what transpired where before you had a gap in time. I want you to begin to bring yourself back to here and now. Count backward mentally from five to one, discovering at the count of one that you can feel very rested, refreshed, and relaxed, as if you have had quite a substantial nap, and able to become once again fully alert and awake without regenerating unnecessary tensions.

ED: (Moderate pause, followed by some movement and stretching and eye opening)

DR. O: Tell me how you feel.

ED: (Deep breath with a quiet pause, looking around the room in orientation) I feel all right . . . I feel very . . . I feel good.

DR. O: You have dislodged some more memories, dreams, or whatever. You can feel more unburdened about things that seemed so mysterious.

ED: The lizards.

DR. O: What do you make of that?

ED: When I was in the rod, on my head, it made me re-
member this incident when I was nineteen years old.
Extremely funny. Just, roll on the floor, funny.
Laugh so hard your teeth hurt.

And then they made me remember when my brother
inadvertently hit—purely by accident—hit a cat with
a club. He was trying to smack a rat it was chasing
but he hit the cat. I was real small. And he killed the
cat. My brother was crushed that he had killed the
cat and I was devastated that he had killed this cat.
And for some reason, they made me remember that
whole thing, the awful feeling I had that the cat was
dead.

And then I was with my wife, making love. And after that I was back in high school. There was this big
event that I organized called Powder Blue Day. It
was a protest against a school dress code. I was a bit
of a rebel, so I organized a protest called PB Day.
All of us, or as many people as I could persuade,
protested the dress code by wearing powder blue
shirts. Pretty mild compared to today when they
would wear no shirts at all. (Laughter)

DR. O: This is one of those memories that was
prompted?

ED: Yes. I was very pleased with myself. That was one
of the forced memories. And then, (pause) your
question was, about the lizards. Having just experienced the terror of the lizards, amazingly enough,
the whole thing with the lizards was replayed. And
the fear that so overwhelmed me was that I was
about to die. I could have saved myself by sacrific-
ing one of those children

DR. O: Do you recognize some similarities between today's regression and the prior ones?

ED: Yes. They forced me to remember different times in
my life but the only memory that was the same was
lovemaking with my wife.

DR. O: But again, a wide spectrum of emotions.

ED: Yeah. The lizards were awful. I don't think they
were a dream or a vision. You know how they seem

to be able to put a vision in your head? I think those two children were there. I believe those three lizards were there. I believe they did that to scare the hell out of me or something. Especially, when it came so close to my stomach. I shoved my shirt over its head.

DR. O: How long or tall are the lizards?

ED: Big!

DR. O: You said big, but I did not know if that meant six feet or sixty.

ED: Well, the hallway I was in was not as tall as this room (eight feet), maybe seven feet. And they stood up. They had huge tails, not necessarily hugely long, but big fat tails. They had me in a corner. One was shaking his head, getting the shirt off, the other two rose up. The blue beam stopped them, and then that corner where I was standing slid open. Maybe a ten-foot wall and half of it slid open, which is where I saw the female.

DR. O: There was one question I did want to ask you. You identified the gender of these two critters in that room very quickly. What was the clue to gender on the female? Was she clothed?

ED: Huh ... Maybe a subtle indication of breasts, but it is strongly in my mind that she was a female.

DR. O: The second critter you immediately identified as male, you said, "He came in." What's your clue there? Do they have hair?

ED: The female had some fluffy white hair. Very soft.

DR. O: Ears?

ED: Very, very small ears.

DR. O: Mouth?

ED: Skinny, kind of like a hole but some shadowy contours around it.

DR. O: I had the impression when she was talking to you, reassuring you, that she was speaking and you were hearing her with your ears, rather than something telepathic such as you have suggested at other times.

ED: Never did they open their mouths to speak.

Dr. O: You were hearing inside your head. She invites you, instructs you, or maybe even pressed you to sit down. On what is it you were sitting?

Ed: A box-looking seat with its back right up against a wall that was cold, and as I touched it with my back, I had the feeling that I would stick to it.

    When all ten of them were standing there, the female also, there was a definite hum about them. Just an ever so subtle hum. It wasn't there before they came in.

Dr. O: And is that hum at all reminiscent of the sounds that you heard? Or is it distinctly different?

Ed: I never heard it before.

Dr. O: This event we believe to have occurred at age twenty-five. Geographically where was that?

Ed: On Beach Boulevard.

Dr. O: Well, to wrap up, what else do you want to reflect on?

Ed: The headgear device was not as traumatic as it was during the May 1, 1988, incident. I did not at the time—having just been saved by the blue beam from the lizards—I was not quite as belligerent. So when she said, "Sit down," there was a certain air of politeness there. They brought me my shirt. It was a little nicer type of thing and I didn't want to offend them because they had just helped me.

Dr. O: It occurs that you may be answering my earlier question of, what do you surmise was the purpose of the lizards?

Ed: Possibly, or the immediate recall of that for these little critters to experience terror of the choice to give up your life for somebody else. You can't get more emotional than that.

Dr. O: Maybe you will reflect on this later. It seems there is a quest for emotions about parenting and saving the children yourself was an emotion about parenting.

Ed: There was a nuance in the telepathic message, "the news must learn."

Dr. O: Also observe that you said that the intensity of

this event was less than the one at age forty-one. Possibly you are desensitizing and can get into these memories without reliving great emotion.

ED: Or the incident on May 1 was so recent.

DR. O: Okay, it's 10:47 A.M., August 16, 1988.

Later that night Frances and I sat together and played the videotape of this regression. My agonized hypnotic reactions, so clearly recorded, prompted a rush of memories and I turned my head, half in denial, half in fear. Again I could see the eyes of the children. I could feel their small fingers squeezing my arm. Frances held me closer while tears filled her eyes.

The videotape repeated my answers to Dr. Overlade's questions but there were unspoken memories. The feel of the gritty wall, the smell of the heavy-laden air, the panic of certain death, were captured not on the videotape but in my very being. As the tape recounted minute by minute, second by second the hypnosis, my body went numb. I could feel it; there was more to be uncovered.

On August 29, 1988, I would join Dr. Overlade again and once more he would jar open my subconscious memories.

Frances's Account

With each new session Ed had with Dr. Overlade, he answered some old questions and raised new ones. We both felt that what he was learning was important. We just wished we understood it better. But even more than those answers, I wished I had an explanation for the strange events taking place in our house. Although none of us saw any more "fingers," there were other things.

One morning I was in our bedroom changing out of my nightgown when I heard the distinct sucking sound of our front door opening, followed by the magnetic click as it closed. Thinking Ed had returned for something he'd forgotten, I called to him. No answer.

If Ed hadn't opened the door, who had? Dannie had left

early to go to the beach with his girlfriend. Laura had spent the night with Becca. If it had been either of them coming in, they would have answered my call to their father. Cautiously I eased through the house to check the front door. It was locked and dead-bolted.

Telling myself not to let my imagination and some commonplace sound spook me, I returned to my bedroom and finished dressing. When Ed came home for lunch, I told him about my mysterious door sounds. He assured me it was probably just the air conditioner coming on. Somehow, from our bedroom, it had sounded different than it usually did.

I gladly accepted his explanation. Bony fingers hanging over the house eave were enough weirdness for me. I didn't want to add a front door that somehow opened and closed while it was locked. But what I wanted and what I got, were not the same. The door sounds continued. Not every day, and sometimes several times a day. And it didn't matter where in the house I was, it sounded the same. Before long I had learned to recognize the sound of the air conditioner kicking on. It didn't sound like the front door opening and closing.

Neither Ed nor I told Dannie or Laura about the mysterious door sounds. Since neither of them had mentioned it, we assumed they either hadn't heard it, or didn't think anything of it. Then one night Ed and I came home late. Dannie met us at the entrance to the living room armed with a baseball bat. He had heard the door open and close, but when he checked it out, he found it locked. Just as I had.

Only partly reassured by my verification that I'd heard this same thing myself, he went on to tell us about other things he'd experienced recently.

"A lot of times when I wake up in the morning, my watch has been moved."

"You mean like you bumped it during the night?" Ed asked.

Dannie shook his head. "No, I mean moved. It's not the way I left it. Sometimes it's turned kind of sideways. Other times it's lying partly on top of a book. Like somebody picked it up and when they put it back down, they didn't do it right."

Ed shrugged. "You probably did it yourself, or just forgot how you'd laid it out."

"Mom." Dannie looked at me with his "you-explain-it-to-him" expression he always got when he felt like what he had to say just wasn't getting through to his father.

"Honey, you know how Dannie is. Everything important to him has 'its place.' "

Dannie had begun his habit to make the morning rush to get ready for school easier. Then he discovered a side benefit. He could tell if Laura or any of her friends had been in the room and moved anything. He had gotten so good that he could tell me what I had moved when I cleaned his room. If he said his watch had been moved, I believed him. So did Ed, and he wasn't happy.

Over the next few weeks what Ed, Dannie, and I referred to as "the weirdness" continued. Finally Laura asked why she would hear the door open and close when no one had gone in or out. By then I had seen shadowy figures seeming to dart from the living room sometimes when I would get up to check on the children at night.

All of this added to the strain caused by reporters, debunkers, investigators, and the continuing hypnosis sessions. Although we had built our house with the intention of staying in it until Laura graduated from high school, we seriously began to consider moving. By the time Dannie left for college in late August the decision had been made. His trip home at Christmas would be to a new house.

CHAPTER 11

THE INTERRUPTED CANOE TRIP—AGE 33

The next suspicious event to be covered with Dr. Overlade was a canoe trip in Texas. Before undergoing hypnosis, I discussed in detail with Dr. Overlade what I consciously remembered.

I was thirty-three years old when we had recently returned from living in Costa Rica and set up housekeeping in Corpus Christi. In need of a day of relaxation and privacy, I went out on a solo fishing/canoeing trip, hoping to catch a fish or two.

The wildlife along the coastal barrier islands was spectacular. I thought I should have taken a camera instead of a fishing pole. The water cut cleanly beneath the bow of the canoe as I slowly passed hundreds of brown pelicans nesting in and around the trees of the protected islands. The waterway I was in was deep, about fifty feet, and quite often I could see porpoises breaking the surface of the water.

At about noon I was drifting with the current and decided to see what Frances had fixed for my lunch. As I reached into the bag, the bottom of the canoe hit something, then was suddenly still, as if I had run aground. But the sound was like metal on metal. Before I could lift my paddle, the canoe drifted free and continued on.

I looked back, but saw nothing in the clear water that could have snagged me. Turning around, I saw a stream of bubbles stretched out in front of the canoe, racing ahead of me. My attention was no longer on the banana nut bread in my hand, but was glued to the strange bubbles. This was no porpoise.

Only thirty feet away I could make out a green glow beneath the water. Very big and getting bigger. I tried to backpaddle. The current carried me forward, closer to whatever was rising ahead of me.

Suddenly, and with no memory of what had happened, I found myself sprawled in the bottom of the motionless canoe. I looked up to find I was beached near the mouth of the channel, miles from where I had last been. A barge passed by into the Gulf. My food had flies on it, and my watch read five o'clock.

The five hours of missing time was in itself unusual but when related to the odd circumstances of the underwater glowing "object" it was certainly suspect.

DR. O: Okay, do you think there are any other bits of memory that you haven't recorded just now?
ED: No.

When this happened to me, so many years ago, I had convinced myself I had suffered a heatstroke. Now that I knew better, I was ready to uncover whatever more I could under hypnosis.

DR. O: Okay, I think it would be appropriate now if you would continue to relax. (Pause) Recall for me which digit of your left hand signals "yes." Okay. (Noticing a flick of my index finger) Which is "no?" . . . Okay. (Noticing the thumb movement) And, "I don't want to answer." (As before, my little finger moved.) (Pause) Consider the desirability of becoming as deeply relaxed in the next twenty breaths as if you had begun to relax twenty minutes ago.

Dr. Overlade encouraged me to fall into the heavy peaceful trance, his presence calming, reassuring.

DR. O: As soon as it would be all right for me to have conversation with your unconscious mind via your left hand, the "yes" digit will jump. (Pause about two minutes)

Be aware of bodily movements. (Pause) Hand, it will not be required that he relive or reexperience anything. I would like to communicate with you now about the time lapse. And, if it would make it easier, safer, or more permissible, it is quite all right for him, at some level, to see these actions on a screen. And to be in a projection booth watching himself in a theater watching the screen. And as soon as it would be all right to communicate, the "yes" digit will jump.

ED: (Pause . . . heavy breathing, followed by a quick reflex of my index finger)

DR. O: Hand, now I would like to ask you to go back into the unconscious archives and there to review below consciousness the events that transpired between the time of opening the banana nut bread and regaining awareness—signaling your entrance into that review by movement of the "yes" digit and conclusion of that review by movement of the "no" digit. Real time is not required; this can be a highly accelerated review below consciousness.

ED: (Pause . . . followed by a rapid movement of the "yes" and then the "no" digits)

DR. O: Thank you; again please.

ED: (Pause . . . with another "yes" . . . "no" movement)

DR. O: Again please and attend to any words spoken or unspoken. Okay, thank you. Hand, now in the interest of understanding, would it be all right to recall consciously that which you have reviewed unconsciously? (Pause . . . without a "yes" or "no" response)

Okay, please review yet again below consciousness. Thank you, there is no need to reexperience; you can interrupt at any time. You are safe and under control. You can stop the action. Now, hand, you can view this as if it were happening to somebody else, as if you are watching yourself watch it on a screen. Would it be all right to review this same scene consciously?

Dr. Overlade was persistent in his efforts to break into my hidden memories and, as his voice hung over me, I began to feel the movement of the canoe. I had the sensation of my mind gently rolling back on itself as if from one consciousness to another and the horizon above the canoe's bow focused picture perfect to my memory.

My canoe paddle stroked the emerald green water with droplets falling on my legs as I cross-paddled in the tidal current. A glint of sunlight sparkled and danced in a drop of perspiration that clung to my right eyelash. My headband was soaked from the sweltering exertion of repetitive paddling as I guided the canoe quietly between the nesting islands of the brown pelicans and pink spoonbills. I felt small and almost invisible in comparison with this panorama of nature around me.

Crossing the ship channel, I headed for a cluster of trees at the water's edge, near one of the closer island sanctuaries. Their trunks were bent, twisted, and pointed to the west from the unrelenting coastal wind. In a battle with erosion their roots arched into the water like huge spider legs holding firm to the shifting beach sand.

At midchannel, and only several hundred yards from my tree-shaded resting place, I let the current push me. I was hungry and could already taste the banana nut bread that Frances had packed in my lunch. I had pulled open my lunch bag when the canoe bottom scraped on something, something that sounded like metal.

DR. O: Tell me what you see. You can speak without
        otherwise disturbing your relaxation. (Pause) Ed,
        are you in the canoe?

ED: Yes.

Dr. Overlade's voice pushed into my mind and raced my
memory forward. I didn't mention the stream of bubbles
that churned the water and seemed to block my path.

DR. O: And you have opened your lunch?

ED: Yes. (Pause . . . distressed breathing) There is a tube
     sticking out of the water.

DR. O: There's a what?

ED: There's a tube. It's glowing.

DR. O: Describe the size of the tube.

ED: About . . . maybe . . . maybe a foot . . . sticking high
     above the water.

DR. O: A foot in diameter?

ED: Yes.

DR. O: About how high out of the water?

ED: Higher than my head.

DR. O: And at what distance from you do you perceive
        this tube?

ED: In front of the canoe about twenty feet from me,
     maybe five or six feet from the front of the canoe.

DR. O: And is this tube cylindrical?

ED: Yes. It's glowing.

DR. O: It's glowing.

ED: Yes.

DR. O: What else can you tell me? (Pause)

A stillness fell over the water. As if a vacuum had
sucked the motion from everything around me, nothing
moved. The wind felt hollow and my breath echoed back
into my face. A flight of pelicans to my left seemed frozen
in a starched white sky. The emerald green water was suddenly sterile and bleached colorless. My canoe no longer

moved with the current, and the wind-driven chop of the water was now mirror-glass flat. A white glowing sheen surrounded the tube that surely caused this disturbance. Only a few seconds had passed before I started to fall.

ED: Something white . . . something white hit me. It hit my head. (Pause)

DR. O: And then?

ED: I think it came from the tube.

DR. O: And then? (Pause) . . . (Noticing a grimace, Dr. Overlade reassured.) You can interrupt it at any time you need to. It's not happening now.

I began to realize that I was lying on my back staring up at a sloping angular ceiling. I thought, this has to be a dream but the reality of the almost choking lack of air and the bright ceiling structure slammed into my consciousness. I bolted upright and was shocked to be face-to-face with something, someone. I reflexed backward with a brilliant flash of white light flooding my eyes. I tried to open them again and felt something pressing on my cheek.

ED: (In a whisper) There's somebody touching me.

DR. O: Say again.

ED: There's somebody touching me!

DR. O: Somebody touching you and—?

ED: It's so bright.

DR. O: Where are you being touched?

ED: On my chest, on my neck, and on my cheek.

DR. O: Describe how the touch feels.

ED: Very gentle, very soft. There's a person, there's two, there's two people. They're not really people.

As my vision once again cleared, I saw a figure standing to each side of me. This moment is frozen in my memory. The female to my left and a male to my right looked down toward my face. They did not move except for a slight forward and backward rocking motion. Their eyes commanded my attention and I looked back and forth between them. Their eyes were dark, navy blue and very large, surrounded by crescent white rings. I could see no sign of eyelids (see drawing E). The female was touching me and I started to recoil and push her away but I did not.

ED: What are you doing? (Pause showing uneven breathing)

DR. O: What are you experiencing?

ED: There's a female standing here on my side and there is a male standing here.

DR. O: Tell me how you distinguish their gender?

ED: I don't know. (Pause) Very small breasts and she acts like a female.

DR. O: What's your posture in this room just now?

ED: I'm lying down flat.

DR. O: On your back?

ED: Yes.

DR. O: So the female is to your left and the male is to your right?

ED: Yes. (Strong muscle reflex)

DR. O: What's happening?

ED: She's touching me and I ask her, who are they? Who are you? What are you doing? She said, "He is of the thirteen."

DR. O: He is . . . ?

ED: Of the thirteen.

DR. O: Of the thirteen. Okay.

ED: And he is of my code.

DR. O: He is of your code?

ED: Yes.

DR. O: Does that have meaning to you?

ED: No.

This reference to thirteen has since been correlated with the memories that I had recalled from my sleep. (Later detailed in Chapter 14)

The male figure was not threatening and his manner seemed familiar to me. Even more astonishing was my passive compliance by allowing the female to softly touch my chest and face. I was not repulsed or fearful and my curiosity was piqued.

ED: She says that she knows my spirit. She knows my fear. She knows my will. He is of my code. She is of my spirit.
DR. O: She is of your spirit? Is that what you said?
ED: Yes.

These two figures were unemotional, yet penetrating with their presence. Somehow I knew them, and their touch did not offend me. With the exception of their eyes and the complete lack of hair, their features were almost human. Each had very small ears, a nose much like that of a baby, and a hint of thin lips. At no time did I see their mouths move as they spoke to me. Her words were clear and she spoke to me with thoughts.

She said that she knew my spirit, my fear and my will. Was this because she could read my mind or was she, too, from my past? Could she have been one of the small, infantlike beings who had been connected to me with that strange rod? Did she know my spirit because she shared my emotions?

ED: She said my spirit is old and I know this is true.
DR. O: Is it she or you that says this is true, about the age of your spirit?
ED: She says.
DR. O: Does that have meaning to you?
ED: No. She said I can remember. She said it is true, I know, and that I can remember.
DR. O: She says you can remember?
ED: Yes.
DR. O: What is it that you can remember?

ED: I don't know. (Pause) She keeps touching me. (Pause) She keeps touching me.

With each stroke of her fingers on my forehead images started to form. These visions may have been an illusion invented by my captors, but in startling detail I began to feel and live an experience completely foreign to me. I was on a horse and I knew its name. The hat on my head was heavy with sweat and I looked down at my arms. They were cut, scratched, scarred and . . . black. I recognized nothing about this body yet knew every detail.

I could hear Dr. Overlade's voice and knew that I was safe and in his office, but the vivid detail of what I was reliving shocked my senses. I could feel, taste, and smell everything about this body that I sensed was, somehow, me.

I knew that the pain in my left buttock was the remains of a festering boil that I had cut open the night before. My left little finger had been cut off by Deacon Baker in front of a church congregation when I was twelve because I stole a chicken. The feelings of that memory were interrupted as my bedroll snagged on a branch, pulled open, and flopped over the side of the horse, Bayboy, who kept his slow, cautious gait over the rocks and against the thick brush that grabbed at us.

The images continued. Mixed with the sound of Dr. Overlade's questions about the female alien, I was completely absorbed with the feelings of this black man. Real or illusionary, I didn't know, but so graphic was the setting that I was completely swept away by what seemed to be reality.

I felt myself dismount, the thump of my empty canteen made me pull my dried lips open and curse at the clawing thickets that bloodied the horse's forequarters. I knew that somewhere ahead was a place called Twister Crossing, a river, if I could find it. I wrapped the blanket in a tight roll, tied it with a double knot, and strapped it to the saddle . . .

These images shot through my consciousness in exquisite detail. But I did not know if they were illusions or the real memories of the torment of a black man in the West, of killing or being killed. Real or not, my emotions were awash with the anger he had died with. The anger flowed from my eyes and edged down over my temples where the female being gently pressed her fingers into my tears.

Again she said, "You can remember." My mind was pushed open once more and flooded with images. Feelings and senses overwhelmed me and I knew that I was once again experiencing the astonishing reality or vision of another's life. The emotions of a person foreign to me took control of the moment and the images closed around me.

My right hand and forearm were suddenly bitterly cold. I pulled an empty trap from beneath a rain-swollen creek. Snow swirled around me, collecting on my frozen beard. The stench of this unknown body penetrated the layers of fur hides that fought off the cold.

My reflection in the creek revealed a deep scar on my face, a reminder of what had happened. My mother was white, my father a Cheyenne who had kidnapped her twenty years ago. I was conceived in rape, consumed by hatred, and lived for revenge . . .

The vision of this tormented life burned in me with vivid recall. These images of places unknown to me opened a curtain that death had closed, tightly concealing another life that may have gone before. But whose life and death was unclear. I had already experienced the aliens' ability to create graphic illusions when they had shown me Laura choking. Perhaps this was another example of their mental manipulation.

I felt the male being touch my right hand, drawing me once again into the reality of the brightly lighted room.

ED: The male is looking right into my eyes. He is very familiar. He touches my hand. (Pause) She asked me to get up and sit up.

DR. O: Are you sitting up now?

ED: Yes.

DR. O: And you are sitting on a . . . ?

ED: A table or something.

Dr. O: With your legs hanging down over the end?
Ed: Yes.
Dr. O: Look there at the end of the table and see if you
see anything distinguishing. (Pause)

The edge of the table was curved, with a polished gleam
that seemed to disappear into the brightness. I could see
nothing at the end of the table. A row of small gray figures, twelve feet away, posed at the far wall. They stood
as if they were mannequins, each holding a fragile, infantlike being.

Dr. O: Now what transpires?
Ed: She's touching my cheeks. Telling me to be still. Sit
still and remember. The male is different from the
others.
Dr. O: What others? Are there more than the male and
the female?
Ed: Yes.
Dr. O: How many others would you estimate?
Ed: (Pause) Twelve.
Dr. O: And what are they doing?
Ed: Just standing there with little ones in their arms.

Because of the similarity in events between an earlier
hypnosis session and this session, Dr. Overlade interrupted
to address my deeper unconscious memory.

Dr. O: I address this to you, hand. Hand, is what he is
recounting now, is this from the day with the canoe at Corpus Christi? There are some similarities obviously between this experience and the
one in Jacksonville. Is that correct? Okay. (He ac-
knowledges the "yes" digit reflex and continues
on.)
Dr. O: So the male is holding your hand and she is
touching your cheek . . .

ED: She is putting something on my head.

DR. O: Putting something on your head . . .

From above me, an odd, four-pronged device was lowered. Attached to a slender rod it looked somewhat like a
double audio headset but the tips fit over my head and
tightly pressed on my temples, on my forehead between
my eyes, and at the back of my head at the base of my
skull. I tried to jump up but I couldn't make my legs react.

ED: She says to be still. (Breathing heavily) I told her I
       didn't want this. I asked, who are you? She said,
       (pause) "I am of the thirteen."

I suspect and strongly suggest that this female was one
of the small beings that had been "emotionally linked" via
the headgear during an earlier event, possibly as early as
the incident when I was eleven.

ED: I asked, where do they come from? (Pause) She says
       she comes for the renewal. I said, where?

She passed her fingers over my forehead and I felt different. The bright, angled room faded as my mind flick-
ered with confusion and my stomach groaned. I was
different. Once again I was experiencing the life and consciousness of another person, but this time I was small and
afraid.

Through eyes unknown to me, I stood quietly next to a
burned out fire and watched dogs fight over the charred
remains of a human forearm. A rock hit near the dogs and
a familiar voice yelled out. I ran for some broken tree
limbs and looked down at myself. I was young, maybe
twelve years old, brown, barefoot, and skinny, with a tat-
tered cloth wrapped around my waist and between my

legs. I pulled at the edge of the cloth where it stuck to a chafing rash.

Somehow I knew that the village was dying. I could smell the morning breeze, sour with the smell of death carried on whiffs of parched smoke. Only a few others of my age were left and they too attended the fires. The sickness seemed to be everywhere. First, it would reach into you and tear at your stomach. That was its sign. My stomach groaned again and I was afraid ...

The visions of the black man, the half-breed, and the Indian boy are an absolute mystery to me. How they should be interpreted depends on your philosophical beliefs. How they are rationalized along with the UFO abduction phenomena, I will leave to others. But since they are a part of events I recalled while under hypnosis, I include them as possible real events but I also recognize that they may have been alien manipulations.

Dr. Overlade's voice unknowingly directed me back to the bright room with the small beings.

DR. O: What is happening now?

ED: They've got the thing on my head and I'm remembering.

DR. O: What are you remembering?

ED: I'm remembering Nicaragua. (Pause with visible stress) He's going to kill all those people ... all those children ... he's going to kill all those children.

DR. O: Is this a memory from your own history?

ED: Yes.

DR. O: Of what year?

ED: I was twenty-nine.

DR. O: Who was in power?

ED: Somoza.

The headgear glowed red and I stared into the eyes of a small, infantlike being. I could suddenly feel, smell, and touch a memory that welled up inside me with fear and sorrow. I was in Nicaragua on what turned out to be an unfortunate business trip.

The humble clapboard house that I was in sheltered three generations of the Diego family. The children were fascinated with me and laughed at my attempts to converse in my rudimentary Spanish.

The country was in turmoil, with daily skirmishes between the National Guard and the Sandinista revolutionaries. My luck, or lack of it, had placed me in an adjoining bedroom, on the way back from the toilet, when a Sandinista burst into the living room. He shouted Spanish that was so slang-ridden I only understood how desperate the moment was.

I stood frozen, feeling the fear of those captured helplessly in the other room. Through a crack in the curtain covering the doorway between the rooms, I saw the fourteen people huddled in the center of the floor.

Frantic, I looked around the cot-filled room. An open window offered me possible escape. A single-shot, bolt action .22 rifle lying partly covered on one of the cots held me there. A part of me shouted "run," there were surely other guerrillas close by who would hear the shot. But I couldn't just let these people be slaughtered.

I crept over to pick up the gun, then carefully crossed the room back to the doorway. The guerrilla was still shouting, waving his gun at the terrified people in the room. From my undiscovered location only fifteen feet from him I fought for control of my racing heart. I steadied the barrel of the rifle on the edge of the doorframe, aimed, and fired . . .

The rest of the incident in Nicaragua was not a part of this induced memory. Only the agonizing decision to shoot a man—so the children and others might be saved—was replayed over and over with the emotionless eyes of a fragile alien infant looking into mine. If it was absorbing my emotions, there was no sign.

Somehow these beings knew of the most powerfully emotional moments in my life and repeatedly jerked me from the depths of fear and sorrow to the heights of love and passion. From the uncontrolled joy of tear-soaked laughter to the rich inner glow of pride, I was forced to relive both emotionally wrenching and exquisite times of my life. All of this seemingly for the benefit of UFO beings who would not be denied. The emotions continued.

DR. O: (Observing a smile) Are you being tickled?
ED: No.
DR. O: What's happening?
ED: Taking a shower on the mountainside with my wife.
DR. O: Where and when is this memory?
ED: At our coffee farm in Costa Rica.
DR. O: And that would be about what year?
ED: Nineteen seventy-seven. (I had jumped forward in time, from one memory to another.)
DR. O: And then?
ED: I'm building a thermal syphoning water heater. Lots of people from the village are watching me work.
DR. O: This is still Costa Rica?
ED: They can't believe water is circulating uphill.

Surrounded by a circle of Costa Ricans, we splashed the hot water over our hands and flinched at the high temperature it had reached. A sense of satisfaction welled up in my chest and I smiled at the looks of amazement glued on the faces of the visitors from the village. Rumors of my solar water heating device had brought the curious to witness water circulate uphill without the aid of a pump.

It's a very simple principle of nature that hot water rises as long as you give it a path to flow. There was no mystery to it, but the local people were impressed so much that a few children laughed and called me *"gringo brujo"* (gringo witch).

I was happy to share with these new friends any and all information that might help them since most didn't have hot water heaters in their houses. Flattered by their smiles and laughter, I proudly demonstrated the simplicity of the system, hoping to encourage them to build one for themselves.

ED: They have no hot water.

DR. O: And then?

ED: (Pause) Caressing my wife, holding her close to me.

DR. O: And the next memory?

ED: (Stressful) They're going to kill the children. I have to stop him. If I can't stop him, they'll all die.

DR. O: Are you back in Nicaragua?

ED: Yes. If he hears me ... If he hears me ... he'll shoot. I have to stop him ... I have to stop him.

DR. O: Who is it that you have to stop?

ED: The guerrilla. (Rapid breathing and stress) He's going to kill them all. (Long pause)

DR. O: (Noticing another reflex) And this memory?

ED: I'm taking a shower.

DR. O: On the side of a mountain again?

ED: Yes.

DR. O: I can't tell if you are replaying these memories or if somebody is asking for replays.

ED: They're going over and over.

DR. O: Well, let's get to the last one and see if you can determine what happens after that. Is the device attached to your head attached to others?

ED: Yes.

DR. O: To the twelve.

ED: Yes.

DR. O: Is it attached to the twelve or to the ones that the twelve are holding?

ED: To the little ones.

DR. O: To the little ones that are being held?

ED: They stand them up ... they stand them up and put their heads into the headgear, and it turns red ... and when it turns red, I start to remember. And they do it again and again.

DR. O: And the little ones are held standing with their heads in the headgear?

ED: Yes, I don't think they can stand by themselves.

Gulf Breeze UFO witnesses assembled at the South Santa
Rosa Recreation Center on October 14, 1989 for
on-camera interviews.   *Photo by Duane Cook*

Photo 1. Taken on November 11, 1987, the UFO crossed over my Gulf Breeze neighborhood. Seven independent witnesses reported seeing the same UFO on that day. Notice that the tree blocks part of the UFO's image thus ruling out the possibility of simple trick photography.

Photo 11. On December 2, 1987, a small dark being fled from my backyard while the UFO hovered over the high school soccer field and shot a blue beam to the ground.

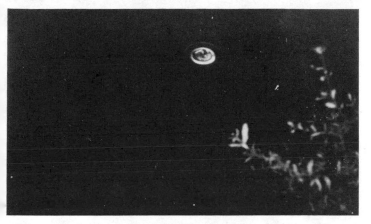

Photo 17. On December 17, 1987, Frances and I managed to take this photograph. We huddled beneath a small oak tree as the UFO passed overhead showing its bottom "power ring."

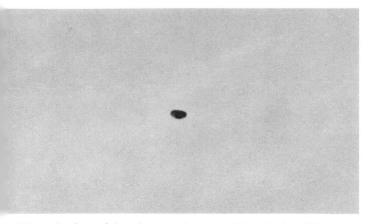

Photo A. One of the photographs sent with a blackmail letter to the U.S. Army and the media in an effort to gain the release of six soldiers arrested in Gulf Breeze.

Photo 38R. This is an enlargement of one of the photos taken with the SRS camera used to calibrate the size and distance of the UFO. The larger object is approximately 14 feet in diameter and 475 feet away. Notice the second smaller UFO in the upper right. This smaller UFO is called the "probe craft."

Photo 25. This is a super-enlargement of the "probe craft" that shows up in Photo 38R. Photographed with a 35mm stereo camera, it's size was confirmed and later reconfirmed with the stereo SRS camera. For the first time in history specialized stereo cameras were used to document the size and distance of UFOs.

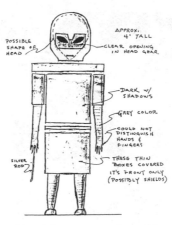

Drawing B. Under the clinical supervision of Dr. Overlade, hypnotic memory vividly retrieved the moment by moment recall of these beings with their silver rods. In unison, twelve of them circled around me on May 1, 1988. This was the same small shielded being that Frances and I saw on our back porch on December 2, 1987.

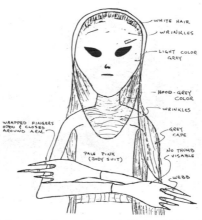

Drawing C. In early September 1988, Budd Hopkins asked me to draw the "principal" alien in as much detail as I could. Most peculiar to me were the hands that seemed to have no thumb. Budd confirmed the thumbless hand with a drawing documented ten years earlier by Leonard Stringfield.

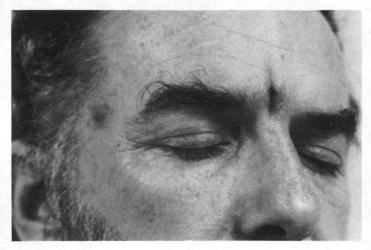

Photo D. This photo was taken several days after my struggle on the beach and the hour and fifteen minutes of "missing time." The red abrasion points and bruising on my temples and between my eyes happened during the "missing time."

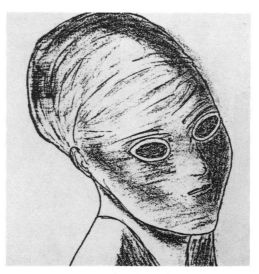

Drawing E. On my left the female "being" pressed her hand on my forehead and I began to remember...

Photo F. This 14-foot diameter circle of flattened grass remains unexplained. It was discovered in Shoreline Park where UFO sightings were frequent. The bottom ring of the UFO shown in Photo 38R is verified by the stereo camera to be 14 feet in diameter.

Drawing G. Close to me, the head of a huge lizard came into view from behind an opening in the wall. Slowly, deliberately, three of these swaggering giants headed toward me.

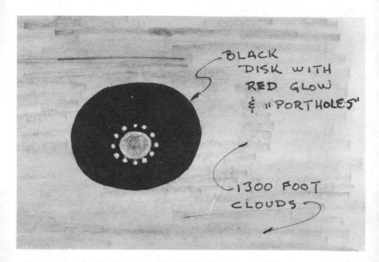

Drawing H. On January 8, 1990, Frances and I, along with a group of Gulf Breeze residents saw this flying disk for twenty minutes. Photographs *(see below)* were taken and increased the already overwhelming Gulf Breeze UFO evidence.

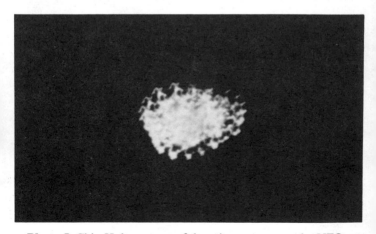

Photo I. Chip Holston, one of the witnesses to see the UFO on January 8, 1990, took this picture. Slightly blurred due to the movement of the UFO, it shows the red "power source" and a surrounding ring of lights. Minutes later, helicopters arrived in the area.

NOVEMBER 15 1991   THE ISLANDER NEWSPAPER

UFO Investigators Photograph Unidentified Object Over Beach

By Gary Watson

On November 5, an unidentified object was seen and photographed as it hovered over Gulf Breeze. A dozen witnesses and several MUFON (Mutual UFO Network) investigators saw the UFO from the south end of the Bay Bridge.

Photographs were taken by Patti Weatherford and Anne Morrison who used a 440mm lens and fast action 3200 ASA film to capture the image of the "crown" shaped object.

The object seen on this night is believed to be the same type UFO first reported by Ed Walters and scores of other witnesses in 1987. The configuration of "portholes" and the very bright bottom "power" light resembles the outline of the UFO that Ed Walters described in his best selling book "The Gulf Breeze Sightings."

The UFO sightings in Gulf Breeze have been occuring at a record pace since the first of the year, but recently the UFOs have displayed a variety of effects. Before the eyes of scores of people who gather nightly at the Bay Bridge, spectacular rings of lights have appeared from "out of thin air." These rings of light are made up of separate points of light that often hover making no sound and then suddenly vanish in a clear sky. Often the witnesses can see the structural shape of the object as it travels across the sky and blocks out the stars as it passes. This was the case with this latest sighting when one very skeptical witness looked through his binoculars and said, "Hold on here, I can see something black around it." Another witness, Bland Pugh said, "I could see a definite curved structural shape above the blazing red light at its bottom."

On November 5, 1991, Anne Morrison and Patti Weatherford took 21 photographs of the UFO when it appeared as a red ball of light and transformed into the crown-shaped "Gulf Breeze" UFO.

Photo K (top right). This photograph, taken by Patti, shows the bottom "power source," five center "portholes" and a top "beacon" light.

Photo J (bottom right). This photograph, taken by Anne moments after Photo K, shows the bottom "power source" and the top "beacon" light but only four center "portholes."

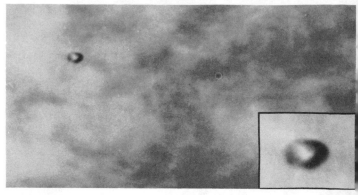

Photo L. Taken in Green Bay, Wisconsin, this UFO displays a blast from its "power ring." The enlargement *(inset)* shows that the clouds are overlaying the UFO which convinced me that the UFO was many thousand feet in elevation. Also, the "white balls of light" described by the witness can be seen shooting from the UFO.

Photo M. At 7:55 PM on September 12, 1989, I arrived at the Church where the meeting had begun. Toward the east, as I got out of my truck, I saw the now familiar red glow of the UFO. With my 110 Instamatic that I carry in my truck, I took two photos and ran to call others to come outside. Several dozen people rushed out into the parking lot to see the UFO ascending.

Photo N. This second photograph taken in Green Bay, Wisconsin, along with its enlargement *(inset)*, also shows the "energy ring" that the witness reported bursting from the UFO and rattling the windows of her house.

Photo N-1. This is the computer image analysis of Photo N verifying that there is no evidence of a hoax. The energy released from the UFO was scanned and outlined.

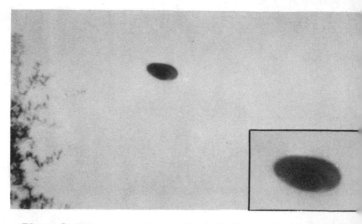

Photo O. Taken in Rochester, New York, on July 15, 1989, this UFO photo shows remarkable detail. The sighting resulted in four hours of "missing time" for the witnesses. In the enlargement *(inset)*, the "power ring," although not radiating its brilliant light, is very clear.

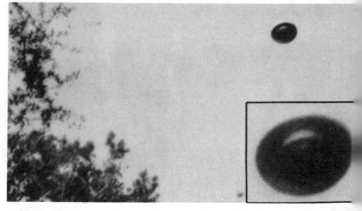

Photo P. Experts have tried to replicate this photo using the same type camera with a 1/3-second shutter speed. In every case, when a Frisbee-shaped object was tossed into the air, it was severely blurred. This object is only slightly blurred, even in the enlargement *(inset)*, indicating a slow hovering speed. The size ratio of the UFO image and the trees indicate that the object is large and distant.

Photo Q. Taken in South Bend, Indiana, on November 6, 1989, this UFO photo, and its enlargement *(inset)*, show a silver disk and the same type bottom "ring" that is documented in the Green Bay and Rochester photos.

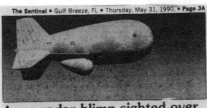

The Sentinel • Gulf Breeze, FL • Thursday, May 31, 1990, • Page 3A

Army radar blimp sighted over Pensacola Bay

A radar blimp like this one (above) can be seen in Pensacola Bay and, according to the Army, will be here for six weeks.

The U.S. Customs Service has several similar radar carrying blimps that track lowflying aircraft near the Mexican American border and over Puerto Rico. But Harry White, spokesman at NAS, said the ship pulling the blimp, Carlton Tide, is U.S. Army and is running sea trials. The Army released no information as to the mission of this special radar in our area.

In January 1988 the same type radar was deployed in Pensacola-/Gulf Breeze for over three months. At that time, George Roberts, Eglin Air Force Base public affairs, said the Army was conducting research. The attention as to the purpose of this special radar was in part due to the record set-

ting UFO sightings that had begun a month earlier. As the UFO sightings continued, 150 foot portable radar towers were deployed and also received local media attention.

In midApril 1990, reports, photographs and video tapes of UFOs flooded our area. Witnesses reported seeing helicopters and jets arrive within minutes at the locations of the sightings.

The UFO sighting reports have continued and we are now once again visited by a special radar blimp, the Carlton Tide. During and after each UFO sighting the Military denies having any aircraft in the area, even though dozens of witnesses have seen and even videotaped the UFO and the arrival of the helicopters and airplanes. The sightings continue but the military has "no comment."

Media attention focused on the continued UFO sightings, and on the deployment of radar blimps and portable radar towers that circled Gulf Breeze.

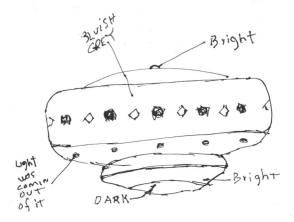

Drawing S. From Saudi Arabia, Abdur Rahman Ahmad said, "Here is my drawing of what I saw. It was beautiful!" The similarities between Mr. Ahmad's drawing and the UFO seen in Gulf Breeze *(see below)* are obvious.

Photo 19. Taken on January 12, 1988, in Gulf Breeze, this photo is an enlargement showing the UFO hovering above Soundside Drive in Gulf Breeze, Florida.

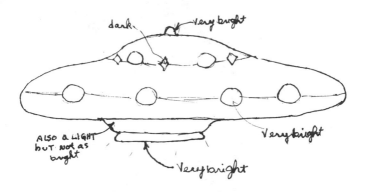

Drawing T. From Florence, South Carolina, Paul Garrett said, "Three years ago I saw this UFO flying close to my home. Just before dark, it came from beyond a patch of trees and disappeared behind some others."

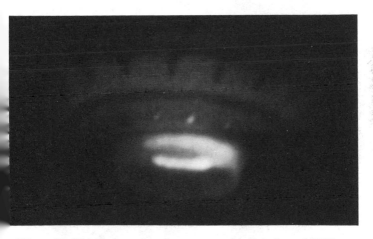

Photo 22. This is a super enlargement of a disk shaped UFO that I photographed on January 26, 1988. This type of glowing red "energy ring" is very common in the skies of Gulf Breeze and has been photographed by many witnesses.

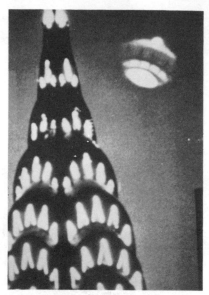

Photo U. This is an example of a debunker's hoax UFO photograph that was used to try and discredit the Gulf Breeze sightings.

Photo V. This is the 9-inch model that was used by an unknown prankster/debunker in an attempt to influence the news media.

They have skinny legs and a real skinny neck. They stare at you. (Pause) They left.

These four memories raced through my mind with vivid clarity and replayed precisely over and over as each small being was placed in the headgear. The memories, inducing the same emotions of sorrow, joy, pride, and love, could not be denied. The vacant stare of the "infant" showed through the red fluorescent-type, glowing haze that surrounded the connecting rod. That thin, broom handle–size rod apparently engaged the memories and possibly transferred the emotions.

The larger beings who held the infants also seemed oblivious to their task and moved their charges in a seemingly appointed routine. Soon, the final infant of the twelve, who had patiently waited its turn, was carried away. The other male followed, leaving only the original female standing close to me.

DR. O: Who left? The twelve?
ED: Yes.
DR. O: The twelve with the twelve little ones?
ED: Yes.
DR. O: And now who remains in the room?
ED: Just the female.
DR. O: The male has departed?
ED: Yes.
DR. O: And what happens now?
ED: She's touching me. (Pause)

The pressure on my temples eased while a curious whistle rang out, echoed, and then muted quickly as if it had come from the wall behind me. I turned my head away from the female . . . I was confused. I closed my eyes.

How I was returned to the canoe, I don't know. I only remember a sudden flood of sea air filling my lungs and the cry of the gulls that swarmed around a passing barge.

I raised my head from the canoe bottom. A slight rocking movement mixed with the grinding of sand against the hull.

I sat in the bottom of the canoe for a moment and looked around. The canoe was beached at the inlet to the bay, several miles from the nesting islands where I had been, it seemed, only moments before. My lunch had spilled from its bag and flies partly covered the banana nut bread. Over the side of the canoe, along the edge of the beach, were hundreds of undisturbed fiddler crabs, but no trace of footprints.

My head ached, I was stunned and talked aloud to myself. "How did this happen?" My only explanation was maybe I had suffered a heatstroke. I really didn't believe it, but I couldn't think of any more reasonable answer.

Darkness was closing in on the coast as I gathered my strength and paddled the canoe toward home.

Frances's Account

While Ed continued his sessions with Doctor Overlade, the media interest in the Gulf Breeze events raced on. Even though Ed was still keeping his identity from the public, hardly a day went by without Duane Cook at the *Sentinel* or one of the UFO investigators calling to relay another message from some reporter.

Most of the time Ed gave them permission to use the UFO photographs and agreed to be interviewed as long as they promised him anonymity. He also encouraged the reporters to talk with the other witnesses. Most of the time the reporters did talk with as many people as they could. But once in a while, even if they had done extensive interviews, the articles would have some inaccuracies, or worse, would be written tongue-in-cheek. It was hard for Ed to know when to say "yes" to an interview request.

One morning he came into my home office and I could tell by his expression he was debating something. "Honey, I just got off the phone with the people at 'Unsolved Mysteries.' They want to do a show about what's going on here in Gulf Breeze."

I stopped typing and looked at him. With newspaper, magazine, and radio interviews, it had been easy enough to keep his identity a secret. He simply refused to let them use his name or a photograph of him. But this was television he was talking about—the visual medium. How in the world could he talk to them without "going public"?

"What did you tell them?"

"That they can use our UFO photos as long as they focus on all the other witnesses."

"We wouldn't be on?" The thought terrified me. My heart pounded every time I had to give a report at a PTA meeting even after years of doing it.

"Nope." He shook his head. "We would talk to them off camera and go to the location shoots to be sure they got everything that happened right."

"Oh, okay." This I could handle. And it would be interesting to watch the film crew in action. "When are they coming?"

"Soon. They plan to use this early in the new season."

Before long the "Unsolved Mysteries" team arrived in town. For days they reenacted our sightings, as well as those of other witnesses, and conducted a multitude of interviews. The amount of video footage they shot was staggering. I wondered how they would ever edit all of those hours of film down into a twenty-minute segment for the show.

Finally it was time to shoot Robert Stack's introduction for the show. Dozens of witnesses gathered at the Pensacola Yacht Club for a day of filming. While the television crew set up cameras and lights, Robert Stack circulated through the ballroom talking with people, posing for photographs, and in general helping put everyone at ease.

Ed, Laura, and I were there. It was the first time we met most of the witnesses. One after another they shared what they had experienced. Jeff Thomas and his son told of seeing the UFO, describing exactly what we had seen, but in a daylight sighting. Listening to our fellow Gulf Breeze residents relate their own sightings and events was chilling yet at the same time we felt a bond with these people we hadn't known before.

Several weeks later it was the production crew for "UFO Cover-up Live" who were stringing cables and hoisting lights. They set up a Washington to Moscow to Gulf Breeze satellite link and invited local UFO witnesses to join in the live telecast from the Gulf Breeze auditorium. So many witnesses arrived for the show that they more than filled the auditorium. The television crew moved the overflow crowd to a separate large room with a big screen TV so they could watch the show. Since Ed and I were still withholding our names from the media, we watched the live telecast from the auditorium balcony, out of reach of the television cameras.

As we exited the auditorium after the show a Miami TV crew "ambushed" us. Ed had given them a lengthy interview earlier in the day after receiving their assurance that his identity would be protected. Whether it had been their intention all along to renege on their promise, I don't know. But caught in the glare of a handycam's spotlight, a microphone thrust in our faces, questions being shouted at us as we ran for our car, it didn't matter. Premeditated or not, we both found it an unnerving experience. We'd always been a bit leery of the news media. Now our opinion of the ethics of some reporters sank to rock bottom.

CHAPTER 12

MOVE AWAY FROM
THE HOUSE

December 1988
Frances's Account

Since our new house was only a few blocks away from our old one, we made the move in stages. Nonessentials were either moved first or left for later. Midway between Thanksgiving and Christmas we reached the point where we could finally spend the night in our new house. I called Dannie to let him know which house to come home to for Christmas and gave him our changed telephone numbers. They were all unlisted and I could just imagine how he'd feel if he tried to call and couldn't get through.

We hoped that moving would put an end to the "strangeness" we'd experienced in our old house but we avoided mentioning that reason for our move. Laura didn't like the fact we'd moved, no matter what the reason. She missed living so close to her friends. Hoping to make our new place seem more like home, I took the time to put up our Christmas tree and hang some other decorations, even though boxes still sat in every room waiting to be unpacked. Soon the spiciness of Christmas potpourri mingled with the smell of fresh paint and new carpet.

Christmas and New Year's came and went without clicks, shadows, moving watches, or anything else unexplainable. I felt relieved. We had apparently left our "strangeness" behind. Then Ed came home from a Chamber of Commerce meeting with news that made me feel even better. The chamber board wanted him to conduct a treasure hunt like the one he had made up for the city's silver anniversary celebration back in October of 1986.

I knew another treasure hunt would be a lot of hard work, but I also knew Ed would love doing it. More importantly, it meant that these people, most of whom had figured out that my Ed was "the" Ed, still saw him as they had before the UFO sightings started. That kind of community acceptance and support helped us through the months of sightings, and we still took comfort in it.

Shortly after New Year's, Dannie went back to college and we tried to readjust to being a family of three again. Early Saturday morning the week after he left, Laura thundered down the stairs and ran into the kitchen calling my name.

"Mom! Guess what? A barge hit the bridge about daylight and knocked it down!"

"Now who told you that?"

"Becca. Her dad started for work but couldn't go because the bridge is closed."

Better than a lot of people I knew how rumors could get started and grow. I called Brenda Pollak. As a city councilwoman, if anything had happened, she would know. A few minutes later I had at least partial confirmation of Laura's report.

A barge had hit the bridge connecting the Gulf Breeze peninsula to the mainland and Pensacola. While none of the roadway had fallen into the water, the collision knocked out a support pillar, causing enough damage to close the four-lane span. Overnight we became what Gulf Breezians jokingly called the world's largest cul-de-sac.

One tabloid had fun with our plight, running an article with the headline: "UFO Aliens Transform Village into Ghost Town!" They quoted some unnamed UFO experts as claiming that the nineteen-knot wind and rough seas which had forced the tug captain to lose control had seemed to come out of nowhere. It was as if someone or something had made it happen. Not for a minute did anyone in town take them seriously. And, faced with months of making an hour-plus detour to drive to what we could see three miles across the bay, we didn't find the joke particularly funny.

But our family, along with other people in the area, did have a sense of humor about UFOs. A few businesses in town used sketches of craft in their ads. One artistic fellow designed a tee shirt adorned with a UFO and beach scene which proclaimed that people from everywhere knew how great our beaches were. And then there was the Mardi Gras parade out at Pensacola Beach.

Ed, Laura, and I went. We could hardly believe it when we saw a huge, homemade UFO, complete with portholes, coming down the street. As the first place winning float, done by the Pensacola Beach Flamingo Club, drew closer, I glanced at Ed. What would his reaction be to someone having fun with what we considered so serious? The UFO-topped float passed us and he read the logo aloud.

"Now You Know." Ed looked at me and smiled "Well, at least people are thinking about it."

We drove home from the parade, still talking about how humor had its place in helping people open up to the possibilities surrounding the UFO phenomenon. Once home, eager to get inside and warm up, I hopped out of the car and hurried to unlock the front door, Laura right behind me. We stepped into the foyer and stopped. The house was freezing.

Wondering how something could already be wrong with a heater only two months old, I hurried over to check the thermostat. The unit had been switched from heat to airconditioning, the temperature set on thirty. I looked at Ed.

"Could a power surge or brownout have caused this?"

He glanced at Laura then back at me and shrugged. "I don't know."

"Maybe it's warmer in my room." Laura turned and headed up the stairs.

With each step she took we heard a distinct click. She paused and looked down at her father and me, her expression strained, then ran the rest of the way up the stairs. Ed and I exchanged disappointed glances. The "strangeness" had moved to our new house with us.

Ed's Account

The hypnosis sessions had come to an end. The memories released to my conscious mind were staggering but I still had not managed to make sense of it all. Two, sometimes three, times a week I continued to "dream" of the green valleys and mountains around Tamacuari.

There seemed to be no direct answers and I had little time to study the puzzle. With each day came events that swept me along with them. We had moved to a new house to escape the prying eyes of the media and the ever present "strangeness" that manifested itself as shadowy figures, clicks, and "fingers." But our new house and unlisted telephone number made no difference. Investigator interviews and rude news reporters were the order of the day. My construction business was holding its own, the "strangeness" continued, and so did the UFO sightings. On March 30, 1989, the *Sentinel* newspaper ran a report of a UFO sighting by a retired Air Force F-4 pilot.

> "I was able to snap 3 photos in rapid succession before the object departed to the west. I'm not sure what I photographed but it wasn't one of our local aircraft. This thing made no noise and climbed away like a rocket. My truck would not start for about 5 minutes after the object left and I noticed that I had built up a pretty stout static electric charge when I touched the door handle."

Witness reports such as these were satisfying from the standpoint of knowing that others were seeing the UFO, but Air Force and Navy spokesmen continued to deny any knowledge of the UFO that was now so commonly seen over Gulf Breeze.

CHAPTER 13

HISTORICAL ON "IN SLEEP YOU KNOW"

by Dr. Dan C. Overlade

I found it fascinating and intriguing that Ed feared others would deride his "in sleep you know" memories, that others would find his dream enlightenments the only unbelievable part of his entire incredible story! Actually, he had—on his own—stumbled onto a technique that had been applied by many highly intelligent people for centuries.

The dreams of René Descartes, the French philosopher, provided him the fundamental ideas that guided his work in physics, metaphysics, algebra, and philosophy.

Mahatma Ghandi, through a dream, was guided to his technique of civil disobedience, that ultimately moved India to self-determination and liberation from British rule.

Elias Howe was able to perfect his invention of the lockstitch sewing machine when he had a dream of natives hurling spears which had a hole (eye) in the point of the spear instead of in the shaft (like an ordinary needle).

The nineteenth century German physiologist, Hermann von Helmholtz, acknowledged that many of his original ideas came to him following sleep and after he had searched unsuccessfully for answers in his waking state.

The 1936 Nobel prize in physiology and medicine went to Otto Loewi who, in his sleep, designed an experiment that demonstrated the chemical nature of neurotransmissions.

D. B. Parkinson, a telephone engineer, helped develop a potentiometer to improve the accuracy of telephone transmission measurement. In a dream he was shown his invention on an antiaircraft gun which brought down every plane at which it fired. His dream inspiration led to the development of the first all-electric gun director, which in one week in August of 1944 downed eighty-nine of ninety-one German V-1 buzz bombs aimed at London.

From dreams, Richard Wagner wrote the opera *Tristan und Isolde,* Steve Allen wrote his most successful song, "This Could be the Start of Something Big," and Robert Louis Stevenson wrote *The Strange Case of Dr. Jekyll and Mr. Hyde.* Many other writers, composers, and inventors have learned from their dreams and Carl Jung called attention to the inspirational and creative functions of dreaming. Mary Arnold-Forster, an English psychologist writing in 1921, told of using autosuggestion to direct the content of her dreams and to become conscious of the fact she was dreaming.

San Francisco psychologist and dream researcher Gayle Delaney views all dreams as proffering solutions to problems and answers to questions. Asserting, "It *is* possible to direct your dreams by conscious intent,"[1] she recommends the "incubation" of dreams by deliberately posing questions to the "dream producer" within oneself just before going to sleep and writing down recalled dreams upon awakening for later introspection and interpretation. Delaney believes that dreams offer "insight, understanding, and inspiration (and that) they do not parrot what you already understand. They come to show you something you have not yet fully grasped. They serve a purpose and have a message."[2] She believes that defining and describing events and images of the dream will clarify its meaning.

Without any conscious knowledge of this existential view of dreams, Ed had happened upon a closely parallel procedure.

---

[1] Gayle Delaney, *Living Your Dreams* (San Francisco: Harper & Row, 1979), p 8.
[2] Ibid., p 34.

CHAPTER 14

"IN SLEEP YOU KNOW"— THE MEMORIES

Each memory recall detailed in this chapter occurred during the five months of UFO encounters described in *The Gulf Breeze Sightings,* three months before I underwent hypnotic regression. I have studied these memories and my comments about them were arrived at by considering the hypnosis, telepathy, and the "sleep memories."

The facets of what I now call my "in sleep you know" memories could be an important source of clarification when studied along with the clinically controlled hypnosis. These memories hold a wealth of information hidden in short disconnected phrases that I recall moments after awaking from a peaceful sleep. To understand these phrases and how they were stumbled upon, first a brief background.

As a child I played a "game" each night when told to "go to sleep." For me to fall asleep as quickly as my parents might have liked was not possible until I learned the "black cloud game." I have no memory of how I learned this sleep technique, which allows me to almost immediately fall into a deep sleep, but I'm reasonably sure neither of my parents taught it to me. The question can be posed as to a possible connection of the "black cloud" with a UFO encounter, but I have no confirming anecdotal details to confirm or deny the suggestion.

Simply put, I imagined a black cloud touching my toes and slowly moving up my body, engulfing me in relaxation until it reached my head, at which point my mind seemed to roll over into deep, peaceful sleep. Unknowingly I had developed a type of preconditioning that I now recognize as self-hypnosis. But I thought that I was very clever.

The routine reinforced itself each night and as the years passed I began to shortcut the system. No longer did I start the cloud at my toes. As a teenager I moved the cloud quickly from my chest to my head and I eased into slumber within less than thirty seconds. During my twenties I further reduced the time needed to fall asleep and began to think the word "peace" just before the black cloud closed over my mind.

A nagging sore throat and cold prompted me to add another word, "healing." Many a fever or cold had been eased when I awoke in the morning after using the "black cloud" to carry me into slumber the night before.

The years have allowed me to program my senses to fall to sleep when I think these two words together. These "sleep words" do not affect me when spoken by another, but the reaction is quick and undeniable if I sit for a moment and concentrate on them. I don't claim that the result of thinking these sleep words is an unusual talent. I am quite sure that most people who took the time could eventually condition themselves in a similar way.

This uncommon sleep procedure also has produced another effect. I can address a problem or question in my mind, say my words, then fall asleep promptly; I awaken in the morning with what appear to be answers surfacing to my conscious mind.

I first recognized this when I was faced with many very difficult problems during our early years of living in Costa Rica. For instance, we couldn't supply water to the house site from a spring over half a mile away, a spring that was five hundred feet lower than the house, because we had neither electricity nor a gas pump.

How could I solve the problem? Perhaps I could devise a kind of wind-driven pump, or possibly sink a well closer to the house. I needed to solve the problem quickly because hand-carrying water from the spring was a difficult chore. I thought about my options just before turning in one night.

In the morning my mind was a rush, filled with ideas of using a gravity-powered pump. This type of pump is called a "ram" pump and it uses the force of falling water to pump a part of that water to extreme heights. The method to make and set up this pump was crystal clear in my mind. The details of how much fall versus the volume in order to "ram force" water five hundred feet up the mountain to our house were clear in my mind and I began writing the notes as quickly as I opened my eyes and could grab a paper and pencil.

Several days later I learned that another North American living in the area had installed a similar system on his property. Although the distance he had to pump water was far shorter, I talked with him anyway. His information on sources for material saved me hours of experimenting and construction, enabling me to complete our system more quickly.

This incident may seem peculiar at first but I still don't think there is anything psychic or unnatural about it. How often have you heard people say, "I'll sleep on it," to solve a problem? I rationalized that somewhere in the reaches of my mind I had obviously been exposed to the idea of a ram pump. By concentrating on the problem before going to sleep I must have unlocked those memories and used them to solve the problem.

This "sleep memory recall" has come to be a normal part of my life and is often very helpful. Could I use this "sleep memory" to help answer some of the "why" questions about the UFO? During the early months I didn't think so because I wasn't willing to consider that there was anything there to remember. I didn't suspect any previous contact; therefore, there should be nothing to recall.

Others didn't take this "sleep recall" ability as lightly as I did and urged me to experiment further. Even the few MUFON investigators who knew about it encouraged me to make a concentrated effort. I was neither eager nor reluctant; during those early months I just didn't believe I had been exposed to any earlier information that would help. The argument for at least trying was tied to the telepathic message I had heard on January 24, 1988, while with Duane Cook.

That incident was very traumatic and was videotaped by Duane as it happened. The message spoken to me telepathically was "In sleep you know." Conjecture and speculation on the side of experimenting with my "sleep recall" were obvious, so I agreed.

The results, below, of my first concentrated effort to obtain any information by way of my sleep recall, or "in sleep you know," were unclear. The recalled thoughts were direct and I had no trouble writing the words. They pushed their way into my consciousness when I awoke in the morning after concentrating on the question the night before. My recall was full of information, yet it was lacking completeness. All of the following "in sleep you know" memory recall took place before I met Dr. Overlade and underwent hypnosis.

March 31, 1988—11:00 P.M.

QUESTION #1: When was the first time I was contacted?

I chose this question assuming there would be no recall and my argument would be supported. No recall of a first time contact meant there were no previous events to remember. I gave the process a fair chance and concentrated intently on the question just before saying my "sleep words" and allowing myself to fall into a peaceful sleep.

In the morning my mind was reeling with thoughts, very disconnected, but what I remembered was certain in my mind. I wrote the words as they came to me and here is the exact order and content.

RECALL #1:
At eleven years—from house to light in street.
I broke the wave—will could break.
I ran and gave to brother's need.
No block out and came.
With news I have no fear.

Five news to learn.
Return and know to light.

So there it was. My sleep memory recall had revealed "at eleven years" as the answer to my question of when I had first been contacted. I was stunned. Not only was I wrong about no possibility of earlier events in my life but my brother was somehow involved.

Under hypnotic regression many months later my brother's presence was confirmed as part of an incident when I was eleven. During that hypnosis I relived an encounter that startled my senses.

My brother and I were asleep but I awoke and became terrorized by a light coming through the bedroom window. I ran from the house toward the bright light at the corner of the street where I would be safe. This hypnosis memory seemed to fit with the sleep recall memory of "from house to light in street." Again and again the recall under hypnosis supported my sleep recall detail by detail.

"I broke the wave—will could break," possibly implied that I broke free and "ran and gave to brother's need." The rest of the sleep recall phrases meant nothing to me but, with words like "five news to learn," and "with news I have no fear," I was eager to try again.

I sat and considered the ramifications of these memories and what question I should think about next. I couldn't wait until nightfall and decided to try again that same morning. The "wave" seemed to be a noun, something that could be broken. "News" could be a reference to "five news (items I had) to learn" but I wasn't sure; therefore, I concentrated on this question.

April 1, 1988—8:00 A.M.

QUESTION #2: What are the "wave" and "news"?

Although I had only an hour earlier awakened from seven hours of sleep, I quickly fell into deep slumber after repeating my "sleep words" several times. When I opened my eyes, three hours later, the words bombarding my memory only added to the speculation.

> RECALL #2:
> Eio stri echo force—dual pull bientoc.
> Monorod neuro control.
> Our young with theirs.

This sleep memory recall used words unknown to me and basically added to my confusion. But, under hypnosis months later, these cryptic phrases underscored the implications of the "news." I could only speculate that I was repeating words I had heard used to describe the "wave," words not of my vocabulary, with the exception of "force" and "neuro control." So, was the "wave" some type of "neuro control"? Was this "wave" used to induce amnesia and/or effectively neutralize an abductee?

Within RECALL #1 was, "I broke the wave—will could break." Did I somehow break out of the "neuro control wave?" An eleven-year-old boy might not be expected to resist strongly. I speculate that I did resist, just as I resisted the UFO time after time, beginning with the November 11, 1987 sighting.

Also within RECALL #1 was "I ran and gave to brother's need." How my brother was involved in this abduction, I still don't know, but I interpret this to mean that I somehow broke the "control wave" and ran only to be recaptured. The "no block out and came" could refer to this recapture but without the use of the "block out wave."

The second part of RECALL #2 addressed the second part of my question, "news." "With news I have no fear" and "five news to learn" were part of Recall #1. What did "news" refer to? The RECALL #2 was very clear, "our young with theirs." Clearly, the word "news" referred to here was a noun, but not news as of an event or yesterday's news.

"Our young with theirs" was very disturbing. Had I seen something called a "new" during my abduction at age eleven? If so, I apparently had "no fear" of them and for some reason five of them had something "to learn."

At eleven years of age I could be considered "our young" and "with theirs" obviously meant their young. But if the recall is taken literally to what is a "new," then the answer "our young with theirs" implies a connection or a joining. This speculation led me to try more recall about "news."

April 1, 1988—11:30 P.M.

QUESTION #3: Is there anything more about news?

RECALL #3:
News were the past.
Best of both end decline.
The body needs function.
The mind new movement.

By using these "sleep memories" to help explain parts of previous recall memories I was piecing together a better picture, and RECALL #3 added more troubling speculation.

Did this mean that a "new" was a being from the past? If we consider the "our young with theirs" and place it with "best of both end decline," therein arises a very disquieting idea. "Best of both" what "ends decline"? Is the answer "our young with theirs"? Could it be that a "new" is in fact a new being that is the "best of both," the human being and another being?

My speculation may have been leading me in a wrong direction so I needed to make sure that a "new" either was or was not a new being.

April 2, 1988—7:10 A.M.

QUESTION #4: Are the "news" a new type of being?

RECALL #4:
New but the life of their past.
Life of our future.

There it was. A "new" was a type of being. Again there was mention of the word "past," which seemed to mean that the "new" was not a new life-form but "life of their past," and to further confuse the analysis, this life-form was the "life of our future." How could this be?

If a "new" was the "best of both," then in order for it to be the "life of their past" and the "life of our future," it suggests the possibility of genetic altering. Perhaps the best genetics of a being on the UFO were being molded with the best genetics of humans to "end decline."

The third line of RECALL #3 seems to make some sense if this genetic joining is taking place. "The body needs function" and "the mind new movement" implies a body lacking function and a mind that is stagnant.

Are the beings on the UFO in need of a body with better function? How could an advanced species need a body with better function, let alone a mind with "new movement"? These concepts seemed directly opposite. An advanced race with a poorly functioning body and stagnant mind just did not make any sense. Yet, there was a strange phrase in RECALL #1 that might explain this contradiction, "five news to learn." Somehow that phrase hinted at a connection with "the mind new movement."

(Later, when my theories and suppositions on all this were being discussed, another interpretation for "the body needs function" and "the mind new movement" was put forth. It was suggested that this meant the alien body needs function and human intelligence needs to advance or both species may become extinct. That could well be. Even though I have drawn my conclusions from what I've learned, other interpretations are possible and may further broaden the scope of information and our understanding.)

April 5, 1988—12:30 A.M.

QUESTION #5: What does "five news to learn" mean?

RECALL #5:
Five at 11, eight at 17, ten at 25, twelve at 33, twelve at 41.
News gain neurosplice.

As I woke that morning those numbers were racing through my mind. Over and over they repeated as I hurriedly reached for my pen to record the numbers and the three word phrase. The numbers "five at 11" could have been a coincidence but considering the question was about five "news" and that my age at the first contact was 11, I was spellbound by the other figures.

I had experienced a loss of time at each of those ages—17, 25, 33—and I was now 41. It was also easy to assume that each age was accompanied by a number equaling the number of "news." This seemed to be the first insight suggesting other abductions and for some reason they were each associated with a particular number of "news."

The accompanying three-word phrase immediately gave me a quick shiver as I understood that in some way these "news" had gained a neurosplice with me. What a neurosplice was, I didn't know, but the words "neuro control" had come up before in RECALL #2. However, I couldn't believe that there was some "neurosplice" controlling me, or accept any explanation similar to that.

I looked again at the question I had asked, "What does 'five news to learn' mean?" The recall had detailed four dates in my life when I had experienced missing time. Each one of the dates was accompanied by a number of "news." The key word in the recall was "learn." Did these five "news" gain a neurosplice with me to learn something? Was this the case at each following abduction? Was there something about me that so interested the UFO beings that they returned every eight years to gain a neurosplice?

April 5, 1988—7:30 A.M.

QUESTION #6: What does "mind new movement" mean?

RECALL #6:
Return feeling and challenge.
Learn what is lost.

This was another bombshell. Was I to understand that these new beings were learning "feeling and challenge" from me? That, somehow, the UFO beings were creating "news" from the best of both human and alien beings was a staggering revelation. Was it possible that these "news" had to be "neurospliced" to learn "feeling and challenge"? If so, of all people . . . why me?

April 5, 1988—11:30 P.M.

QUESTION #7: Why me?

RECALL #7:
News learn will, solve, and care.

Through my study of these powerful phrases it seemed to become more and more obvious that indeed these "news" were being created by using the "best of both" but lacked basic human emotions; will—the will to live, will to succeed, willpower to meet a challenge—problem solving and caring. All of these are natural for humans, to one degree or another.

The answer to "Why me?" was fairly direct. I possessed these human emotions; therefore, I could serve the aliens' needs.

April 6, 1988—11:00 P.M.

QUESTION #8: Can I stop contact?

> RECALL #8:
> With the will and passion.
> Link set to ninety-six.

More important at the time was my immediate problem of keeping my household normal. Solving all these speculative questions took a backseat to trying to resist the UFO and its frequent appearances. The morning recall to this question was again vague with what could be a reference to 1996, which fit into the 1988 to 1996, eight-year cycle consistent with the pattern of time between most contacts. To me, this was not a bright thought, having to mark off the years until I might be again snatched from my car or bedroom. At least if some kind of link had been set to take place in 1996, then I had time to consider how to prepare and possibly avoid it.

April 11, 1988—11:30 P.M.

QUESTION #9: Where does the UFO come from?

> RECALL #9:
> No name.
> Old line to pass.
> News to build.

This was a question that would be considered high on the list of questions and yet I apparently had no recall of a name. Having no memory of a name, my subconscious apparently released two more very suggestive phrases that I had most likely heard during an alien incident. If an older generation of aliens is passing on, "old line to pass," and a new line or generation is building, "news to build," then the ramifications are truly incredible. How involved in our culture are they and how deep does this building of a new generation go?

April 12, 1988—7:00 A.M.

QUESTION #10: A place with no name. Where?

RECALL #10:
In years and years to find in 483 minutes.
To meet and join.

Once more I tried to stimulate a memory recall of where the UFO was from, but the intriguing phrase of how long before they might be found came rushing to my mind. As strange as it may sound, the 483-minute figure seemed to me to be the length of time in travel before we were "to meet and join."

Four hundred eighty-three minutes is clearly not enough time for any space travel as we know it within our current rocket propulsion technology. So, either they are a lot closer than we know, or can travel a lot faster than our physical laws allow us to understand.

April 15, 1988—11:30 P.M.

QUESTION #11: It has been thirty years since I was 11. How old are the five at 11?

RECALL #11:
Five at 11 are small and 10,512 minutes at two years.
Speaker tells of 1 to 100.
Two years plus 30 divided by 2 times 10,512 equals how old now.

I was troubled by the idea that each earlier abduction involved a certain number of "news" and the earliest seemed to be when I was eleven years old. What happened to those small beings I had seen thirty years ago when I was eleven? Were they now mature, possibly thirty-year-old, creatures that continued to pursue me?

The math equation seems to indicate that 10,512 minutes is equal to two years, as if to say the "news" were equal to two years, therefore 5,256 minutes would equal one year. If you multiply the number of minutes in the average year, you will reach 525,600. This is a proportion of 1 to 100. I believe that this means that these beings have an approximate 1 to 100 life span. That is to say, for every one year we live that would be equal to 5,256 minutes for a "new." Or, for every 100 years that passes in our time only one year passes for a "new."

With these figures in mind, I gave more thought to the information disclosed in RECALL #10. Were the 483 minutes our minutes, or "new" minutes? Either way—eight hours and three minutes, or roughly thirty-three and a half days—still seemed too fast for anything we could manage to travel.

April 17, 1988—1:30 A.M.

QUESTION #12: Who is the Speaker?

RECALL #12:
An old one, white hair, soft, dark blue eyes, sick, shakes.

Each memory recall brought about more questions and I began to piece together answers. In the previous recall I had written "the speaker tells," so the normal question of "Who is the speaker?" was obvious to me.

By now, with rudimentary analysis, no one could see patterns developing and surmise that the answer to my question would be some type of special being, so my recall tried to describe the speaker. The image of an old, white-haired, sick being came through very clearly. The central alien figure during my May 1, 1988, abduction was wrinkled, with white tufts of hair, as I indicated with my drawing. Was this "the speaker"?

April 17, 1988—8:30 A.M.

QUESTION #13: Have my contacts been for genetics?

> RECALL #13:
> Early at 17.
> I stood up—no.
> Helpers run.
> Speaker, female needs help.
> Thick air.
> Rod to head.

The question of genetic experiments or direct manipulation went to the heart of what seemed to be the underlying trend of the abduction phenomena. Bob Reid, investigator, prompted this question during a meeting with several researchers.

An earlier recall, "best of both end decline," certainly implied that genetics was involved. No matter how distasteful, the possibility had to be considered. This recall answer was just clear enough for me to understand that something possibly related to genetics had happened when I was seventeen, something that caused me to stand up and the helpers to run, and further involving "thick air" and a "rod to head."

April 17, 1988—11:00 P.M.

QUESTION #14: What is "Rod to head"?

> RECALL #14:
> No harm. Calm. No. They must know.

At this time, three months before the start of hypnotic regression, I had no idea what "rod to head" meant. I tried to recall any further memory about this curious phrase. The resulting memory was definitely of words spoken to me as I reacted defiantly.

My memory allowed me only flashes of an event in which small beings were around me and spoke to me issuing orders. There was the certain image of a device being placed on my head and connected with another head only an arm's length from me. This was a very strong memory and I sketched the headgear device that I saw.

April 18, 1988—7:00 A.M.

QUESTION #15: Was the creature on the porch a speaker?

This question was in reference to the small shielded being that Frances and I had seen on our back porch on the night of December 2, 1987.

RECALL #15:
Synthetic job being.
Job beings produce.
Synthetic Biological Unit (SyBU).

One of the few direct answers, this definition of the four-foot-tall, shielded creature added weight to the speculation that life was being manipulated. Synthetic certainly means fabricated or somehow genetically produced. This answer was even specific as to what their purpose was. "Job beings produce." They have a certain function, or job, designed for them.

Does the possibility of genetic engineering sound like a science fiction dream? Having seen the unbelievable and experienced what seemed impossible, my mind was open. Later I came across an article by Carol Kahn in *Omni* that proclaims, "The era of cloning has arrived, says Jim Robl of the University of Massachusetts. Cloned cows and sheep may have ranchers buzzing, but could the age-old dream of human cloning ever take place? In fact recent startling accomplishments suggest that cloning of people may soon be here."[1]

---

[1] Carol Kahn, *Cloning, Omni* Magazine, January 1990.

The assumption that a vastly advanced civilization of aliens has mastered the techniques of cloning and genetic manipulation is not unreasonable. But what problems could surface after hundreds of years of selective breeding of aliens by aliens? The natural variation of genes in human reproduction creates a diversity of spirit and of individuals that specialized cloning would certainly inhibit.

April 18, 1988—11:20 P.M.

QUESTION #16: Where are the five at 11 now?

RECALL #16:
At 17 unseen only eight new.
Large room.
Walls hum.
Back wall stuck in cold with arm.
Wet are pulled.

If I could, I wanted to know more about those beings called "news." What happened to them after the emotional linkup that they experienced with me? Where did they go from there? Did they return to a distant home or do they share this planet with us? None of the answers to these questions were revealed, only more vague, seemingly isolated bits of data that teased my desire for complete sentences.

These "in sleep you know" memories were enormously suggestive and I could not deny how they seemed to fit together. Yet, a "new" somehow being developed from the best of mankind and the best of an alien race was beyond credible thinking. Add to that a "neurosplice" that allowed the "news" to learn, and even more outrageous, to learn something from me, and my mind boggled.

I could hardly think about these revelations which took place late in my six-month-long encounter with the UFO. After all, couldn't this be explained away as dreams? I decided not to talk about any of what I had learned and written down from these "dreams" with anyone other than the investigators who had encouraged me in these attempts. Seeing and photographing the UFO was enough. Suspecting a motivated connection with the UFO beings seemed way out of line.

My attempts at denial failed to stop these recall memories and thoughts of the telepathic messages from churning in my mind. The extensive disclosure under regressive hypnosis has proved to be the only way to tie together all of these suggestive phrases and try to answer, "Why?"

Frances's Account

When Ed was first encouraged to pursue the "in sleep you know" theory, I was as skeptical of anything coming out of it as he was. Yes, all my life I'd heard about "sleeping on it" as a means of solving a problem or reaching a decision, but that, in my opinion, didn't apply here. First, like Ed, I didn't want to admit that there could be anything to recall. And second, if there was something, I wasn't certain I wanted to know about it. But the investigators were insistent, and Ed's curiosity finally got the better of him.

When he "received" his first memory, I was stunned. What I hadn't wanted to believe was true. There was more to this UFO incident than what we had recently undergone and were still experiencing. Since the night Ed and I had seen the creature on our back porch, when it seemed to ignore my presence entirely, I had been afraid Ed was the focus of the entities' attention. Not only did his sleep memories seem to verify that, but apparently their interest was long-term.

The thought that "they" had been popping in and out of his life, and later our lives, for years, shook me. Even more disturbing was the apparent fact that, while they might go away for years at a time, they always came back. Would they, as Ed's sleep memories indicated, be back in 1996? I hoped not, but I couldn't, and wouldn't, worry about it now. Ed had asked for my help in understanding the strange information he was "receiving" and, although he hadn't asked for it, I knew he was counting on my emotional support as well. I could hardly offer him that if I let myself worry about something that might happen years down the road.

So, each morning after Ed wrote down his sleep memories, we discussed them. I found that the cryptic words and fragmented sentences rarely made sense, not if each memory was taken alone. But, after several mornings, when we sat and pieced all of the phrases together—"what iffing" and "supposing that"—at least part of it did convey some understandable information.

What I didn't understand was why the entities didn't simply ask for the help they apparently needed instead of terrorizing Ed and the rest of our family to get it. Had they tried that straightforward approach before and been turned down by some frightened human, perhaps even by Ed himself? Was that why they had adopted these commando tactics to achieve their goals? And lastly, just how much of what came out of Ed's sleep recall could we believe?

Months later, when Ed underwent regressive hypnosis with Doctor Overlade, we received answers to some of our questions, primarily about the "news" and Ed's repeated contacts with them. It was also clear that Ed had never been a cooperative "guinea pig." Since he had always resisted the encounters, it made sense for the entities to assume he would continue to do so. But I still wondered if they had ever tried asking. Nothing in Ed's subconscious recall indicated that they had. But at least we knew there was truth in his sleep memories. And that worried me.

What would people think when they heard about this? Would Ed be cast in an unwanted "guru" role? On top of everything else, that was the last thing we needed, or wanted. Ed's sleep memories were just that, memories. True enough, they were memories from past encounters with the UFO's occupants, but there were no "messages" from "space brothers," benign or otherwise.

We didn't want or expect any messages and avoided using the word, going so far as to correct others when they referred to Ed's memory recall in that way. Once word of the accuracy of much of Ed's sleep recall got out, he found himself time and again stressing that he was merely relaying information and events he had been exposed to—somewhere, somehow. He couldn't tell anyone how to save the planet, cure anything, or predict the winning numbers in the state lottery.

The revelations which came through Ed's sleep recall and under hypnosis added to the strain we had been under, even months after they had come to light. Added to that was the media coverage, which seemed to ebb and flow with no discernibly logical pattern. A week would go by without a telephone call from a single reporter. Then, suddenly, three or four would call on the same day with the resultant flurry of interviews in newspapers and on television. All of this lent a surreal quality to our lives.

We were delightfully "brought back to earth" when Ed was told he'd been nominated to receive the Southeast Regional Builders' Aurora Award for his design and energy efficient construction of our house. We were invited to attend the regional banquet in Orlando, but couldn't go. Instead Ed accepted his award at the local banquet hosted by the Home Builders Association of West Florida. I was so proud of him. And I knew he was pleased to be recognized for his outstanding work and to be receiving a different kind of attention.

My obligations and duties as president of the high school PTA also helped keep our lives on an even keel. I once jokingly told Ed he had Dr. Overlade, I had PTA for my therapy. But there was a great deal of truth in what I'd said. I understood and shared the concerns of most parents—how to finance a college education, what to do about teenage drug and alcohol abuse, and how to prevent date rape. These were all problems I could confront head-on, with at least a chance of having a positive impact.

Planning and chairing meetings and programs, acting as liaison between parents and the school, and the everyday routine that was part of the office of president made it possible for me to sometimes forget—for a little while—all about UFOs.

CHAPTER 15

PRELIMINARY CONCLUSION

By the time Dr. Overlade and I ended the hypnosis sessions, we had uncovered an astounding history of interaction between the alien beings and me. The answers we found were not complete and for those things left unresolved I can only suggest possibilities. I continue to consider many theories as I struggle to learn the meaning of what happened during the abductions.

I realize that the disclosures I have written in this book go beyond the normal limits of science, beyond the traditional reaches of possibility. But I ask that you, as I have, consider the objective facts.

Hundreds of witnesses have reported sightings of UFOs in my hometown. Thousands of people have reported events throughout the world. The photo evidence I obtained is exceptional and is corroborated by the photos and videotapes of other witnesses. Witnesses have come forward and reported seeing the blue beam and even more have reported unexplained periods of missing time. Clearly, something happened in Gulf Breeze—and continues to—something that, as yet, cannot be fully explained.

After months of study and thought, I have arrived at my answers to the "why" questions. Key to those answers is the alien interaction with humans involving emotional and, maybe, genetic transfer. The alien motivation seems to be a rejuvenation of their race or possibly the creation of a new race by using the best of human attributes, both physical and emotional. In my case, their interest seemed to be in the emotions of love, joy, sorrow, and pride.

The emotions and memories that I was forced to relive,

for the apparent use by the "news," were real memories from my life. The events that I relived while under hypnotic regression were for the most part known and real events even though during portions of those events certain "control" visions were placed in my mind.

For example, the image of my heart exploding from my chest was used by the aliens to reinforce control over me. The vision of my daughter suffocating was used to distract me as I struggled with the shielded creatures on the beach. Those visions were not real, only illusions. Also, the visions of the black man, the half-breed, and the Indian boy may or may not be real, even though I later uncovered what is possibly a connection between the Indian boy and my recurring dream about the Venezuelan jungle.

The confrontation with the lizards seemed to be an emotional test that was physical in every way. I touched the lizards and held the children. They seemed real, but given the aliens' ability to create lifelike illusions, I can't be positive. However, the four red dots on my forehead, neck, and temples after the May 1, 1988, abduction convinced me that the emotional transfer rod was a real object from a real event. I have no doubt of that.

Based on the massive volume of mail, I believe that there are hundreds, perhaps thousands, of people being subjected to physical and emotional alien contact such as I have reported. I propose that the alien interaction in my life is not the exception but, rather, a common experience suffered by many.

There remain many other unanswered questions for researchers to explore. I look on the Gulf Breeze sightings as a piece of the puzzle and not a definitive answer. Only when aligned with the myriad of other worldwide sightings, events, and reports, will the answers one day become clear. For myself, based on what has happened to me, I've formulated some answers of my own.

Do UFOs exist?
Yes, there is no doubt in my mind.

Do UFOs come from "outer space"?

Maybe, I don't know; it certainly seems possible.

But whether these beings are from outer space, another dimension, or our own future—they are "alien" to our time, our culture.

What is the purpose of alien abduction?

Based solely on my experience, I must answer—interaction physically and emotionally to rejuvenate or develop a "new" species.

These conclusions spring from the personal encounters that I have disclosed openly in this book. My answers are possibilities which to me seem acceptable. The things that I saw and heard I have interpreted only on the basis of my own personal intellect. Philosophically, I see myself as neutral, but I also acknowledge that I have, like everybody, certain preconceived and subjective ideas that may color my conclusions.

These subjective ideas can cause two witnesses to see and hear the same event and later report very different stories. For example, a devout Muslim might describe an event in terms completely opposite from those of an atheist. Likewise, if a person who places heavy emphasis on a single interest in his daily life has a UFO encounter, he might interpret the event with overtones of that single interest.

As we approach the twenty-first century—spiritualism, religion, the environment and ecology, the lingering threat of nuclear holocaust, and other fears are all very powerful forces and concerns. Are they connected in some way to this wave of UFO encounters that people from all over the world are reporting? Do the aliens care what we do to ourselves, our planet? Or do some witnesses (including myself) subconsciously interpret an alien abduction in the context of ideals more meaningful to their own personal philosophy? That I can't answer.

Are the abductees and UFO witnesses seeing and experiencing the same aliens? Some descriptions of the beings vary from one case to another, but is this explained by the ability of the UFO occupants to produce vivid, lifelike visions? Might a small gray alien figure portray itself as a handsome, blond human and therein calm the emotions of an abductee? On the other hand, where there exists one type of alien being, with such advanced technology, might there not exist another and even another?

I understand that by disclosing these experiences I may be ridiculed, but as outrageous as they may seem, I report them in good faith. UFO sightings have been scoffed at by some who label UFOs and alien contact as some very remote fantasy, while others ease their thoughts by assuming that this could only happen in the future.

Before my awareness of these events that have thrust their way into my life, I, too, thought that perhaps only in the distant future might such encounters be possible. I wasn't ready today for something that we, humanity in general, didn't expect until "tomorrow." I tried to reject it, forget it, hope it would go away—close my eyes and be safe from the future. These astounding alien encounters have awakened me to the fact that the "future" has arrived.

CHAPTER 16

A PLOT TO DECEIVE

Our November vacation to New York City in 1988 was effectively a tranquilizer, a relief from the nonstop prying eyes of the media and the UFO investigators. The excitement of the Big Apple pushed thoughts of debunkers out of my mind. Little did we know that even our vacation would not go unassailed.

At about this time Manuel Fernandez, a New York photographer, had read about the Gulf Breeze sightings and decided to see if he could make some UFO photos that resembled the object seen in Gulf Breeze. Manuel approached the question as a test. How difficult would it be to fake UFO photos? His efforts produced several variations of a Gulf Breeze–type UFO hovering above the New York Chrysler Building (see photo U).

The results of his tests were unconvincing and several weeks later he discussed and shared copies of his work with a well-known New York journalist, Antonio Hunneus. Antonio had also been following the news about Gulf Breeze and the controversy generated by the critics. As a journalist, Antonio was interested in both sides of the story and, in the interest of research, decided to send copies of Manuel's test photos to the Gulf Breeze critic, Mr. Jones. With a cover letter identifying Manuel Fernandez as the photographer of the test photos, Antonio mailed the copies to Mr. Jones in late February 1989.

Antonio said, "I gave little thought to the test photographs until a month later when I saw a copy of a letter sent out by Mr. Jones."

This was only one of several letters sent out by Mr. Jones. It began, "Here is a copy of one of the photos allegedly taken by Ed Walters in New York." Attached to the letter was a copy of one of Manuel's test photos (see photo U).

Of primary importance to a debunker, Mr. Jones in this case, is to contrive a way to discredit the real UFO photographs and hope the scores of other UFO witnesses would be ignored by the media. His plan was simple. He would circulate the fake UFO photos made to look like the photos I had taken. He would insinuate to the media that they were photographs taken by me and that he could prove they were fake.

Mr. Jones mailed the fake photos, and his letter suggesting they were taken by me, to Jim Moseley, editor of *Saucer Smear*, the gossip tabloid of the UFO media. Upon receipt of the "New York UFO" photos, Jim called me to ask if I had been to New York recently and if I had taken any UFO photos while there.

Skeptical of all UFO sightings, Jim agreed to send me a copy of the photo showing the Chrysler Building and the UFO hovering above. I was outraged but I could only deny taking the UFO photo. I remember saying that the photographer would have to be nine hundred feet off the ground to take such a photo. At that point, it was my word against the insinuation of "Dr." Jones, who at the time had not yet been exposed for inventing his Ph.D. degree in physics.

Who was the media to believe, me, a UFO witness, or "Dr. Jones"? I have learned that the critic need only cast doubt and the media will repeat a critic's story in the name of balanced journalism.

The typical news reporter has little time to sort out conflicting claims and accusations and the debunker is counting on this not only to spread his debunking plot, but also to get his name recognized so other unsuspecting reporters will call on him for a negative statement. A normal example of "balanced journalism" when reporting on a multiple witnesses UFO sighting is to use half the article to interview the witnesses and the other half to allow a debunker, who was not there during the sighting, to explain it away as an airplane, helicopter, balloon, or hoax.

Unfortunately debunkers are not often caught "red-handed" in their efforts to discredit UFO sightings. But in this Chrysler Building UFO fake photo example the debunker was exposed. Jim Moseley talked to Antonio Hunneus and to Manuel Fernandez. Manuel made a complete report to the media and Antonio exposed the debunker's dirty trick in the *New York City Tribune*.

Manuel Fernandez publicly denounced the debunker. He released the numerous letters he had received from Mr. Jones, who had requested additional fake photos to be made under the pretense of research. The details of his debunking plot were amazing. At one point Mr. Jones managed to take photographs in my front yard and forwarded them to Manuel to have fake UFO images added.

Manuel did not know the purpose intended by the debunker and assumed the photos that he was asked to make were for valid research. Before the plot was exposed, these front-yard photos were completed by Manuel and mailed to Mr. Jones, who quickly began to use them in his fake photo evidence hoax.

Certainly the motive of the debunker was to distract and confuse the media and gain public attention for himself. The impact of the genuine UFO photographs would have been undercut had the fake photos not been exposed. Manuel Fernandez, Antonio Hunneus, and Jim Moseley deserve the credit for uncovering Mr. Jones and his debunking plot.

Out-of-town newspapers continued to report bits and pieces of the Gulf Breeze UFO story. Unfortunately, they usually felt the need to handle the events in a "tongue-in-cheek" manner. I read quotes attributed to me in columns from all over the country, as if the reporters had actually talked to me. In a Washington newspaper, columnist DeWayne Wickham reported,

> There's at least one man in Gulf Breeze, Fla.
> who says he can predict the arrival of alien visitors. When they are nearby he gets a humming

on the right side of his forehead—an alert he believes results from an alien listening device that was secretly stuck into his head.[1]

DeWayne Wickham has never spoken to me. So I can only wonder where he got this "listening device" story. It is an interesting idea but I never stated it as an explanation. A few times I did hear a humming sound during and before a UFO sighting but many sightings occurred with no humming.

Those kinds of misquotes were an aggravation but, most likely, Wickham did not intend any malice, so I refused to spend my time responding to the Wickhams of the world.

As did I, my community and business associates also ignored these absurd accusations and misquotes being printed by out-of-town newspapers apparently unwilling to check their facts. I was honored when the Gulf Breeze Chamber of Commerce asked me to organize an upcoming community activity. A citywide treasure hunt was decided on, much like the one I had organized a few years before to celebrate the Gulf Breeze Silver Anniversary. I was proud of my fellow Gulf Breeze residents who had not been swayed by the negative attacks on my reputation.

Witnesses continued to call in UFO reports to the *Sentinel* but to the "debunkers" and the "tongue-in-cheek" out-of-town news reporters, that made no difference. They were persistent as they continued to focus on me and my family and I agreed to interviews only on the condition that my name be withheld.

One day a *Miami Herald* reporter came to town. She arrived at our front door, unannounced. She asked for an interview and agreed to withhold my name.

I'm sure that all newspaper reporters should not be judged by using this woman as a standard. After reading her article in the paper, I have to say that when she came to my house she left her ethics at home.

From the start of the interview I should have been sus-

---

[1]DeWayne Wickham, *Gannett News,* May 20, 1989.

picious of her. She acted very nervous and almost never looked me in the eyes. The headline on her article said, "FLASH! UFOs Are Real!—Is Mr. Ed Giving Us The Horse Laugh?"[1]

Remember the agreement to withhold my name? Well, here is what she said, the fifth sentence into her article. "The new improved Mr. Ed is not a horse, of course, of course. He is Edward Daniel Walters, alias Daniel Edward Walters, alias Daniel Walters, alias Edward Hanson."[2]

I'm still not sure why she scrambled up my name and inserted "alias, alias, alias" but whatever her reason, it is clear that she came to town for a funny story about Mr. Ed the Talking Horse and not a serious report about the UFO that so many people were seeing.

[1]Sydney P. Freedberg, *Miami Herald,* August 6, 1989.
[2]*Ibid.*

CHAPTER 17

THE UFO SIGHTINGS CONTINUE

The personal UFO encounters that my wife and I documented in *The Gulf Breeze Sightings* ended on May 1, 1988. My last words in that book's Epilogue and my last thoughts were focused on a desire to know what had happened to me during the last encounter, when I experienced an hour and fifteen minutes of "missing time."

The three questions most frequently asked of me: first, was I put under hypnosis?; second, what happened?; third, have the UFO sightings continued?

The following represents a small sampling of area UFO sightings that continued after my May 1, 1988, encounter.

May 10, 1988
Eyewitness Report

Ray Poole, a professional engineer, and his family visited Shoreline Park and were shocked to see the Gulf Breeze UFO hovering over some nearby trees. He said, "It was very clear. I know what I saw was the same thing so many others are reporting. We watched it for about a minute before it disappeared."

July 18, 1988
MUFON Investigative Report

"Fenner and Shirley observed a round craft with lighted windows and a large white beam shining on the water.

'It was the exact craft that had been printed in the paper . . .' "

September 12, 1988
The Sentinel Newspaper

"At 8:00 pm, a woman watched from her car as a huge elongated object seemed to tow a smaller circular object. There was no noise . . ."[1]

November 22, 1988
Pensacola News-Journal

"Two miles east of Gulf Breeze, James Larkin reported seeing a UFO at 10:45 pm hovering twenty-five feet above the tree tops . . . Another man reported a similar sighting at the same time . . ."[2]

December 4, 1988
The Sentinel Newspaper

"Jackie saw a light pass his window and looked out to see a UFO, that looked 'like the pictures' of the Gulf Breeze UFO, crossing the sky . . ."[3]

February 8, 1989
Pensacola News-Journal

"Jeff watched a small lighted object, about three feet wide and two feet high, descend near his home at 3:30 am. He walked to within thirty feet of the object before, in a flash, it just disappeared . . ."[4]

---

[1]Duane Cook, *Sentinel,* September 12, 1988.

[2]Michael Burke, *Pensacola News-Journal,* November 22, 1988.

[3]Duane Cook, *Sentinel,* December 4, 1988.

[4]Michael Burke, *Pensacola News-Journal,* February 8, 1989.

March 8, 1989
MUFON Newsletter

"Maxie and Jane were driving home at 10:30 pm when they noticed a bright light pacing them from beyond the trees on the side of the road. As they rounded a curve, they could see it hovering over the road just ahead of them casting its reflection on the road . . ."[1]

April 17, 1989
The Sentinel Newspaper

"While in Shoreline Park, Lynn, Charles, a fisherman and two police officers watched a silent UFO through binoculars at 10:00 pm . . ."[2]

September 12, 1989
Multiple Witness Sighting

September 12 was a Tuesday and I was committed to three seven o'clock meetings: PTA at the high school, a committee on the city/school natatorium, and the MUFON meeting at the Unity Church in Pensacola. My wife, Frances, was president of the PTA and understood that I could only stay for a moment before I was off to the natatorium committee. After almost an hour of discussions and some recommendations I excused myself and drove the five miles into Pensacola, arriving at the parking lot behind the Unity Church meeting hall at about 7:55 P.M.

My concerns over a UFO encounter had long since disappeared since my last sighting had been on May 1, 1988. I angled to a stop about sixty feet from the meeting hall entrance door, turned off the engine, and climbed out of my truck. Closing the door, I turned around and caught sight of a glowing, red object approaching rapidly from the east. I was suddenly staring at a boiling, glowing object that I had seen so often sixteen months before.

---

[1]Rex Salisberry, *MUFON* Newsletter, March 8, 1989.
[2]Duane Cook, *Sentinel*, April 17, 1989.

I was caught off guard, but this time it was different—I was excited but I didn't feel threatened. I opened my truck door and reached into the glove compartment for the small 110 Instamatic camera that I carry. The red glow continued to move closer and closer toward me. I backed up a few feet, turned on the flash switch, and pressed the shutter button. The flash still hadn't had time to warm up before I advanced the film and hit the shutter button again.

Still a block or so away, the object remained steady in its course. I turned and ran for the meeting hall but stopped a few steps inside the door. I wanted to yell out to all who were sitting quietly before the guest speaker, but my past encounters with UFOs made me hesitate. For me, UFOs had a history of leaving quickly. What if this glowing red object had already departed? What if I called everybody outside to see . . . and the UFO were gone? I'd feel like a fool.

The yell froze in my throat. I caught Gary Watson's attention with a wave of my hand and with an anxious look I motioned him to follow me outside. Within seconds we both rounded the corner of the building as I finished my excited description and pointed to the red, glowing UFO. Ascending rapidly, the UFO was now smaller but still very clear.

Gary fixed his gaze on the glow and said, "Hurry, go get Don Ware."

Almost as a reflex I responded and rushed back into the quiet meeting. I signaled Don to follow me and returned to the parking lot. By now the UFO was even farther away, but the red glow was still visible. After a moment of study Don sent me to ask all those in the meeting hall to come outside.

Minutes had passed since I'd first seen the red, boiling energy of this UFO, which had been only several hundred feet away. Now, as more people rapidly filed outside (see photo M), the red glow was several thousand feet away and reaching the cloud cover. A dozen of those first into the parking lot managed to spot the UFO's glowing bottom and documented what they saw for the record.

The next morning the newspaper headline said, "35

Witnesses Spot UFO Over Pensacola." I agreed to allow my name to be included with all the other witnesses and for the first time (with my permission) I was publicly a UFO witness.

The article quoted Gary Watson as saying, "Something was there and we all saw it. I saw the object for the entire seven minutes. It was bright and hovered very still before it began to move up. Most of the other witnesses saw it before and as it began to enter the cloud cover. I am an experienced MUFON investigator, in fact, I instruct the training course and test the Field Investigator applicants. I saw a true UFO along with the other witnesses and those photos show what I saw."[1]

---

[1] Duane Cook, *Sentinel,* September 21, 1989.

CHAPTER 18

SKY QUAKES AND GRASS CIRCLES

November 15, 1989
Grass Circles

During a UFO-related interview with a local reporter I learned of the first unexplained "grass circle" reported in our area. The discovery of the flattened grass, spiraled into a perfect circle, caused a rush of questions to flood my thoughts. Was it a coincidence that the circle appeared in South Shoreline Park, the site of my May 1 UFO encounter and of so many other UFO sightings?

Duane Cook, the *Sentinel* Newspaper publisher, and I went to the circle location after a WEAR Channel 3 reporter told us where to find it. Most interesting was the undisturbed, surrounding area. Although the circle was easily seen from the edge of the sandy shoreline, there were no signs of pathways leading to the circle through the thirty-inch-tall grass around it.

When Duane and I walked around the area to photograph the circle, the trails we made were obvious. The long grass within the circle refused to stand up and weeks later, even after a flood of spectators and scientists, the swirled grass remained growing in a clockwise circle. A few of our curious local residents even spent the night in the park close to the circle in the hope of discovering what caused this mystery. That night a UFO was sighted and reported with the following headline.

The Sentinel:
Cigar-Shaped UFO Sighted Over Park

November 15, 1989—A Gulf Breeze resident reported to the *Sentinel* this week that he and two other motorists watched a UFO descend into the trees in the Naval Live Oaks east of Gulf Breeze the evening of Wednesday, November 15th. "The witness said he was driving west on Highway 98 near the park about 9:00 p.m. when he saw a beige, cigar-shaped object, with lights on both ends and a light on top in the center, settling down into the trees between him and the Sound. The whole craft just glowed in the dark, said the witness. "It was probably 20 to 40 feet long and made no noise," according to the witness. "We watched it for 5 or 6 seconds. Then we looked at each other and just shrugged our shoulders," said the witness, referring to himself and the other driver.

November 18, 1989
"Sky Quake"

Three days after the discovery of the mysterious circle, the city shook from an equally unexplained atmospheric tremor. These sudden atmospheric jolts were sporadic, very strong and became known locally as "sky quakes."

Pensacola News-Journal:
Officials Can't Explain Reports Of Shaky Ground

A tremor heard and felt by Pensacola residents at about 3:00 p.m. Saturday remains a mystery to authorities. Bruce Presgrave of the U.S. Geological Survey in Golden, Colo., said offices in Tennessee and Alabama did not register ground activity at that time. Presgrave said the tremor probably was caused by a sonic boom.

But spokesmen for the Pensacola Naval Air Station and Elgin Air Force Base said there were no flights or tests at that time that could have caused the shaking.

The National Weather Service, Escambia County Sheriff's Department and Emergency Medical Services received calls about the tremor Saturday, but could not explain it.

Privately, I wondered if the "sky quakes" along with the mysteriously flattened circles of grass were merely a timing coincidence. Almost two years had passed since my first sighting on November 11, 1987, and now the sky quaked in what seemed to me to be a planned anniversary event. Publicly I ignored the "coincidence" and focused on the task of organizing the yearly Gulf Breeze Christmas parade. Representing the Chamber of Commerce and the city, I was honored when asked to be chairman of the parade. Again my community had turned its back on the negative attacks that a few debunkers continued to throw at me.

This year I decided to redirect the focus of the annual parade. I wanted to downplay the commercial floats and encourage the families of Gulf Breeze to participate. The children would not be on the sidelines, not this year. They would be marching in the parade and the adults could cheer them on from the sidewalks. This parade would be for the children and I decided to call it the Gulf Breeze Christmas Tree Parade.

With help of the business community we supplied a Christmas tree to each elementary school classroom. I then arranged to have the trees mounted on small "red wagons." Each classroom proudly decorated their tree and eagerly awaited the start of "their" parade in which every member of the class would march along with the decorated tree.

Parade day was cold but the Christmas spirit was high.

Hundreds of children showed up to march in the parade. Their Christmas trees were decorated in every manner of handiwork, each a first place winner as far as I was concerned.

A week later my Christmas euphoria turned solemn. Stricken with a sudden illness, Dr. Overlade died.

I thought of his cheerful personality so well captured in the way he said hello on the first day I met him at his office when I politely said, "Hello, Dr. Overlade, how are you?"

He smiled and responded, "Fantastic, but getting better."

He often used humor to make serious points as a therapist. In the early 1960s, he was concerned about the lack of professional licensing of psychologists in Florida. To make his point he managed to get F. H. (Fuzzy Hamster) Overlade, his pet hamster, a Florida license. Soon thereafter, his recommended regulations were enacted at the state level.

Dr. Overlade was the past president of the Florida Board of Examiners of Psychology and Florida Psychology Association, positions he was proud of and took quite seriously.

Skeptical at first of UFO reports, it is to Dr. Overlade's credit that he studied the evidence in search of an answer. His help in understanding the UFO mystery will be missed and it is to his memory that I dedicate this book.

CHAPTER 19

GROUP PHOTOGRAPHS UFO

January 8, 1990

Frances and I have learned during the past years how to adjust to the unknown and how to expect the unexpected. With our feet planted firmly on the ground, we refused to be swept away by our UFO sightings and what we knew to be true. UFOs are real. UFOs were being seen in every country around the world. From cities, large and small, across the nation, we were receiving mail generated by the media coverage of the local sightings.

Our evening walks after dinner had become a quiet time for us, a miniescape from the frequent phone calls concerning construction business, the building subcontractors, and the anxious home buyers wanting to change a "very important" detail on their house plans. Phone calls from out-of-town reporters had mostly stopped because my phone number was now unlisted.

On this Monday, the evening breeze was crisp, so Frances and I wore our windbreakers as we set off on our brisk, randomly directed walk. Only a block from our house, while discussing our daughter's upcoming church-sponsored ski trip, we approached the Methodist Church. I turned to look at Frances, froze in my tracks, and pulled her to a halt beside me.

"Oh no, look there." I pointed to our right, off to the south, where a red, boiling light glowed from beneath a black disk (see drawing H).

We stood on the sidewalk, arms locked together, and watched a UFO's silent presence display itself with a pattern of rapid zigzags across the sky. Its darting movement was perhaps seventy-five degrees high and forced us to tilt our heads back to keep it in sight. Only seconds had passed when Frances let go of me and gave me a gentle push.

"Run, call somebody. And get the camera."

I didn't accept the implication that she would stay behind and took her by the arm saying, "Let's go. Come on, let's go."

We sprinted the short distance back to our house and burst through the front door with Frances calling to our daughter, Laura. I ran into my office, fumbled with my phone number index, and began calling MUFON investigators. Charles Flannigan was the first to answer—with his answering machine. I left a quick message and hung up.

The thought of whether or not the UFO was even still there crossed my mind. These sightings were usually brief and I could look quite foolish if people arrived to see nothing but the clouds so brightly illuminated by the full moon. It was a risk I was willing to take.

As the minutes were passing I dialed Vicki Lyons, MUFON field investigator. I got her answering machine. Again I left a quick message and called investigator Gary Watson. I got his pager and again left a message. Ready to give up, I called Duane Cook, *Sentinel* publisher, and Buddy Pollak, both of whom answered their phones and were immediately on their way.

My new 35-mm camera with its 222-mm lens awaited. Still unfamiliar with the complicated f-stop and exposure settings, I opted to leave the camera on automatic, allowing it to select the proper aperture and shutter speed. With tripod and camera in hand I ran back outside. Excited and relieved to see the UFO still overhead, I hurried down the block and closer to the red glowing object.

By pitching my head up and down I managed to keep an eye on the UFO and also attach the camera to the tripod. About that same time Duane pulled up with his wife, Dari, and her son, Chip. Car doors flew open releasing their cries of, "Where is it?"

I pointed, with an excited, "There. There. Don't you see it?"

Chip answered, "Yeah, there it is."

Dari followed his pointing finger and cried out, "I see it! I see it."

I struggled with the 222-mm lens in an effort to catch the darting UFO in the viewfinder. Hovering for a moment, the UFO would dash out of focus before I could lock down the tripod handle and snap the shutter. Its movement was almost impossible to follow. With the sudden turns, stopping, and moving in the wink of an eye, I'm surprised we managed to take any photographs of it at all.

Finally the object paused, motionless, in my field of view, its intense glow clear and still. I hit the shutter button. After another series of dizzying movements, the UFO was still again. I shot a photo, but this time the UFO flashed off to the right while the shutter was open.

Set on automatic, the camera selected a four-second shutter speed and 1.8 f-stop. What I could see through the 222-mm lens was approximately five times the size of what was visible to the naked eye and I hoped for some excellent photographs. I continued my efforts to locate and hold the UFO in the viewfinder long enough for another photo. Suddenly a ring of small lights surrounded the large red circle under the disk. I took a photo and with this ring of small lights still visible, Chip Holston also managed to take a photograph (see photo I).

During this time, Brenda and Buddy Pollack arrived and instantly filled the air with exclamations as they watched the red glow. Brenda was using her 300-mm lens, but was also having trouble taking photographs.

Emotions were running high, with the exception of Duane Cook's, who coolly kept his eye on the object. Expecting and hoping for the object to land, Duane's comments later were of disappointment that it hadn't.

At one point I recall seeing two other men join the group. I assumed somebody knew who they were, and didn't ask. As it turned out, each of us thought the others knew these men and so none of us found out their names.

Approximately fifteen to twenty minutes had passed

when suddenly I could no longer see the red glow. The black disk remained. The red glow had merely disappeared from beneath it. At this time Brenda Pollak took a photograph hoping to catch the black disk. Her photograph remains a mystery. Taken with a three-second exposure, it shows the trail of the object with one hundred ten separate color changes.

Dari said, "It looked like it just turned over."

Others felt differently about it.

Duane said, "The red disappeared and then a few seconds later is when I saw the black disk."

He was suggesting that maybe they were two separate objects. But others, myself included, recalled seeing, with the aid of the 222-mm lens, the disk and the red glow as one object.

A few moments later the black disk, highlighted against the moonlit clouds, which were at a thirteen-hundred-foot elevation, vanished into the cloud cover. What happened next was of great significance to those of us standing there still watching the sky. Only a minute or two had passed when the loud roar of two helicopters beat the air. They sped toward us over the surrounding houses, floodlights ablaze. Again, later, a single chopper hovered over the Methodist Church parking lot and searched the area with its floodlight. Were they looking for what we had seen and photographed? If so, they missed their close encounter by minutes.

The next day, Vicki Lyons checked with the air control tower at the Pensacola Naval Air Station. A Navy spokesman said there was "unusual activity over Gulf Breeze requiring deployment of search and rescue helicopters." When Vicki asked what our military was searching for she was told, ". . . given the nature of things that are going on over Gulf Breeze, take your best guess." When asked the time of this "unusual activity" the answer was 6:30 to 7:00 P.M.

According to my watch our group sighting started at 6:28 and ended at 7:05 P.M. The next night the helicopters were again out in force and witnesses once more reported seeing the UFO. How long could the officials, military and otherwise, keep a lid on what so many of us were seeing? Our local newspaper featured these UFO sightings with a huge front-page story but at the "official" level, not a word was spoken.

The Gulf Breeze witnesses were ready to be heard but only the entertainment TV shows were interested. Where were Peter Jennings or Dan Rather? How could hundreds of people step forward as witnesses and be completely ignored by the network news? Are the national networks so worried about their reputations that they are afraid to mention the word UFO or is there a more sinister motive for the lack of coverage?

Frances's Account

Ed and I arrived home at a full run. While he punched the autodialer on his telephone and gathered up his photo equipment, I dashed up the stairs calling Laura. Since Ed didn't feel threatened or frightened by the UFO, neither did I. It had been so long since we had seen anything, I thought Laura would want to see it too.

"I thought you and Daddy were going for a walk. What are you yelling about?" Laura met me at her bedroom door dressed in a short, sleeveless nightgown. She'd just finished an early shower and water still dripped from her hair.

"We were, but when we got to the church we saw a UFO. Grab your robe and come on. Quick. Maybe it's still there."

I turned and hurried back down the stairs. Laura was right behind me, my advice about the robe ignored. We ran outside and stopped in the driveway and looked up. The UFO seemed dimmer than it had when Ed and I first saw it, but it was still clearly visible. As Laura and I stood looking at it, Ed dashed out of the house with his camera equipment and sprinted toward the church.

"I'm going to get the binoculars." Laura ran for the house before she finished talking.

"Put some clothes on while you're in there. You'll get sick standing out here in the cold with a wet head."

She'd been shivering in the cold January night air, but I half expected her to come back outside dressed as she'd been. I was happy when she came back with more on, but I couldn't help but laugh at her choice. She was brilliant white from head to foot, all decked out in her new ski suit and boots. Ignoring my chuckles, she lifted the binoculars and started a running commentary on what she could, and couldn't, see.

"I can see a black shape above the red light. But it all looks fuzzy. I can't hold these things still enough."

"It must have gone higher, because it looks so much dimmer. If I look away, I have a hard time finding it again." I did my best to assure Laura that neither her eyes nor her ability with the binoculars was at fault.

"We need to be closer. I'm going up on the roof! I bet I can see it better from there." Her words wiped away my humor.

"No!" My order fell on thin air. She was already gone. Seconds later she climbed out her bedroom window and onto the roof of the first story.

"Laura, get back inside right now."

"Why?"

"You could fall."

Binoculars slung over her shoulder, she hoisted herself onto the second-story roof. "Mom, I sunbathe out here all the time; I'm not gonna fall."

I couldn't argue with her on that point, and I hated to tell her my real reason for not wanting her on the roof. Not only was she in the open, and high, but in her white outfit she practically glowed. She was a perfect target for the UFO if they were interested in taking her. Ed hadn't been afraid, and I'd felt secure in knowing that, but now I wished I had my daughter safely on the ground beside me.

"It's gone. At least the red light is. But I can still see a black disk-shaped thing. Can you see it from down there?"

I'd been so worried about Laura, I hadn't even thought to look at the UFO since she'd climbed onto the roof. Now I searched the sky for it. The red light was indeed gone, and I couldn't see the black disk Laura was talking about.

"No. And since you can't see much of anything either, come down."

Soon she was back on the ground beside me and we decided to walk over to the church. Maybe some of the people Ed had called had arrived in time to see the UFO. With luck, Duane would have his camera with him.

CHAPTER 20

MORE SKY QUAKES AND GRASS CIRCLES

January 25, 1990

Sky quake. That's what they have come to be called. The ground rattles like an earthquake and the sky shakes like a silent sonic boom. The newspaper carried these reports.

Pensacola News-Journal:

Mystery Jolt Rattles Area

Puzzled officials were unable to say what or who was responsible, but all agreed something happened . . . The U.S. Navy was calling it "tremors of unknown origin." Geophysicists at the National Earthquake Center in Golden, Colo., . . . pooh-poohed the idea of an earthquake. "We don't see anything on our instruments in Tallahassee," said Willie Jacobs.

Pensacola News-Journal:

No Answers For The Day The Panhandle Shook

The great mystery remains.
Police and emergency switchboards were flooded with calls after something shook the

Pensacola area about 2:10 p.m. Thursday, yet officials are unsure what caused the tremor.

Initially, rumors centered on the military and the possibility of a sonic boom caused by one of their aircraft.

"We're totally in the dark. We know it's none of our stuff," said 1st Lt. Leah Bryant, a spokeswoman for the Munitions System Division at Eglin Air Force Base.

"We don't have indications of it being caused by the U.S. military," said Harry White, a spokesman for Pensacola Naval Air Station.

Geologists and geophysicists swear the earth didn't move and point their fingers back at one of Uncle Sam's supersonic jets.

"All we can comment on is the fact that we didn't detect any earthquake that you would have felt down there," said Georgia Tech geophysicist Dr. Tim Long.

January 25, 1990
Grass Circle

The discovery of another circle of flattened, spiraled grass in South Shoreline Park on the same day as the latest sky quake prompted more questions. Were these circles and the sky quakes somehow related? And did these circles have any connection with the UFOs?

As with so much of this phenomenon, we couldn't answer the questions but when this latest, larger circle (see photo F) was measured, its diameter matched the fourteen-foot bottom ring of the UFO I had photographed with the stereo camera on May 1, 1988.

These unexplained circles and "sky quakes" gave us physical evidence. Something very strange was happening. There was no denying their existence. Even the most skeptical could see the circles for themselves and feel the jolting "sky quakes." But once again there were others who ignored the evidence and tried to ridicule me.

An article in *Woman's World* Magazine quoted a critic as saying, "The Gulf Breeze sightings are just a yarn." The critic accused me of "trick photography" and of "embellishing" tales to reap financial profits.

My community rejected those outrageous accusations and that following week I was reappointed unanimously to serve another two-year term on the Gulf Breeze Planning Board.

CHAPTER 21

THE NINE O'CLOCK UFO

April 14, 1990

Sporadic UFO sighting reports continued and were investigated by MUFON as their manpower would allow, but most UFO sightings were now considered by local residents as commonplace. Discussed with matter-of-fact attitudes at social events throughout town, many sightings were never officially reported.

MUFON investigators were looking into several early-April sightings that had occurred at about 9:00 P.M. All of these reports involved multiple witnesses. Andy O'Daniel, Linda and Lyle Culberson, as well as others reported to the *Sentinel* and MUFON that their sightings happened shortly after 9:00 P.M. Clearly nine o'clock had become the time to have a UFO watch. The question was, Where? MUFON investigators suggested the parking area at the south end of the Pensacola Bay Bridge because of its unobstructed panorama overlooking Gulf Breeze.

On Saturday, April 14, 1990, a dozen people gathered at the bridge. Cameras in hand, they scanned the horizon and filled the time with casual conversation. Suddenly, City Councilwoman Brenda Pollak yelled, "Look over there! Here it comes!"

A red, boiling light was coming directly at them. It made a few zigzags, changed its course, and once again headed straight toward the group. A flurry of commotion swept through the crowd. They began taking photographs and video film of the UFO as it approached and passed overhead.

I had been invited to the "UFO watch" and as I made

the turn onto Highway 98 at the stoplight about three quarters of a mile from the bridge I saw the red glowing ball of light. Grabbing my 8-mm video camera, I began filming through the window as I drove. Not wanting to lower the camera, I never managed to get my truck out of first gear. With my engine racing I reached the group and pulled into the parking area near the boat launch.

The excited sounds of people watching the UFO greeted me when I opened the door. By now the UFO had passed directly overhead, cut perpendicularly across the bridge, and was moving east over the bay. Its distant red glow was still easy to see. I handed my video camera to a bystander so I could use my 35-mm camera to zoom in on the object. A local film producer, Bill Richards, was present and, with his professional Beta camera, he managed to document the very bright outline of the UFO.

The sighting that night resulted in three videotapes and multiple photographs, but this was only the beginning of the "nine o'clock UFO." Every night people gathered at the bridge parking lot but nothing happened until three days later. On April 17 the UFO again appeared and a larger crowd watched it move across the sky toward the southeast. The next night an even larger crowd of area residents took up positions and cameras at the foot of the bridge. Two Gulf Breeze police officers were on duty to oversee the crowd.

From nearby, a woman yelled, "I hear it. It's coming." She grabbed her children in a panic. "Can't you hear it? It's humming."

Suddenly the red object appeared. It was 9:48 P.M. The UFO moved from the east to the west, approaching the center of town. Cameras flashed. The crowd was stunned. Nobody else had heard a humming, yet the UFO appeared seconds after the woman yelled, "It's humming." The crowd fell silent and watched the brilliant red object light up the night sky.

I understood the woman's distressed yell, "Can't you hear it?" But the hum was not audible, it was within her, a hum I had heard many times during my UFO encounters many months earlier.

In almost every sighting the UFO departed the same way. The red glow would fade and be replaced by a sudden flash of white, then nothing; it would be gone. But other times the brilliant red would return after the white flash. Many, many times white, yellow, or red balls of light would shoot out of the UFO.

During these mid-April "nine o'clock UFO" sightings, scores of witnesses gathered to watch. Military aircraft would arrive just before the UFO winked out, yet their presence would be denied the following day by military spokesmen. Also of interest was the return of the special low-level radar blimp deployed in Pensacola Bay (see plate R).

Unfortunately the tabloid newspapers could not let these UFO sightings go unreported. So the sightings and all the witnesses were lumped in with the other tabloid headlines such as, "Held Captive On A UFO—I Was Sex Slave" and "Pigmy Gives Birth To Half Man Half Frog." In with that company, how was it possible for the general public to accept the reality of what we were seeing?

Tabloid reporting and motivated debunking seem to have a common bond: twist the true story to make it fit and if the facts don't fit, simply make up some new ones. But where the tabloid reporters had limits, the motivated debunkers did not and in the following weeks we found out how far they would go.

Frances's Account

Early in our sightings, Ed had been contacted by a book publisher about letting someone ghostwrite the story of our UFO experiences. We'd told them no. The sightings were ongoing, the investigation had just really begun, and we didn't want our names revealed to the public.

Months later, the MUFON investigators brought up the subject of a book being written. Again Ed and I balked, but we did concede that if a book was ever written, we wanted it done in a scientific, non-sensational manner. We'd seen, all too clearly, what the media could do—intentionally or not. Debunkers had often used inaccuracies in the media reports against us, saying we were changing our story.

Finally, after months of agonizing over the ramifications of going public, Ed and I had decided the only way to get the true story on record, once and for all, was to write it ourselves. The book about our UFO encounters was published in March of 1990 and we immediately experienced some positive side effects.

At our first book signing, in our local Gulf Breeze bookstore, people shared their own UFO sightings with us. Not all of them were recent, as ours were. Many of the encounters they told us about dated back years, some as long as ten or twenty years in their pasts.

What amazed Ed and me almost as much as the number and variety of sightings people told us about was the way in which they did it. Hesitantly at first, almost as if they were afraid, even now, to tell anyone, they would lean close to the table where we sat and begin. Once they realized we were interested in what they had to say, that we wouldn't laugh at them, they relaxed and opened up.

There was no "type" of UFO witness that we could discern. Children, adults, grandparents, pilots, active duty, ex-military, white-collar, blue-collar, and retirees—all were represented in those who spoke to us. The one common bond they all shared was that they had experienced something they couldn't explain by ordinary means, though many of them had tried to, often for years. And they hoped that, finally, something would be forthcoming on an official government level to help them understand what we'd all been seeing.

It was after one of these book signings that Ed took off to meet the MUFON investigators at the foot of the bridge to look for the "nine o'clock UFO." I couldn't go with him. Laura had homework and, since I'd been gone most of the day, I felt I needed to stay home and help her. When Ed came in later and told me about the glowing red ball they had all seen and photographed, I wished I'd been there.

As many nights as we could, we joined the crowd of watchers gathered at the bridge. Ed went more often than

I did, since Laura often kept me busy at home, but I had my share of these glowing ball sightings, especially after Dan came home from college in early May.

As the end of the month approached, the sightings had generated new media interest, both locally and from as far away as Japan. And, as we had already learned, any time the media coverage increased, so did the debunking effort. But I didn't have time to think too much about debunkers. Laura and I were going to my niece's wedding.

After driving Laura to school Friday morning, I came home to finish the last minute details for the weekend trip. I fed the dog and the cats, paying special attention to Crystal. While the cats didn't seem to care if they saw us or not, so long as they were fed, Crystal wasn't happy if she didn't see each member of the family every day.

Each time Dan came home from college and then left again, it took her a while to get over it. I knew Crystal would miss Laura and me, although we'd be gone only two and a half days, so I threw a few sticks for her to fetch and played some more with her before I went inside the house to finish packing.

When Laura and I returned home Sunday evening, Ed and Dan told us Crystal was sick. She'd stopped eating and wouldn't even drink water. Worse, she was vomiting when she tried to drink. We all hurried out to the backyard.

Crystal lifted her head when we came outside, and tried to wag her tail, but I could tell she was too weak. She didn't look like the same dog I'd left barely two days earlier. Her ever present energy was totally missing and her eyes had a glazed, feverish look. She seemed to be pounds thinner. As quickly as we could, we took her to the veterinarian.

Ed and I described Crystal's behavior, and how she'd been fine on Friday. The first thing the woman asked us was if we had sprayed our yard with fertilizer or weed killer, or if there were any other toxins around that Crystal could have gotten into. Our answer on all counts was "no." The doctor told us her first suspicion was that the dog had been poisoned but since we felt certain Crystal couldn't have gotten into anything in our yard, she would work on trying to rehydrate her, then go from there.

We left Crystal at the clinic and returned home to face Dan and Laura. Ed tried to reassure them that Crystal was going to be fine. So did I, but in my heart I didn't believe that the dog we'd given Laura as a birthday present seven years before would be coming home. When the veterinarian called the next morning and told me Crystal had died during the night, I was the only one in our family not surprised by the news. But having feared it would happen made me no less heartbroken than the rest of them.

Ed and I drove to the clinic to get Crystal. He kept blaming himself for not realizing how sick she was. I tried to remind him of the other times she would skip a day or even two of eating when she had a virus or something. She'd always gotten better before; he'd thought she would this time.

At the clinic, the doctor told us it was unusual for a healthy dog like Crystal to go into such a rapid decline. She asked us if we wanted her to perform an autopsy to determine, without a doubt, what she suspected—that Crystal had been poisoned. I told her no.

The only way Crystal could have eaten something poisonous was if someone intentionally gave it to her. If that was the case, I didn't want to know. I didn't want to believe that there was anyone cruel enough to do that to an animal whose only "sin" was that she wouldn't let strangers into our yard. And, as long as I didn't know that she hadn't died of natural causes, I wouldn't have to lie to Laura.

We buried Crystal in the backyard, near Laura's late parakeet and goldfish. Just before Ed covered her with dirt, Laura leaned down and ran her fingers through Crystal's white coat one last time. As Ed spaded dirt into the hole, Laura turned away and hugged me, hiding her face against my body.

The next week went by in a blur as school drew to a close. At one time or another, every one of us would forget Crystal was dead. We'd look outside, expecting to see her, and the pain would hit us again. But we couldn't dwell on it. Ed and I were helping out with Project Graduation again this year and the all-night party for the newly graduated students was coming up that weekend. A few days after that, Laura would be off on a trip to Six Flags Over Georgia with the church youth group.

It was probably because we were all so busy that Ed didn't discover that the album of UFO photographs was missing until the day we saw Laura off on the trip to Georgia. He kept the album in his desk drawer, handy if anyone should have a question about a particular photo or if they simply wanted to see them.

They were professionally made copies and anyone who didn't know better would have mistaken them for the originals. The original photographs were locked away, taken out only when someone like Dr. Maccabee needed them for analysis. The copies had been made at his suggestion to protect the originals from being damaged by too much handling. Now it would seem they had possibly protected them from being stolen.

"When's the last time you remember having the album?" I sat across from Ed in his office, wondering if he'd have any way of recalling.

"About the time you left for the wedding. When that Japanese TV crew was in town. I took the album over to their hotel so they could shoot some footage of the photographs."

"Are you sure you brought it back with you?" I didn't doubt it. Ed was almost as careful with the duplicates as he was with the actual photographs.

"Absolutely."

The doctor's questions about Crystal and poison flashed into my mind with an impact like a fist to my stomach. Suddenly short of breath, I tried not to think about it, but couldn't stop. The album had disappeared sometime in a two-week period, most likely after Crystal had died. Was it a coincidence? As much as I wanted to think so, I couldn't.

CHAPTER 22

FAKE MODEL CAUSES
MEDIA BLITZ

National media attention was focused on an upcoming conference, the 1990 Mutual UFO Network International Symposium, scheduled for July 6, 7, and 8 at the Pensacola Civic Center. Reservations made from around the world quickly sold out the much talked about event.

UFO experts would present their theories and latest UFO evidence. Frances and I agreed to address the symposium and present an update on the continuing UFO sightings in Gulf Breeze.

The local MUFON chapter responsible for organizing the symposium appointed a committee to deal with the many details of such an international event. The possibility of dirty tricks being played by debunkers was recognized when, on April 28, 1990, an ad was placed in the *Pensacola News-Journal* proclaiming "Hoax UFO balloons should be reported."

The intention of the ad was to distract, to make a false explanation that the hundreds of UFO sightings in the Pensacola/Gulf Breeze area were "Hoax UFO balloons." Directed at the media and at those who had not had a UFO sighting, this attempt at misinformation was only a hint of what was to come. A debunking attack, driven by the scheduled presence of national media at the symposium, was a certainty. Most of the local MUFON members assumed that we would see the sky flooded with the debunkers' "UFO balloons." We were all caught off guard by the massive media coverage of the surprise UFO "model."

The huge headline on the front page of the Sunday, June 10, 1990, *News-Journal* proclaimed:

"Gulf Breeze UFO Model Found"

A photograph of a nine-inch UFO model accompanied the article and clearly the insinuation was that the UFO photographs that I had taken were nothing more than photographs of the model. In the rush to print the story, little attention was paid to the obvious differences between the model and my photographs. But later when the model (see photo V) was compared with my photographs, the model was quickly recognized as a debunker's "dirty trick."

The *News-Journal* editors did not note that the size ratio of the model was too flat and wide. A missing bottom row of "portholes" from the model was also of little concern to the news reporter, as was the number of "portholes" across the top of the model. There are seven of these "portholes" visible on the model and only five on the real UFO that I had photographed. Another important detail that received no coverage was the manner in which the model was found. A complete investigation revealed that this is what happened.

In December 1988, Frances and I built a new house. We moved and placed our previous house on the market. For ten months the house remained open for potential buyers to freely look through the house. In November 1989, we sold the house. Eight months later, June 1990 (fully eighteen months after we had moved out), a *News-Journal* reporter walked up to the front door, rang the bell, and asked the new owner three questions. "Have you seen any UFOs? Have you found any photographs? Have you found a model?"

The new owners of the house commented on how odd it was to have a reporter "drop in from out of the blue and ask, 'Have you found a model?' It was almost as if he knew the model was there."

I strongly echo that comment. The circumstances suggest those of a reporter who received a tip, but a tip from whom? My answer is, a tip from the person responsible for making and planting the model in the house attic sometime during those ten months after we moved out and before the present owner moved in.

When questioned about the tip, the reporter denied that he had received one. The reporter also refused to take a lie detector test.

For three days following the front-page "model" story the *News-Journal* rejected all requests by other newspapers to see the UFO model. I was also turned away by secretaries who said that all the editors were on "retreat." The local television stations were also refused access to the UFO model.

When the model was finally released, to the owners of the house, the reason for withholding it from examination was clear. Not only did the model not look like the photographs that I and others had taken of the UFO in our skies, but it was actually made out of material that could be dated.

Dating when the model was made proved conclusively that the UFO model was a debunker's dirty trick designed to discredit the Gulf Breeze UFO sightings, a dirty trick timed to have the maximum impact on the upcoming International MUFON UFO Symposium.

This is how the model was dated. A complete examination was performed on the model and the experts were surprised to find that the center section was made with a two-inch-wide by approximately twenty-eight-inch-long strip of blueprint paper. I am a house designer and builder and I immediately recognized the writing on the paper as mine. It was covered with drafting lines, dimensions, and, most importantly, the notation of the living area and slab area of a custom house plan that I had designed.

With the exact square footage of both the living area and the slab area the plan could be traced back to the house and the owner. The owner was located but the house had never been built. The owners, a Mr. and Mrs. Thomas, were very helpful and presented copies of the house plan that I had custom designed for them. When the Thomases were asked for the date that the house plan had been drawn, their records and memory agreed, September 6, 1989. A critic tried to press the Thomases to change their statements and here is how Mrs. Thomas answered.

> The 2,393 sq. ft. slab area might be the same as that of another house or the 1740 sq. ft. living area might be the same. But the possibility of both being the same is nearly impossible. Even if it were planned it would have been difficult. With us telling him [Ed Walters] what we liked etc. *That* I know would have been impossible. It [the UFO model] certainly could not have been used for any pictures before Sept. 6, 1989. The first time we met or spoke to Ed.
>
> I'm sorry if this is not what you wanted to hear but it is the conclusion I have reached. I do know my own writing and I do know what was on the paper [plan] when we brought it home.

This date, September 6, 1989, certified by Mr. and Mrs. Thomas, was conclusive proof that the model, made with the Thomases' blueprint paper, did not exist until almost two years after my first UFO sighting and photographs. Whoever made the model had tried to use a discarded piece of blueprint paper to tie the UFO model to me and this same piece of blueprint paper was the conclusive evidence that proved the model was built after September 6, 1989. All of my photographs were taken between November 1987 and May 1988.

We still did not know who made and planted the model but we had exposed another "dirty trick" that had backfired on someone. The UFO model created a lot of talk and controversy but when the smoke cleared the UFO model itself proved that the debunkers were still at work. Along with the fake Chrysler Building UFO photographs, the model gave us additional evidence supporting my theory of an orchestrated UFO cover-up.

Photo Reenactment Test

During the past years I have learned that when a UFO witness makes a report, the scales of justice are reversed. The witness is expected to prove that the UFO sighting happened. It is generally accepted that a skeptic need not prove that it did not happen—merely offer a standard explanation of "heat inversion," "helicopter," "Venus," "hoax," etc.

In a case involving photographs of clearly defined UFOs, the hoax accusation is quickly spread by the debunkers. In other words, the witness/photographer must prove that the UFO sightings and photographs are real. This means that the photographs and the photographer must be examined completely—the photographs computer analyzed and the photographer lie detection tested.

I have taken four different lie detector tests, given by three different examiners. I have passed them all. Not a single lie detector test has been taken by a debunker. Yet every time a negative accusation is hurled at me, I have been expected to take another test.

One hoax allegation that followed a few weeks after the "UFO model story" was that the model was suspended over a flashlight and photographed with a double exposure to produce photograph 19 of the UFO hovering over the road.

Photographic test experiments by the media are the exception in the news business because television news and newspaper deadlines seldom permit such time-consuming tests. Fortunately, an ABC reporter was interested enough to spend some personal time and set up a photo experiment to test this latest hoax allegation. At the exact location where I took photo 19, he suspended a small model over a flashlight and, with the help of assistants, set up the conditions as per the accusation.

The flashlight lens was covered with an orange filter and mounted several inches below the model so as to shine up onto the model. The position of the flashlight was arranged to create the illusion of a reflection on the road, which was really the head of the flashlight shining up and onto the bottom of the model.

Many test photographs were taken of this model and flashlight experiment. Based on the principle that a source of light is brighter than its reflection, the results of this re-enactment are conclusive. Every photo clearly shows that the light "reflection" coming from the road (the flashlight) is brighter than the model.

The same brightness test was performed on my photo 19 and shows the exact opposite. As it should be, the UFO in my photo 19 is brighter than the reflection on the road. In other words, the source of light is from the UFO and not a flashlight mounted below a model. The hoax allegation was proved false.

Frances's Account

On Saturday, the twelfth, Laura returned from her trip to Six Flags Over Georgia with the church youth group, eager to tell us about every ride, the trip there and back, and who did what to whom—all in minute detail. We stayed up late into the night, talking and laughing, even though I knew I'd be up early to see how the *News-Journal* would handle the story about the model. I didn't tell Laura about it; she was just too happy. I'd have plenty of time to explain to her on Sunday what little we knew.

The tone of the Sunday morning headline and article in the *News-Journal* didn't surprise me. The reporter involved had made his opinion about UFOs in general, and Ed and me in particular, well-known to us and others. Still, I was upset that they had managed to twist the facts while giving the appearance of writing a balanced story. And the next day, when a friend called to tell me he'd heard about the model on the Paul Harvey radio show—with a few mistakes added—I wished there was some way we could fight back. But we couldn't. I had quickly learned that talking with most newspaper reporters was a waste of time.

At one time I'd had a rock solid, probably naive, faith that if you read it in the newspaper, then it must be true.

No longer. I had first person experience with how a reporter can alter the meaning of what a person says by paraphrasing a statement or using a quote out of context. Suddenly I found myself wondering how widespread this practice of manipulating the news was. How many times had I been influenced about a candidate, an accused, an issue, by biased reporting? And the worst of it was, unless you personally had access to all the facts, you didn't know you were being fed a skewed version of the truth.

I explained all this to Laura, as well as I could, and drove her to her first Driver's Education class at the high school on Monday morning. We had been through so many rough spots since the UFO sightings had begun, and each time something new hit the media, I held my breath waiting to see how the other kids would treat her. What they'd say. This time, since the article had been so negative, I was more anxious than ever. I wasn't as concerned about Dan. The people at the nephrology clinic where he was working for the summer stayed too busy with dialysis patients to do much gossiping.

As it turned out, I worried for nothing. Laura's friends were too nervous about getting behind the wheel of a car, many for the first time, to talk about UFOs. And the kids weren't the only ones with other things on their minds. Later in the day, when I took my contribution for dinner over to the church, no one there mentioned the newspaper article either. But the model—who could have made and planted it, and if we could hope to prove that—never left my mind.

Days later, when Ed and I finally learned what was written on the strip of drafting paper used in the model, we went to work. In addition to the square footage figures, we had the name of the road the house was on. We'd built several houses on that road and had one lot still vacant. We spent hours going through Ed's files of blueprints. None of the houses on that road, nor any of the other houses Ed had ever built, had those square footages. Nothing matched. But we knew something should have. That's when we remembered Ed had designed a house for some people from out of town. It had been planned for that last lot but the house was never built.

It took a minute for us to remember their names, but when we did, Ed knew why he couldn't find the blueprint. He had thrown it away after the Thomases called and said they wouldn't be building the house after all. He couldn't even find any of his preliminary drawings. The Thomases had been given a copy of the graph paper drawing, but would they still have it after all this time? Especially since the house could only be built on a lot that sloped as radically as ours did. It was a long shot, but it was worth checking into.

Finding the Thomases turned out to be harder than we imagined. We had only their names and the name of a rather large city. Directory assistance turned up no matches in the city, but by checking the surrounding areas they came up with three phone numbers. Ed dialed each in turn and finally found the Thomases we were looking for. And, glory be, they still had the preliminary drawing Ed had done for them. He asked Mr. Thomas what the square footages were. They matched!

Naively, I thought establishing the date on the drafting paper used in the model would prove something to the debunkers and the news media. The debunkers tried to convince the Thomases that it wasn't their plan. The media chose to ignore it. Subsequent stories made no mention of the fact the model had to have been built more than a year and a half after Ed's last UFO photograph, nor did they mention any of the other discrepancies between the model and Ed's photographs.

While the model took center stage with the media, a few other UFO stories were also printed. The June 14 *Gulf Breeze Sentinel* carried an article about a sighting on Friday, the eighth.

At 11:30 P.M. on the eighth, the Bridges family of Navarre Beach, east of Gulf Breeze, saw a UFO light display out over the Gulf of Mexico. A total of twenty to thirty lights appeared to be low over the water approximately ten miles away, south southeast of their home. According to the Bridges, the lights would at times seemingly join together in a circular orbit, then shoot out in many directions. Some of the flight paths were smooth arcs, while others jagged with sharp turns and abrupt stops. The UFOs would then randomly regroup and repeat the process.

Another group of approximately twenty people also saw the lights. Because of the extreme speed of the movements, sharp turns, instantaneous reversals, and abrupt blinking out, the witnesses decided this was not a natural phenomenon such as fireworks, naval gunfire, flares, or lights from a ship. The sightings lasted for about thirty minutes.

Two weeks later the *Sentinel* briefly reported two sightings on June 21, a Thursday. There had been two calls to the MUFON hotline by two sets of independent witnesses, who may have observed the same UFO, but at different times.

The first sighting, by two adults, occurred at 2:30 P.M. They were driving east on Highway 98, approximately four miles from Navarre, when they noticed a white round object in the sky above the road, heading west to east. At first they thought they were seeing a blimp, but then they realized it wasn't, because of its shape and relatively fast speed.

Later, at 6:00 P.M., a woman and two teenagers were driving north on West Bay Boulevard. They saw a white, round object hovering above the road at treetop level. Within seconds the object shot off to the west and disappeared from view. Because of its appearance, low flight path, and high rate of speed, they knew it was not a conventional aircraft.

In all, during June, there were four daylight and two nocturnal sightings reported to MUFON. Every report made Ed and me feel better. The planted model and the subsequent media hurrah had been intended to discredit us, to put an end to all the news coverage and talk about UFOs in the Gulf Breeze area. But whoever was responsible for the model apparently had no control over the UFO. No matter how much the debunkers and certain members of the media wanted to, they couldn't stop the sightings.

CHAPTER 23

SOLDIERS FLEE TO GULF BREEZE

On Saturday, July 14, 1990, "Kathy,"* a classmate of my daughter, asked to come to our house. She was tearful but didn't explain what was wrong. When she arrived, she emotionally detailed a riveting story. My instincts told me her UFO story was true and, at the very least, a major event. Her voice was soft and her emotions tangled in details uncertain to her.

That morning she had been awakened at gunpoint and handcuffed. FBI agents swarmed through her house. Along with her mother and their visiting houseguests, six U.S. Army soldiers, they were taken to the local police station and questioned. Several hours later both mother and daughter were released but the six soldiers were charged with desertion. News of this incident did not leak until four days later, when the *Pensacola News-Journal* front page proclaimed:

"Six Soldiers Held in Spying Probe"

The events detailed by "Kathy" were far removed from a "spying probe." The six soldiers had secret clearances and were stationed in Augsburg, Germany, at a secret Army electronic listening post. Trained in cryptography, the soldiers had suddenly abandoned their stations, evaded authorities, and reentered the United States undetected.

---

*Kathy is not her real name.

Was it just a coincidence that two days later they arrived in Gulf Breeze or were the UFO stories that they told—later repeated to us by Kathy—what motivated them to desert? With the exception of a confidential conversation with our local police chief, Frances and I decided to say nothing to the news reporters.

One day later, on the front page of the *Pensacola News-Journal,* the headline read:

"Cult Linked to Desertion Arrest"

There it was. A cover story in the making. The six soldiers had embarrassed the U.S. Military and something very odd was going on. What Kathy had repeated to us took on added meaning.

From experience, I had learned that the official cover story of choice is the "cult." If the six soldiers could be branded "cult" members in the eyes of the general public, then they would have no credibility. It was a replay of the first attempt that was made to discredit me after the Gulf Breeze UFO sightings, but this was big national news. The major networks carried a news conference with a Pentagon spokesman explaining it all away as "just six members of a cult known as The End of The World."

Oddly enough the media never questioned why six so-called cult members would be trained in cryptography and have secret clearances. Nevertheless, the "cult" explanation was spread on the national wire services and one day later the cult story was being further exploited with this headline:

"Six Soldiers Here to Kill Anti-Christ"

If that didn't fan the flames of national media attention, nothing would. The Antichrist in Gulf Breeze! I couldn't believe the extreme extent of this cover-up story. These six soldiers either had earthshaking classified information or this was the most bizarre case of overreaction by the military in recorded history.

Three days and three headline stories, and no mention of anything to do with UFOs, as I had heard repeated from Kathy. But on the fourth day the UFO story began to show up. The headline:

"Soldiers Were to Expose UFO Cover-Up"

Within the article it was reported that the soldiers were in Gulf Breeze "to meet with an unidentified author who had written about UFOs" and to "expose a government cover-up of reports that aliens have visited Earth." Based on the Antichrist story and the UFO cover-up connection the electronic media flooded my front yard. I was the only UFO author in town. Reporters yelled to me from the road, "Are you the unidentified author?" "Were you contacted by the soldiers?" "Are you the Antichrist?" I answered no, no, and no to all such repeated questions.

Only four days had passed since the "Spying Probe" headline and the media had now been driven into a frenzy by the "Antichrist" and "UFO Cover-up" stories.

The six soldiers were under arrest and being held in the Fort Knox stockade. On that fourth day they were allowed to speak briefly to family members. What we learned from the families showed up in the headlines of the newspapers on the next day.

"Soldiers Deny Being Spies or Cult Members"

On approximately July 23, 1990, only six days into the intrigue, an anonymous letter accompanied by UFO photographs (see photo A) was mailed to the U.S. Army and the media. This is what the letter said:

ABC, NBC, CBS, AP, UPI

US ARMY:
FREE THE GULF BREEZE SIX.
WE HAVE THE MISSING FILES, THE BOX OF
500+ UFO PHOTOS AND THE PLANS YOU WANT
BACK. HERE IS PROOF WITH CLOSE-UPS CUT
OUT. NEXT WE SEND THE CLOSE-UPS AND
THEN EVERYTHING UNLESS THEY ARE RE-
LEASED. ANSWER CODE AUGSBB3CM

I learned of this letter from our local newspaper publisher and later saw an original which had been sent to CBS reporter Lea Sinclair. The letter was not reported on the nightly news by any of the recipients. Mark Curtis, a reporter for WEAR, an ABC affiliate, said the decision had been made to "wait and see." The general opinion was that the letter was a prank and that the military would never capitulate, even if the letter was valid. Therefore, a refusal to release the six soldiers would call the bluff of the extortion letter. So, if the UFO photos, plans, and files did exist, then all the media had to do was wait, confident that the military would not bow to such a threat.

Four days later, the six soldiers were released. Coincidence? The July 28, 1990, headline read:

"Army Releases Soldiers Charged with Desertion"

All six were given a general discharge. Three of the soldiers returned to Gulf Breeze directly from Fort Knox and continue to insist that they are not members of a "cult." They resist any comment on UFOs.

Frances's Account

I guess I should have known from the minute we heard Kathy's message on Ed's answering machine that something strange was going on. It wasn't just that Kathy sounded so upset, almost hysterical. It was the fact that she had called Ed's private telephone number instead of the family number.

From "day one" all the kids knew that Ed's phone number was strictly off-limits to them except in cases of a genuine emergency. And Kathy, probably the most respectful and reserved of Laura's friends, would be the last one I'd expect to abuse that rule. Still, I never dreamed that what had prompted her call would turn out to be so bizarre.

As soon as we finished listening to Kathy's message, I called her back. Although more than two hours had passed since she had called us, her voice was still shaky, as if she was on the verge of tears. The first thing she asked was if she could come over. I quickly explained that Laura wasn't home, then told Kathy she was welcome to come to our house anyway and wait for Laura. Kathy asked if I could drive over and pick her up. It wasn't that unusual a request. Since neither she nor Laura was old enough to drive, I often acted as their chauffeur.

It took me only five minutes to reach Kathy's home. As I pulled up at the curb, she and her mother, "Anna,"* came out the front door. I got out to meet them and noticed that Kathy's eyes were red and puffy, as if she'd been crying for hours. But it was her mother's appearance that shocked me.

Anna's normally perfect hairstyle and makeup were nonexistent. And instead of her usual well-chosen clothes and jewelry, she looked like she had dressed in the first thing she could put her hands on. Like Kathy, she'd been crying. As soon as I was close enough, Kathy hugged me. When it became apparent she wasn't going to move away, I kept my arm around her and looked at Anna. What was

---

*Anna is not her real name.

going on? I didn't voice the question in my mind, hoping Anna would supply the answer without my having to ask.

Instead, she said, "Frances, after you get to your house and Kathy tells you what this is all about, if you want to bring her back, I'll understand."

What I wanted was to ask Anna for an explanation, but she kept looking down the street, then back at me. I had the feeling she was anxious for us to leave.

So, instead of asking anything, I heard myself saying, "Whatever the problem is, Kathy can stay with us. And don't worry about her."

Anna hugged her daughter, promising to call her later. Kathy and I got into my car. I drove forward to make a U-turn on the dead-end street. Looking in the rearview mirror, I noticed a dark blue sedan, with two men in it, pull up to the curb where I'd just been parked. As we passed Kathy's house she gestured at the two men now standing in the yard talking to her mother.

"The one without a jacket is the FBI agent who was here early this morning. I don't know who the other one is."

FBI? At Kathy and Anna's? I almost ran off the side of the road trying to get a look at the men. A thousand new questions ran through my head, quickly followed by a disconcerting realization. My license tag number had been clearly visible to those men for more than long enough for them to write it down. Whether Anna told them who I was or not, they'd find out easily enough. Just what was I, and my family, getting into?

Kathy waited until we got to my house before she told me anything more about what was going on. I saw no reason for her to have to tell the story twice—once to me, then again for Ed. As soon as we were inside the house, seated in the living room with Ed, she started.

She was hesitant at first, but soon her words tumbled out almost on top of one another. I sat in stunned silence as Kathy related being shaken awake to find a man standing beside her bed, his drawn pistol pointed at her. He identified himself as an FBI agent and made her go stand in her front yard, handcuffed, dressed only in her nightgown, the object of the neighbors' stares. I thought my anger would choke me. For heaven's sake, she was a fifteen-year-old girl. The same age as Laura. And, like my daughter, she was a normal suburban teenager. Not some hardened criminal. Just how much of a danger did these agents think she could possibly be?

Her answer to my question of "why" didn't lessen my anger. Some soldiers, wanted for desertion, had been picked up by our local police. Her mother had met one of the men a year or so earlier when he'd been stationed in Pensacola, and some of the soldiers had been staying with Kathy and her mother. I didn't treat desertion lightly but I didn't see it as justification for the treatment Kathy had received.

"They searched the apartment. Took my mom's computer and all her disks. Finally they told us they were taking us all to the police station. I asked them if I could go inside and dress. They said no, but one of the agents brought me a pair of blue jeans. I had to put them on in the front yard."

Knowing what a private, modest person Kathy was, my heart ached for her. She had to have been humiliated. At least when they reached our little Gulf Breeze police station, things got better. Kathy told us that our officers convinced the FBI agents to remove her handcuffs. And later, when the agents were threatening to fly Kathy and Anna to Fort Benning with the soldiers, our policemen insisted that wasn't necessary.

Once Kathy finished recounting her ordeal to us, she told us why the FBI had come to her home. The story she told us had nothing to do with the version later given by the Pentagon spokesman to the media. She mentioned nothing about spies, a cult, the rapture, or the Antichrist. The only words she used which later appeared in the newspaper were UFO and government cover-up. According to Kathy, some of the soldiers had accidentally gained access to top secret information on those subjects. And what they had learned had frightened them—and the other soldiers they told—so much, that they had deserted and fled to the United States.

Later that afternoon Kathy's mother brought her some clothes so she could spend the night with us. Anna confirmed everything Kathy had told us. She added that she was afraid of what was going to happen to the six soldiers and maybe to Kathy and herself. "This could be a matter of life and death. Promise me you won't repeat to anyone what we told you."

Ed and I promised, and we've kept that promise, even with our closest friends. What we've revealed here—all of which has by now been reported in the media—is the extent of what we plan to tell unless the circumstances should change. Better than most, we understand the strain of unrelenting media attention.

Anna moved away later that summer. The soldiers, after their discharges, went their own ways, some together, some separately. Kathy is going to the local junior college now. The way Ed and I see it is—it's their story to tell one of these days, if they want to.

And the media, as it always does, went on to other stories. One, in the August 23 *Sentinel*, was of particular interest to us. On Sunday, August 19, MUFON investigator Joe Barron had received a call at 8:55 P.M. from a prominent local family. They reported seeing a "UFO" at a very low altitude. All of the witnesses were adults and all had used binoculars.

When Joe interviewed the witnesses the next night he concluded that what they had seen was a parachute flare. In all likelihood the flare had been launched from a flare gun fired from the ground since the activity of aircraft in the immediate area didn't correlate with the flare's trajectory.

Joe's report, routine for a MUFON investigator, was interesting. It showed that investigators could, through routine questioning, determine whether a UFO was truly unidentifiable or if it could be explained away as a known, man-made object. But equally interesting to those of us who knew about it, was the fact that on the night the flare was seen, a well-known debunker was in the area, a debunker who had recently said that the UFOs the local people were seeing were nothing but flares.

CHAPTER 24

RED UFO RETURNS

November 23, 1990

The weeks passed, with frequent UFO sighting reports coming from area residents. Frances and I decided to avoid the large groups which assembled to watch for a UFO, but the fascination of seeing the UFO often overruled that decision. We felt it was important for the media to focus on the scores of other witnesses. But, often a UFO would show up when Frances and I were present at a "sky watch," so people made the incorrect assumption that I was the catalyst, a "UFO magnet."

One example of this happened on the Friday after Thanksgiving, 1990. Bruce and Ann Morrison called and asked if we would drop by the Three Mile Bridge Park that night to say hello to a few of their visiting family. They had planned a "sky watch" in the hope of seeing the UFO. Our schedule for that evening was very full but I agreed to stop by for a moment after dinner.

When we arrived the Morrisons and their relatives were braving the strong north wind. Suddenly, after several minutes of polite conversation, a UFO appeared out of thin air from the south. Soundlessly it burst into sight over central downtown Gulf Breeze. Within seconds the dazzling white circle of light turned a brilliant red.

Dr. Adams, Mrs. Morrison's brother, later said, "I'm a flight surgeon and I'm very familiar with all types of aircraft. What I saw was not a fixed wing airplane or a helicopter, nor was it a balloon or a flare. Flares and balloons don't hover perfectly still in a fifteen-mile-an-hour wind. I had a fix on it, relative to a nearby flagpole, for approximately two minutes. The object didn't move, until it turned into a small white ball of light and disappeared."

November 25, 1990
UFO Video Taped Again

Word spread about this sighting and quickly swelled the ranks of UFO watchers arriving nightly at the Bay Bridge.

With his video camera in hand, a local bank executive, David Cary, and his wife Andrea stood by skeptically watching the sky and the frequent navigational lights on airplanes coming and going from local airports. Along with a group of MUFON investigators, I was facing south in the direction of the last UFO appearance, two nights ago. Hours passed when abruptly Andrea pointed behind us and yelled, "Look, what's that?"

Gary Watson echoed her words and the group spun around to see a UFO directly behind and almost overhead. A spectacular red, it radiated a glow that reflected off the low-lying clouds.

Marsha Athey stepped backward, insisting the UFO was coming closer. I agreed and edged closer to the opposite side of a parked car. Patti Weatherford, Gary Watson, and all the others remained steady, describing out loud what they were seeing. With video cameras running and cameras flashing, exclamations filled the air for about two minutes until the UFO collapsed into a white ball and, seconds later, disappeared.

Frances's Account

Each new sighting, of what became fondly known as the "red light UFO," brought more people out to look. Some of them had had other sightings, but many of them were new people, drawn by the coverage in the *Sentinel* to come out for a sky watch and the hope to see for themselves.

Not all of them were "believers," in fact a number of them were quite skeptical. But none of them, once they saw the UFO, could dismiss it as "some excited fool's" misidentification of some normal, earthbound object.

Without fail they all knew what it wasn't. It wasn't an airplane, a helicopter, a flare, or an illusion caused by mass hysteria. It was deciding what it was that was difficult. Was it from another planet in another solar system? Was it from another dimension? Was it from our own future? Or was it something our own government had made and was testing?

The theories were sometimes tossed out with all the seriousness of confetti on New Year's. Other times they provided hours of serious discussions at a local restaurant, The Bay Window Deli, as we all tried to warm up with hot chocolate and coffee after hours of standing watch in the bitter cold.

And then one night we had an "earthly star" to add to our "sightings." And a little excitement of a different kind was added to our watches.

A made-for-TV movie was being shot about sixty miles to the east of Gulf Breeze, in San Destin. One of the screen writers, Jesse Long, had a longtime interest in UFOs and called Ed to find out if anything was going on in the area. Ed told him about our frequent sightings of the glowing red UFO and the next night Jesse drove over from San Destin to watch with us.

As we usually did when we were standing around in the cold, trying to stay warm and watch the sky at the same time, we talked about all sorts of things. After discussing UFOs for awhile, someone asked Jesse to tell us about the movie he was working on. We all knew Kelly McGillis was the star and we wanted the inside scoop. To our surprise, Jesse said he'd try to get Kelly to come over one day after they finished shooting.

I don't think any of us missed those next few watches. But although Jesse came back, Kelly was never with him. He said she had wanted to come, but the movie required her to be outside, often in the water, and she was so cold and tired by the end of the day, she just wanted a hot bath and bed.

Finally Jesse told us they would wrap up filming the next day. If they finished early, he'd come see us one more time before he left for California. And, once again, he promised to try to bring Kelly with him. By now we'd all pretty much given up any hope of ever seeing Kelly McGillis anywhere but on TV and in the movies. Still, we were all there the next night, although not a person would admit that it was the hope of seeing Kelly as much as the UFO that brought them out into the freezing weather.

Then, just as we thought we wouldn't even see Jesse, a van drove up. Jesse climbed out, followed by a half dozen other people, one of them Kelly McGillis. For a few minutes we all virtually ignored her. I think we were afraid of looking like star-struck fools.

Finally Ed and I walked over to say hello and found ourselves talking to as down-to-earth and friendly a person as you could ever hope to meet. Soon others from our sky watch group wandered over and listened to stories about life on the set from Kelly and the other members of the cast and crew.

Unfortunately, we didn't see the UFO that night. It would have been great for Kelly and the others. But those of us who met them had a different, equally interesting memory to compensate us for those long, cold hours spent at the foot of the bridge.

For Ed and me, all our time out in the cold didn't take place at night at the foot of the bridge. Ed had been asked to be the chairman for the Gulf Breeze Christmas parade and I had volunteered to help him. Each evening we checked the weather, not only to see if we'd freeze on sky watch, but hoping for a warming trend before parade day.

Mother Nature didn't cooperate. The night before the parade the temperature plummeted. We awoke to overcast skies, a biting wind, and temperatures so low we wondered if anybody would show up—to watch the parade or be in it. Our only hope was that by the 11:30 A.M. step-off time the weather would be better.

Because the parade route had been changed, no longer going up busy Highway 98, Ed had added something new. Each class, in every grade of the elementary schools, had been given a four-foot artificial tree to decorate. The trees would be mounted on wagons and pulled along the parade route by students from that classroom.

Now, with it cold and gloomy, we were afraid our Christmas Tree Parade might fizzle. Ed and I walked from our house to the staging area at the Methodist Church, hoping that our fellow Gulf Breezians wouldn't let the unseasonable cold keep them home.

At first in a trickle, then in a flood, adults and children filled the church parking lots and drives. Shiny red wagons bounced along, their tree passengers bedecked with homemade ornaments of every shape and color, steadied by anxious young hands. Walking presents accompanied one tree. A reindeer-antlered dog another. For most of the children, being a participant in the parade was something new. At times it was hard to hear instructions over their excited chatter.

Seeing their smiling faces, and those of the children who lined the parade route, made the hours Ed had put into planning the parade worth it. This was what Christmas was about for him. The children. Not at all to my surprise, the parade was hardly over before he'd agreed to chair it again the next year.

CHAPTER 25

ABC NEWS FILMS UFO

January 2, 1991

The UFO stakeouts continued. The weather was not a factor for the witnesses nor, it seems, to the UFO. Bitter cold or balmy, in a blowing gale or calm, the UFO appeared every two or three nights but without any apparent timing pattern. Many witnesses used home video cameras that slightly but consistently overexposed the brilliant red "power source." The dark superstructure of the UFO blended into the night sky but some photographs, taken with 35-mm cameras using powerful lenses, zoomed in on the perimeter lighting that some witnesses call "portholes."

The video footage taken of the UFO on January 2, 1991, is exceptional because it shows a distinct red ring of glowing energy with a dark center. This ring of light is often called the UFO's "power ring" although exactly what it is, nobody knows. A few of the witnesses described it as a blazing "wedding band" but all agree that it was the same object seen so often over Gulf Breeze, unlike any "normal aircraft" they have ever seen.

Without exception, those of us who waited at the nightly "sky watch" locations were hoping for very close encounters or even a landing. But the UFO frustrated us with overhead flybys and aerial displays prompting the need for bigger and better camera equipment.

The special stereo SRS Camera designed by Dr. Maccabee was needed to determine the size and distance of the UFO. I had used this large specialty camera three times before to confirm the size of the UFOs that I first saw in November of 1987 but now, three years later, the SRS would have to be restabilized and mounted before it could be used to document the size of the red "power ring" UFO.

January 11, 1991
ABC Films UFO

The local television reporter from WALA TV-10, Lea Sinclair, spent as much time as she could with their professional camera equipment but, to our dismay, the UFO did not appear for her cameras. Other out-of-town film crews tried to catch the UFO by setting up cameras during some of the many nightly sky watches. Rick Kirkham, with "Inside Edition," arrived at a UFO-sighting location five minutes after the UFO had come and gone.

One television crew from Washington called to ask what time and where to set up cameras to film the UFO. I explained that they would have to take their chances like the rest of us.

I had hoped that it would be only a matter of time before an out-of-town film crew with professional cameras would document the UFO. A week later, ABC, represented by Jeff Androski of Ohlmeyer Productions, would be the first to do so.

Accompanied by Bob Oechsler, a former NASA Systems Specialist, Jeff Androski and Ron Ladd interviewed UFO witnesses at the most recent and frequented UFO-sighting location and settled in for a long night of watching the sky and waiting. Their assignment to Gulf Breeze had been to cover the unexplained spiraled circles of grass that appeared in a local park. The ongoing Gulf Breeze UFO story was an irresistible bonus that fit in with their assignment, so they waited patiently in the night with local residents, hoping. Bob Oechsler was prepared with infrared film. An hour later he was the first to see the UFO appear from the clouds over the center of town. The film footage of the sighting was shown on an ABC special called "America's Best Kept Secrets."

Frances's Account

Those who had witnessed the sighting, both local residents and the ABC crew, had no qualms about telling others what they had seen from the foot of the bay bridge the night of January 11.

Ron Ladd, the cameraman, said, "It was a long distance away illuminating the clouds and traveling very slowly to the east. It just appeared from within the clouds and after a minute or so it disappeared. I caught it on film. It was sometimes very bright and then would fade, maybe because of the clouds."

An earlier witness, Jeff Lawrence, was quite adamant about what he saw. It "looked like the UFO that Ed Walters photographed three years ago."

Bob Oechsler, who has spent years studying the Gulf Breeze sightings said, "I have tried to consider all the options to this Gulf Breeze mystery. I would like to explain it away as a military aircraft, balloons, flares, temperature inversions, or hoax, but none of these options hold up under scientific study.

"Balloons don't travel opposite the wind, flares don't change color or hover motionless, and I can assure you that what I saw over Gulf Breeze was not an airplane or helicopter. I have designed some very sophisticated remote control systems but duplicating the soundless flight and brightness of this unknown object would be next to impossible. I can only say that I don't know what it is."

For so long, those of us who kept the nightly watches had hoped that a crew representing a major U.S. network would catch the UFO on film. Now one finally had and all we could do was wait for the ABC special to air in February.

CHAPTER 26

STEREO AND INFRARED PHOTOGRAPHS

February 4, 1991

Dr. Maccabee, who designed the SRS (stereo) camera that I used two years earlier, had now developed a computer program to calibrate the stereo photographs and establish the size and distance of any object that might show up. The SRS stereo camera was ready to be used, and for six nights Frances and I stationed ourselves with the large camera at different city parks overlooking the Gulf Breeze skyline. We were sometimes alone, but most often we were joined by a group of dedicated researchers who met regularly and at appointed times.

On this night I received a last minute call from Vicki Lyons with a change in the "sky watch" location and meeting time. The new location, Naval Live Oaks National Park, was about two miles from central Gulf Breeze, overlooking the Santa Rosa Sound. She said, "Just take the second entrance past the Welcome Station and look for our cars. We'll be there at seven-thirty."

Frances had a PTA board meeting, so, alone, I turned onto the shell-covered road and only a few feet into the woods, encroaching trees and shadows smothered my truck's headlights. A half mile off the main road I drove into a small parking area covered with a canopy of forty-foot oaks hugging an overgrown picnic area. It was seven-thirty and the park was empty. Vicki and her group were either late or I had turned down the wrong road. On the chance that they would drive up at any moment, I sat on the tailgate of my truck and let my eyes adjust to the darkness. Thirty feet from me the bushes rustled and parted from the presence of an approaching raccoon. It swaggered past me, ignoring my flashlight, inspected a nearby garbage can, and then pushed into the darkness.

Ignoring my uncertainty about this being the right meeting place, I began unpacking the SRS camera. The two-foot-wide camera and accompanying gear filled my arms and hampered my footing on the path leading to the beach. The water was still, a mirror backdrop reflecting streetlights from the distant barrier island. I neared a wooden stairway descending the thirty-foot bluff to the white sand beach.

To the left my eyes caught some movement. Blocked by the forest silhouette, a red light glinted from beyond the oak tree boundaries of the park. A red light like none other, its crimson blaze drew me into a run for the beach to set up the stereo camera. At the steep rustic stairway I stumbled, dropped some measuring equipment, but continued. Again I tripped on one of the uneven stair landings, lurched forward, and landed on the beach sand.

The UFO was moving slowly from north to south at a distance that was difficult to judge. Its brilliance could have been miles away or closer to me over the water of Santa Rosa sound. I spread the SRS camera tripod legs and spun the control lever to aim the viewfinder. What I had seen with my own eyes became a disappointment through the viewfinder, which reduced the UFO's size and sparkle so much I hesitated to take the picture. I wanted a closer shot but I knew that the SRS camera would accurately document the size and distance and that's what was needed.

Once more I looked through the viewfinder. The red light moved slowly with a boiling pulse. Suddenly a ring of bluish green light surrounded the red glowing center. I hit the shutter buttons and took the photograph. Seconds passed while I watched with my naked eyes. The UFO began to fade as if it were passing into a cloud bank. The outer ring disappeared while the red center light expanded into a larger ellipse. I took another photograph just before the red light disappeared and the UFO was gone completely.

Alone, I sat on the edge of the stairs. My heart was pounding and I looked anxiously into the sky. Now, seven-thirty-five, I was getting nervous. The woods and thick brush that outlined the sandy beach sounded alive. My thought regressed to another beach three years ago when a UFO encounter left me facedown, unconscious in the sand. The forest sounds grew louder. *Certainly another raccoon,* I tried to console myself, while moving closer to the cover of a large group of trees behind me. Three or four minutes passed before the oak tree canopy was awash with automobile headlights and I dashed up the bluff-side stairs to friendly faces.

The stereo photographs that I took of the "green ring" that showed beneath the UFO have been studied and calibrated by Dr. Bruce Maccabee. The ring was three-hundred feet distant and six feet in diameter. (For technical scientific details see Appendix 3, Where to Write, Fund for UFO Research.)

March 12, 1991
UFO Captured On Infrared Film

The glow of streetlights cast a yellow hue off the wind-driven clouds. Two young men in a red Camaro pulled to a stop beside me at the traffic-clogged intersection. The deep rhythm of their radio throbbed, "If I could turn back time. . . ."

Cher's voice muted my animated call, "Hey guys, look at the UFO!"

To the north, over the distant tree line, a blazing red glow hovered motionless. So accustomed to the look of this brilliant red light, I knew immediately what it was but it caused no noticeable reaction from the two young men or any of the other passing motorists.

The traffic light changed. Anxious to point out the UFO to someone, I accelerated forward, lost sight of the UFO, and two blocks later pulled into the parking lot at the

Unity Church meeting hall. The seven o'clock MUFON meeting had not begun and I quickly announced as I entered the front door, with my camera in hand, "Hey, I just saw the red UFO!"

Reaction was swift, bringing the dozen people that heard me into the parking lot to survey the cloud-laden sky. The oak trees that partly surrounded the area obstructed much of our field of vision, but I described what I had seen and where it had been.

"Honest, it was over that way." I pointed to the north. "Really, it was there, keep looking . . . I promise . . . it was fiery red . . . really." Embarrassment flooded through me. I stammered and hoped the crowd believed me but they said little because there was nothing in the sky for them to see but clouds. Within minutes most people returned to the meeting hall. Bruce Morrison, Mary Hufford, and I were the last to give up. Suddenly the red light appeared in the sky to the north.

"There it is!" I yelled.

Mary echoed my yell, "There it is, there it is!"

Bruce raced to the meeting hall to alert the others while Mary and I moved toward the road for a better vantage point away from the oak trees. Ann Morrison joined Mary and both stood in front of me as I aimed my 35-mm camera loaded with infrared film.

Chief MUFON Investigator Gary Watson and I had purchased infrared film and devised a plan to use it simultaneously. My camera was fitted with a 50-mm lens to photograph the UFO and any surrounding foreground in order to show where the UFO was relative to the sighting area. Gary had a 200-mm lens attached to his camera in the hope of documenting close-up details of the UFO.

Behind me I could hear the crowd of people beginning to gather. I turned the flash attachment on and excitedly took a photograph before the flash had time to warm up. The red glow of the UFO gave off an irregular pulse and I tried to hit the shutter button when the glow was brightest. Across the road there were half a dozen blinding security lights and streetlights that made focusing on the UFO difficult and, for all I knew, the infrared film might be ruined. The instructions that came with infrared film did not specify an ASA camera setting, a necessity for proper film exposure. In addition to visible light, infrared film captures light that cannot be seen by the naked eye or by normal film; therefore, standard ASA settings do not apply.

The UFO was now much smaller as I took a third photograph and looked behind me for Gary. He was looking at the UFO but had not had time to get his camera. Bruce Morrison stood nearby with his video camera but later complained that the security lights had washed out his efforts to film the UFO.

After a minute of watching the UFO's distinctive red light, it suddenly turned white. I quickly took a fourth photograph followed by another as its white glow faded and disappeared.

Ken Davis, a professional photographer, was also present and watched the red UFO with the crowd. After the sighting, he asked if I had used a particular red filter designed for infrared film and what ASA I had my camera set on. A long discussion followed. He and Art Hufford, a chemical engineer, agreed that infrared film was very unpredictable and only when developed would we know the degree of success, if any.

The following morning I turned the film in for processing only to hear, "I'm sorry, we don't develop infrared. The ASA settings are far too uncertain for us to guarantee any satisfaction."

When I asked for the name of another company that would process the film, there were none available locally. Coast Photo Labs finally agreed to develop the film but with the understanding that they would "simply do the best they could" with no guarantees.

When I returned the next day to pick up the film, I was prepared for the possibility of underexposed or overexposed prints. To my surprise, and to the satisfaction of the lab technicians, the prints were amazing.

I had taken five photographs in all, three of the red glow, one as the UFO turned white, and one as it disappeared. The three prints showing the red glow had captured the distant object as a white ellipse (the infrared film was black and white). But the two prints showing the UFO when it turned white and disappeared were shocking because they showed the UFO's white glow to be at least twenty times larger in area than what we could see with our naked eyes.

Several physicists explained that within the range of infrared light, red is at the lower end and white is at the highest level and, therefore, would show up with the greatest intensity even though it would go unseen by our eyes. I believe these infrared photos to be very significant when studied along with the numerous videotapes that also show the UFO turn white before disappearing.

I conclude that the change in color from red to white is evidence of a power surge. The infrared film documents a huge emission of white energy.

When extreme enlargements were made of the first three photographs, the bright elliptical bottom of the UFO showed along with indistinct structure lines. (For technical scientific details see Appendix 3, Where to Write, Fund for UFO Research.)

May 10, 1991
Japanese TV Crew Films the UFO

American television network news continued to ignore the Gulf Breeze UFO sightings but from around the world reporters traveled here hoping to see the UFO. A Japanese film crew met with success and reported their sighting to the *Sentinel* newspaper with this letter.

On May 10, 1991, I, Jun-ichi Yaoi and my film crew arrived in Gulf Breeze in the hope of documenting the local UFO sightings. NIPON television network, the largest/oldest commercial broadcasting company in Japan, sponsored our investigative documentary to be aired as part of a two-hour special nationwide in Japan.

Bob Oechsler, a former NASA systems specialist,

from Washington, D.C., accompanied us as a consultant to advise and analyze any evidence that we might be able to capture on film.

At approximately 11:30 p.m. Bob Oechsler told us that a red UFO had been sighted to the northwest of the Holiday Inn where we were staying. We were preparing for bed but we quickly got our cameras and set up a sky watch near the hotel swimming pool overlooking the Pensacola Bay.

Fifteen or twenty minutes passed. Then, out over the water, a bright red object suddenly appeared. The sky was clear over Gulf Breeze and the Bay, with most of the rain clouds still visible over Pensacola. What we saw and filmed was amazing! It was brilliant and I must say, beautiful. As recorded on our 36 to 1 zoom lens, the UFO moved to the northeast for one minute and twenty seconds before suddenly winking out and then returning for a few seconds as a small white ball of light which then also winked out.

Our film of the UFO clearly shows a circular ring of red energy with a center glowing orange core. It will be further analyzed to identify any structure. We have interviewed dozens of local witnesses who have taken video and photos of the UFO but we are particularly impressed with the similarity with photographs taken by Ed Walters in 1988.

Signed, Jun-ichi Yaoi, Director

CHAPTER 27

THE GULF BREEZE RESEARCH TEAM

In the absence of any official government participation in the investigation of the unidentified flying objects that appear regularly over Gulf Breeze and the Pensacola area, a private team of researchers has taken on the challenge. Continuously, since November 1990 (weather permitting), the Gulf Breeze Research Team established nightly surveillance watches which successfully documented the technical data during, before, and after over one hundred UFO sightings. Analysis of the videotapes, audiotapes, 35-mm photographs, infrared photographs, diffraction lens photographs, and testimony from hundreds of witnesses has established the undeniable existence of what is commonly called the "Gulf Breeze" UFO.

The Gulf Breeze Research Team works under the guidelines established by The Mutual UFO Network (MUFON), Seguin, Texas.

Dedicated to the principles of scientific study, these are the members of the Gulf Breeze Research Team:

Marsha Athey, Investigator   Bland Pugh, Chief
                                    Investigator
Mary Hufford, Researcher   Carolyn Pugh, Researcher
Boots Eckert, Investigator   Buck Morrison, Video
                                    Documentation

Sue Jones, Investigator

Ann Morrison, Records Documentation

Clopton Jones, Investigator

Topper Jones, Investigator

Gary Watson, Chief Investigator

Patti Weatherford, Media Consultant

Ray Pollock, Optical Scientist

Art Hufford, Chemical Engineer, Pres. of Pensacola MUFON Chapter

Marianne Jones, Researcher

Vicki Lyons, Investigator

For month after month, the nightly UFO "stakeouts" continued and what had begun in 1989 as an informal group of curious residents and a few MUFON investigators, grew into a dedicated seventeen-member research team. Seeing the unexplained red glowing object made all the difference; the curious became serious and the mystery became too compelling to ignore. During June and July 1991, the frequency of UFO sightings was staggering and pushed the total for that year to sixty-five documented reports.

August 9, 1991

The G.B. (Gulf Breeze) Research Team gathered at the Bay Bridge and I was on my way to join them. I had become very much at ease with the Team members and felt comfortable sharing personal thoughts and discussing UFO speculation.

The traffic slowed my access to the exit nearest the UFO watch location and, without warning, my thoughts flashed to a crystal clear picture of a virgin, tropical forest, much like the rain forest of Costa Rica where years before I had spent many weeks camping and exploring the untouched jungle for rare orchids. I could almost taste the humid air as the lush greenery of the jungle image rushed through my mind.

I shook my head to clear my thoughts, turned off the highway, and joined the G.B. Research Team. Briefly, I mentioned the jungle images to Gary Watson as I set up my 35-mm camera. Then suddenly somebody yelled, "There it is!"

From out of thin air, the UFO suddenly appeared; its blazing red color could not be mistaken. The UFO moved across the sky to the north and on this night a rare photograph was taken by Mary Hufford with my camera. Her photograph shows the red UFO in the distance plus other research team members in the foreground—in the act of photographing and filming the UFO. It is often said by UFO critics that a photograph taken of somebody photographing a UFO would be impressive but impossible. Well, Mary Hufford has surpassed the "impossible." Her photograph not only shows the UFO and Bland Pugh taking photos with his 35-mm camera, but also shows Wayne Summerlin videotaping the UFO.

August 15, 1991

The G.B. Research Team decided to set up a second and simultaneous UFO watch location. They chose an isolated beachfront five miles east of the Bay Bridge. Should there be a sighting, the five-mile separation would provide very accurate triangulation measurements. We would then know how big and how far away the object was from our cameras. On this night I joined the G.B. Research Team stationed at the Bay Bridge. Two women, whom I didn't recognize, sat by themselves at a nearby picnic table. In passing I spoke and asked, "Are you here to watch for the UFO?"

"UFO? Uh . . . no . . . are you?" Their answer carried a hint of disbelief, so I politely explained what we were doing. Minutes later their caution turned to fascination when the UFO suddenly flashed into sight. Here are their statements as published in the *Sentinel* newspaper.

Becky Bailey said:

We were sitting on the benches at the end of the Three Mile Bridge waiting for some friends to meet us. We saw these people with cameras set up and assumed they were star watching. This guy comes over to us and asked if we were UFO watching. We say "No, are you?" He tells us that they have seen it and it's a big white light. Then he started walking away and out of nowhere "bam!" is this white light. It then got small and very, very red. It stayed like that for maybe two minutes. It got very faint, and then got big and snow white again and was just gone.[1]

Tammy Dawson said:

On this date, August 15, 1991, I was at Wayside park at about 8:50 P.M. I saw the neatest thing I have ever seen. I looked up and saw a bright white light, then it turned red and then white—WILD! It was the greatest thing I have ever seen, a real UFO![2]

Unknown to us at the time, Bob Reid, USAF Col. Ret., and four other military officers who were interested in solving the Gulf Breeze UFO mystery, had arrived at the opposite side of the Bay Bridge. They also quickly spotted the red UFO as it appeared. USAF Lt. Col. Gary E. Crowther made this statement for the *Sentinel* newspaper.

The following is an account of what I observed on 15 August 1991, 8:53 pm, at the east side of the Pensacola Bay Bridge.

At the above time, a light appeared in the sky to the north. When I first picked it up, it was bright red and appeared to be approaching. Then it stopped and remained in one location for a short time. I was viewing the light with both the naked eye and a pair of binoculars. After remaining stationary for a brief time

---

[1]Duane Cook, *Sentinel,* August 15, 1991.
[2]*Ibid.*

it then moved slightly to my left, then stopped. After a few moments it then seemed to rise. Then the red light started to fade and became white, then seemed to start to streak to the north and blinked out.

Although I did not time it, my guess is the duration of the contact was between 45 sec. and 1 ½ min.

The light was not like any aircraft light I have ever seen. That said, after 26 years in the Air Force. It was deep red in color and seemed to pulsate. It was also larger than aircraft lights.

The above is my best recollection of the event. Gary E. Crowther Lt. Col, USAF (Ret), Ft. Walton Beach, Fl.[1]

Five miles away, at our other UFO watch location, Marsha Athey, Vicki Lyons, and Bland Pugh sighted the UFO and plotted its angle of elevation and compass direction. The results of our triangulation were amazing. In a direct line, the UFO was precisely in between our two groups. We were separated by five miles and the UFO was exactly two and a half miles away from each group. Both groups could see the UFO but neither had an advantage over the other. This was either a huge coincidence or the UFO had delivered a message that it knew we were watching and exactly where we were.

For the next eighteen days and nights the UFO did not show. Theories among the G.B. Research Team to explain its sudden disappearance ranged from the profound and serious to the flippant. Eighteen nights of staring into the sky and seeing nothing but IFOs (Identified Flying Objects) led Marsha Athey to say, "Hey, I know what happened! Remember after the last sighting when Vicki said she was tired of watching the UFO and ordered it to 'land or go away.' Well maybe it was listening."

Vicki spoke up and with a laugh replied, "Oh no, you're not laying this off on me. It was Ann who said that."

Ann defended herself, "No, no—it wasn't me, that was Ed."

---

[1]Duane Cook, *Sentinel,* August 15, 1991.

Idle joking helped pass the hours and we grew to know each other and became friends. Bruce and Ann Morrison were the official record keepers. Bruce ran the video camera and used the parabolic microphone to document the movement and possible sound of the UFO. Even though the equipment could record the single chirp of a bird at over one hundred yards and the sound of a distant helicopter was easily recognizable, no sound was ever detected from the UFO.

Ann recorded the details of each sighting such as direction, elevation, azimuth, weather conditions, and the names of witnesses. Art and Mary Hufford concentrated on 35-mm photography and took some remarkable photographs that show a double ring of structure around the UFO. Art is a chemical engineer and, because of his formal scientific training, he became the spokesman for the Team. Very often, he was invited to give UFO updates and speak at various civic groups throughout town. Local residents, anxious to see the UFO, frequently joined the nightly UFO watches and they were always greeted by Art Hufford, who was prepared to show them his latest photographs.

The local UFO sightings generated so much interest that the G.B. Research Team set up a UFO Hotline so other witnesses could report when and where they saw the UFO. The mystery attracted other professionals who, after seeing the UFO for themselves, also volunteered to help. Ray Pollock, a scientist who specalizes in optical image analysis, joined the Team and was instrumental in answering questions for the newspaper reporters and out-of-town film crews.

September 1, 1991

For the last eighteen days the UFO sightings had virtually dried up. The Research Team decided to move its main watch location from the north shore (Bay Bridge) to the south shore (Shoreline Park) approximately two miles away. A small group of people remained at the Bay Bridge but the majority of equipment went to South Shoreline park, where they set up watch at the end of a two-hundred-foot pier.

It was a beautiful, partly cloudy night. One of the picnic

tables along the edge of the water and closest to the pier was occupied by four senior citizens. Frances and I nodded as we walked past them and onto the two-hundred-foot pier, where ten members of the G.B. Research Team were watching the sky and passing time with casual conversation. The running joke was that whoever did not show up would naturally be the focus of the conversation.

As we came closer, Vicki Lyons called to us with a slight laugh. "Hi, do you feel your ears burning?" Often, humor relieved the serious nature of our research and in this case tempered the stress of our group's having had no sighting for eighteen nights, a frustration compounded by UFO sightings being reported from other parts of town. We joined the group and listened to Gary Watson describe several of these reports that he had received that day on the UFO Hot line. Gary is the MUFON-trained chief investigator for our research group. Monthly, or as needed, he conducts a MUFON field investigator's training course. Those passing the course are then authorized MUFON investigators. The core of the G.B. Research Team is founded on the MUFON guidelines and procedures but even Gary was not immune from breaking the tedium of the nightly sky watches with a joke or humorous distraction.

On one occasion Gary arrived early at the watch site, located that night in the Naval Line Oaks National Park. He parked his car and walked into the shadows of the surrounding woods that hugged the dark pathway to the shoreline. The next to arrive were Marsha Athey and Patti Weatherford. They saw Gary's car and assumed he was setting up his camera at the shoreline site. They walked down the pathway, reached the watch location, but there was no sign of Gary. In the darkness of the woods, Gary could see and hear them. They quickly decided to retreat but this meant crossing back through the long dark pathway where, unknown to them, Gary was waiting. Gary's surprise appearance from the darkness was funny to him but Marsha and Patti did not share his sense of humor.

For months to come, and on this night at the end of the Shoreline Park pier, they taunted him with good-natured threats of revenge.

Boots Eckert interrupted their banter. "Look! There it is!"

To the north the UFO hovered between the clouds. Slowly it began to move to the west. Its ruby color was unmistakable to us. Vicki Lyons's excitement was unrestrained as she described her feelings of what she was witnessing. Her unabridged comments are recorded on the videotape and became a lesson for all of us to be careful what adjectives we used during a UFO sighting. We continued to watch and photograph the UFO for over three minutes before a cloud blowing from the west blocked the UFO from our sight.

During the sighting I called to the people sitting along the shore and said, "Look to the north. Can you see the UFO?" Distant voices yelled back, "Yes! We see it!" But most interesting in this whole event was the attitude of one of the four seniors seated at the picnic table.

After the UFO had disappeared and when asked their opinion of what they saw, three of them were mystified and quick to share their thoughts. But one man sat with his back to where the UFO had been and said, "Bullshit! I don't believe in that bullshit!"

I politely said, "So, I guess you think what you saw was an airplane. Is that right?"

He sharply responded, "I saw nothing, 'cause there was nothing there."

The woman across from him said, "He wouldn't look."

This man had refused to turn his head and look at what all the others around him were seeing. There was something very meaningful and touching about his emotional denial. It was as if his brain rationalized that if he did not look, then he would not have to deal with something that, to him, had to be impossible.

I have no harsh words for this man. It is an amazing attitude, but one that may be more common than we might expect. Quite possibly this attitude of denial may be the motivation that drives the hard-line UFO debunkers. Simply put, they believe UFOs are impossible; therefore, they can't exist; therefore, if one is in the sky behind you, don't look.

At the Bay Ridge other G.B. Research Team members had a closer and unobstructed vantage point for viewing the UFO. "Professor" Pugh, his wife Carolyn, Ray Pollock, and Greg Liss took accurate note of the UFO's elevation and azimuth. Confirming these calculations, Greg used a wide-angle lens to photograph the UFO relative to the Pensacola skyline. And still closer to the UFO were Brenda and Buddy Pollak, who were in their car leaving the Pensacola Country Club and saw the UFO almost overhead. They pulled over and watched as the UFO ejected a bright ball of white light and then simply raced straight upward and out of sight.

A week later I was pleasantly surprised when one of the "founding fathers" of Gulf Breeze, Floyd Smith, a conservative gentleman also affectionately known as Mr. Gulf Breeze, stopped me to say, "Ed, let's talk about that UFO." He went on to say that on September 1, he and his wife were on their dock and saw the UFO. He described the same red object that the rest of us had seen with particular reference to the white ball of light that shot out before the UFO suddenly raced up and out of sight.

September 2, 1991

Fortunately most people do not share the attitude of the man at the picnic bench who refused to look, and on this next night the UFO was back. While the G.B. Research Team filmed the sighting from the Bay Bridge location, others watched with amazement from all over town and from Pensacola Beach, three miles away. Most notable about this sighting was the enormous ball of light that was emitted from the UFO. During a majority of the sightings these balls of light have been witnessed and videotaped but this one was especially spectacular.

Streaking down, the ball of light almost reached the horizon before it hooked to the right and flashed out of sight. These anomalous emissions were a mystery within a mystery and much speculation was focused on what they could be. Ideas ranged from the "purging of holding tanks" to the "dispatch of probes" but anybody's guess was as good as any other.

September 5, 1991

This next UFO sighting was a surprise. We had grown accustomed to watching for the UFO's brilliant red glow, but on this night Ray Pollock called our attention to a motionless arc of six white lights that he noticed over the Pensacola skyline. For several minutes the arc of lights remained very visible and we could easily count the separate lights with the naked eye. We had no idea what the function of the lights were but the convenient description of "portholes" seemed appropriate. The following night the UFO and its "portholes" returned with a close-up show-and-tell display.

September 6, 1991

Frances and I were not present to witness this encounter. While our attention, as chaperones at a school-sponsored weekend dance, was on several hundred middle school students, the G.B. Research Team, along with others, documented this major UFO sighting. As always, the video camera recorded the event and when I watched Bruce Morrison's tape and listened to the dozens of witnesses recount what had happened, I was filled with satisfaction. For over a year the Research Team had documented sightings only by way of the extraordinarily bright red glow radiating from the bottom of the UFO. But on this night the UFO performed a splendid aerial maneuver complete with a beautiful display of a blazing ring of orange "portholes." The UFO's superstructure blocked the stars as it crossed within several thousand feet of the Research Team and did a slow 360-degree loop before it turned 180 degrees sideways, rapidly accelerated, and disappeared. During the four-minute sighting many of the witnesses fell silent in amazement while others cheered with excitement.

September 8, 1991

Witnesses who saw the orange ring of "portholes" during that spectacular sighting two nights before, told their friends, and those friends told their friends, and once again a crowd of spectators patiently waited at the Bay Bridge watch location. Frances and I joined the group but this time I brought my camera and 440-mm lens.

A half hour passed before we were rewarded with a magnificent display. The UFO simply appeared from out of nowhere. Around its bottom we could see an ellipse of eight bright white lights. Several thousand feet from us, it hovered motionless for several minutes and then seemed to just disappear. The sky was clear. There were no clouds to obscure what we saw but the UFO simply vanished into thin air.

The photographs I took show the ring of eight "porthole" lights. My photographs are supported by photographs taken by others and naturally by the videotape that records the astounded reaction many of us have during a UFO sighting.

Often these questions arise from skeptical people who have not seen the UFO but who show up at the UFO watch location out of curiosity. "How do you know it is a UFO? Couldn't you be seeing a helicopter or airplane?" The answer is in seeing the UFO for yourself and also in the photographs and videotapes. When the questioners see the UFO they understand and a single glance at the photographs allows the skeptics to conclude that helicopters and airplanes just don't look or behave like this mysterious object.

During the sky watch "stakeouts," local residents shared their latest UFO sighting stories with neighbors and strangers and the MUFON investigators began to build a complete picture as to how widespread the phenomenon is in Gulf Breeze. Three days passed before the next sighting, which was a red ring of lights, and three days later the UFO once again appeared to the delight of the ever present crowd at the Bay Bridge.

One witness, Dr. Radomski, recounted a sighting he had

had several years earlier during the time in 1987 when I was also dealing with my first sighting. At that time, because of the controversy and the ridicule factor, he chose to keep the details of his sighting to himself. Only when surrounded by scores of other witnesses did he feel comfortable admitting that he had seen the same UFO that I had videotaped on December 28, 1987.

Likewise, other witnesses came forward to describe seeing the same craft that I had originally photographed. Jeff Lawrence and his brother filed a complete report with the MUFON investigators that detailed the same object Frances and I had seen so often.

Hundreds of people were seeing, photographing, and videotaping an unidentified object flying in the sky over Gulf Breeze. Yet, not one word has ever been mentioned, to this date, on the national news. Local news coverage was one of curiosity presented in a tongue-in-cheek manner and the "entertainment news" shows loved to exploit the UFO subject, but serious involvement at the scientific level was left to volunteer groups like MUFON. Fortunately MUFON's credibility attracted some of the best scientific minds in the country. One such scientist is Dr. Bruce Maccabee, Chairman for the Fund for UFO Research.

The local UFO sightings were occurring at a fevered pace, taking place almost every other night. This was a perfect opportunity for Dr. Maccabee. He decided to fly in from Washington, D.C., to spend three nights at the Gulf Breeze UFO watch location. He arrived on September 15, 1991, but there was no sighting that night.

September 16, 1991

Once again Dr. Maccabee set up his equipment at the Bay Bridge watch location. Over forty people stood in small groups watching the night sky. Frances and I talked with a curious skeptic who was sure that we must be witnessing an experimental military aircraft. A half hour passed before Nancy Sharp noticed a hazy dark silhouette cross the horizon in the sky-glow over central Gulf Breeze. She pointed it out to the people standing nearby as the silhouette disappeared into the darker sky over the Bay. About ten minutes later, as the UFO's hazy outline emerged from the darkness, she pointed and cried out, "There it is!" Seconds after her alert, a perfect ring of white lights appeared. The UFO had engaged the ring of lights for all to see.

To the east, and within several thousand feet of our location, it was hovering very still in the hazy night sky. Seconds passed. It moved toward us and began to rise before, to the naked eye, it suddenly seemed to disappear. Others with binoculars tracked the "portholes" as it continued its ascent.

Bruce Morrison's videotape of this sighting is clear and shows the individual lights on the ring. Many 35-mm photographs were taken but Bland Pugh had the best luck with his 400-mm lens, which also shows each light around the ring.

Dr. Maccabee has written a detailed report on this sighting, which is available through the Fund for UFO Research (see Where to Write, Appendix 3).

September 20, 1991

Each UFO sighting was slightly different and at times more complex than the one before, but on this night the UFO demonstrated a feat that almost went unnoticed.

The G.B. Research Team had deployed two portable elevation and azimuth scopes (PEAS) to help with the triangulation of the UFO. Many hundreds of feet apart, these scopes could establish a close approximation of the UFO's location.

Bob Oechsler, a former NASA systems specialist, was in town from Washington, D.C., to pursue further research on the Gulf Breeze UFO. Bob is an expert on robotics and became fascinated with our UFO mystery after first seeing the UFO in 1989. He explained his theories and latest research to a large group gathered around him when he suddenly saw the UFO appear in the sky. Quickly the cameras were directed to the south as the UFO crossed over Gulf Breeze from east to west. Approximately over the center of town, the UFO disappeared into thin air and the exact location where the UFO vanished was locked onto by the PEAS operated by Gary Watson.

Several minutes passed when the group received a bonus. The UFO reappeared to the south where it had first been seen moments before. Once again the UFO traveled across the sky over Gulf Breeze from the east to the west only to vanish before our eyes after two minutes. The PEAS was still locked on the location where the UFO had first disappeared and to Gary Watson's amazement, the UFO in this second sighting disappeared in the exact same spot as the first. At one mile away, that spot, within the visual scope of the PEAS, was only thirty feet in diameter.

I questioned several helicopter pilots as to the possibility of locating the exact same thirty feet of airspace, at night, in a seventeen-knot wind. Their answers were as I suspected. "Very, very remote possibility" and "That would be practically impossible. It would take some very high-tech equipment." To that I agree. We are witnessing some very high-tech equipment, but not necessarily of human origin.

The G.B. Research Team studied the possibilities and once more ruled out helicopters and airplanes. They cannot travel soundless at less than twenty miles per hour. They cannot vanish before your eyes in a clear sky. Weather balloons or hoax balloons cannot travel into the wind. One hard-core skeptic I talked to insisted that UFOs don't exist; therefore, what he saw had to be a hologram. It was pointed out that a hologram projection had to be projected on something and on this night, as with many others, there were no clouds to act as a backdrop. To me the skeptic's hologram theory was more unbelievable than accepting the obvious. We were witnessing a real UFO. Why that is so upsetting to some people is a question for the professionals who study human behavior.

For me, on this night, I looked at the full moon and the star-filled heavens and understood that sometimes people can look at the stars and still not see the light. I may never understand what has happened to me over the past years but I knew that what had happened on this night was no accident.

The full moon dominated the sky while many of us discussed what we had witnessed. Clopton Jones and his wife Sue suggested that a beautiful sight would be to see the UFO crossing in front of the moon. Two nights later their passing comment came true.

September 22, 1991

Marianne Jones noticed a faint white dot to the left of the moon. She pointed it out to her husband, Topper Jones, who called it to the attention of others at the sky watch. Soon all cameras were trained on the speck as it grew bigger and bigger. Within seconds the dot raced downward, stopped still in the sky, and then turned ruby red. Slightly below the moon, the glowing red UFO moved to the right and ascended until it reached the full moon, where it slowly crossed in front of the bottom of the moon.

We could not believe our eyes. The structural outline of the UFO was more than five times greater than the size of its red glowing bottom. Angular in configuration, its silhouette was darker than the craters on the moon. At first Bland Pugh proposed that maybe we were looking at a parachute flare and Bruce Morrison joined him in that train of thought, but they quickly realized that this object was ascending and traveling into the wind. Objective investigators make a point of trying to explain all UFO sightings until the facts force them to conclude that the object was truly unknown. Later, when the distance measurements were confirmed from three sighting locations many miles apart, the triangulation documented the glowing bottom ring of the UFO to be two miles away and approximately ten feet in diameter.

Was it a coincidence that Clopton and Sue Jones had talked about wanting to see the UFO cross in front of the moon, only to have it happen two nights later?

October 5, 1991

Ann Morrison's log of sightings for the past twelve months numbered over eighty cases involving the "red UFO." Now, the "porthole" UFO was becoming more frequent. The G.B. Research Team debated if we were watching the same object, but the fact was that we had not seen the red UFO simultaneously display any "portholes," so the question remained open.

The crowd at the Bay Bridge steadily grew as the sun began to set. Darkness fell and, as always, a sense of electricity was in the air. Friends greeted friends and welcomed new arrivals; some were from out of town and had traveled cross-country in the hopes of seeing the UFO.

At about eight o'clock a call sounded from Sue Jones, "Look, there it is!" She yelled for others to look in the direction she pointed.

The crowd echoed her words. "There it is!" "To the south, look everybody!"

Bruce Morrison scrambled to his video camera. Greg Liss focused his 500-mm lens camera. "Professor" Pugh, Ray Pollock, and dozens of others began taking photographs.

The UFO was hovering in the sky to the south over Gulf Breeze. Brilliant red, it remained in one spot and then suddenly displayed a bright ring of "portholes" that outlined its central pulsating red light. It began moving to the west, into the wind, before disappearing three and a half minutes later in the clear sky.

The sighting on this night established once and for all that the ring of "portholes" and the brilliant red UFO were one and the same object. During the remainder of the month the Research Team documented ten more sightings.

November 5, 1991

The most frequent question asked of the Research Team is, "Why Gulf Breeze?" At no time in history had UFO sightings been so persistent and semipredictable at one location. What is it that is so interesting to the UFO about the Pensacola/Gulf Breeze area?

For the news reporters and the curious who consistently asked this "why" question, we had no answer.

Unfortunately or fortunately, depending on your point of view, a string of psychics passed through Gulf Breeze and delivered various messages that, to their satisfaction, explained everything. Ranging from a "loving federation of planets here to watch over us" to "evil creatures here to dominate us," the predictions were interesting but less than satisfying for those of us documenting these unprecedented events.

On the opposite end of the spectrum from the psychics were the show-me skeptics and I always enjoyed the occasions when one or more would join a sky watch. After listening to witnesses who had seen the UFO, the skeptic would often respond with, "Well, how do you know what you saw wasn't a helicopter, airplane, etc . . ." The answer from the witnesses was always a strong, "When you see it, you know."

On this Tuesday night, November 5, the Research Team planned to meet at the Bay Bridge. The sky over Gulf Breeze was softly backlit with the glow of the high school football stadium lights.

Patti Weatherford and Bland Pugh were there when I arrived. Bland already had his camera set up so I joined him and tripod-mounted my 35-mm camera for use by the Research Team. A half hour passed while others arrived at the Bay Bridge site. Bland Pugh spotted a red glow in the distant sky and announced, "Show time!"

The red glow grew brighter as it approached and soon began its familiar irregular pulsing. Patti Weatherford used the 440-mm lens that I had loaned to the Research Team. With 3200 ASA black and white film, she began taking photographs of the UFO as it flew across the hazy backlit Gulf Breeze sky. During the sighting, Ann and Bruce Morrison drove up, accompanied by Ann's son, Scott.

Scott was a skeptic and enjoyed a good debate, hoping to explain away the unidentified object as a helicopter, airplane, or flare, but on this night what he saw with his own eyes made him say, "Hold on here, I can see something black around it." Above and around the bright red center, he described what others also saw.

Bland Pugh said, "I can see a definite curved structural shape above the blazing red light at its bottom." Ann Morrison agreed with Bland and also used the Research

Team camera to take several photographs while Patti watched with binoculars.

Ann and Patti took twenty-three photographs that show the very bright bottom of the UFO. Also in three of these photos, they caught the outline of the craft showing its "portholes" and top "beacon" light. The first of these three outline photos shows what seem to be the UFO's early stages of materializing. (This is only my speculation based on the odd distorted image.) The second, photo K, shows a clear outline, and the third, photo J, shows the same outline but with a missing center "porthole."

What happened next demonstrates a truly advanced technology. For five seconds the UFO gave off a huge burst of white energy that, fully five times the diameter of the UFO, blocked out its outline. Ann Morrison took a photograph as the burst of energy engulfed the craft and moments later the UFO's red "power ring" disappeared.

As the months passed the UFO sightings continued. Many first-time witnesses were exhilarated. Most of them were happy to have personal confirmation that the UFO was real. It wasn't unusual to hear them say, "I wouldn't have believed it if I hadn't seen it for myself."

As for me, I was frustrated. Over the years all I had for an answer was speculation. The hypnosis memories, odd sleep recall, and my recurring dream were not enough.

I wanted solid answers but the harder I tried to put the pieces of the puzzle together, the more scrambled they became. And there was always that recurring dream of Tamacuari. I began to wonder if the answers could be found in Venezuela, somewhere near Tamacuari. More and more I thought about how my dream of the jungle might be a clue. If I went to Venezuela, possibly I could put an end to my recurring dream. If I could walk in the jungle below the Tamacuari mountains, maybe I would find the answers that eluded me.

CHAPTER 28

TAMACUARI—THE QUEST?

People from all over the world were now traveling to Gulf Breeze in the hope of seeing the UFO. Nightly, the vigil continued, sometimes with extraordinary success and sometimes with weeks of seeing nothing.

Many years had passed since my November 11, 1987, UFO sighting and still I struggled to understand. My weekly and sometimes nightly dream of looking down on a vast savanna and soaring over a tropical jungle made me anxious. Inside my heart I cried out to know what it meant. I wanted to go to the savanna that seemed so much a part of me. I longed to touch the earth that I could see in my dreams. I wanted to stand on the mountainside and bask in the panorama that was so clear in my mind.

When I closed my eyes and thought of Tamacuari, a granite mountain standing 7670 feet high over the jungle, my senses reached out. I could smell the pure mountain air and I knew that I must go to this place, that I must walk in the canyon below the mountain. Something in the jungle was reaching out to me. I could feel the jungle; it was a part of me.

My announcement to Frances that I wanted to go to Venezuela and search for Tamacuari was one full of enthusiasm, but Frances looked at me in disbelief. She was quick to point out that, aside from being in the southern part of Venezuela, I had no idea where it was. She ended her "are you crazy?" argument by saying, "Jungles in South America were not big on roads; I suggest that you think about what you are saying."

With my most confident voice I reassured her, "Surely I can find it. It can't be that hard."

She insisted, "No way, it's crazy. Drug smugglers, snakes, spiders, and who knows what kind of Indians, that's what you'll find."

Frances was determined but so was I. It couldn't be that bad, so off I went to the library to check on the location of Tamacuari.

The library research department was quiet and I leaned over the atlas of Venezuela. I was stunned and a loud whisper broke from my lips. "What the Hell?" The southern part of Venezuela was called Amazonas and not a single road crossed into this territory. Along the southern border with Brazil the map showed a mountain range called the Sierra de la Neblina, but there was no mention of a mountain called Tamacuari. After hours of digging through books and maps I left empty-handed. I had not found Tamacuari.

The next day, after checking with Duane Cook to find out where he had originally documented the existence of Tamacuari, I was off to the University of West Florida library. Success! Tamacuari is a part of the Sierra de la Neblina and was described this way: ". . . belongs to the Roraima Formation and presents a fantastic vista of mountains rising up from mountains, of vertical walls and impenetrable forest, and of a great canyon, which rivals the Grand Canyon of North America."[1]

There was also this small footnote about the Indians living in the area. "The fierce Yanomamo, living on the southern frontier with Brazil, are an isolated people with a primitive culture that includes the use of *yope,* a drug that is snorted through the nose, like cocaine."[2]

This bit of information was exactly what I didn't want Frances to know. Not only are there "fierce" Indians living in the area but there are fierce Indians who use drugs.

Things could have looked better. Not to put too fine a point on it, I was a little depressed about the "no roads." But on a more positive note, now that I knew about the great canyon that had to be crossed, and the impenetra-

[1] Ben Box, *South American Handbook,* Prentice Hall Press, 1990.
[2] *Ibid.*

ble forest occupied by drug-crazed "fierce" Indians, how much worse could it get? I kept reading and planning and my next step was a letter to the Department of Tourism in Caracas.

Weeks passed while waiting for an answer to my letter, an answer which never came. I was fascinated by the possibility of going to Tamacuari. Even the threat of the "fierce" Indians made little impression on me. I thought of the memories uncovered by Dr. Overlade, the hypnosis recall of the small Indian boy in the dying village. Could it be that the boy was a Yanomamo Indian? Is that why I was so interested in the jungle? And what did all of this have to do with the UFO? I wanted to go to Venezuela.

My motivation was simple. At best I would uncover a hidden connection between the dream and the UFO or between the dream and the "Indian boy." At the least, by going there, I hoped the dream would stop and my nights would once again be peaceful.

I continued my research. Any book I could find that mentioned the Amazon, I read.

The five years we lived in Costa Rica had taught me to speak "countryside" Spanish and my rain forest and jungle camping experience there would be invaluable. But the more I read about the Amazon, the more respect I gained for the magnitude of my quest.

Costa Rica is civilized. Even the jungle is not life threatening if you are prepared. Venezuela's Amazonas, by comparison, is a throwback in time. Ants two inches long with the sting of a scorpion command respect. Foot-long centipedes and poisonous snakes that drop from the trees dominate the lush forest loam, not a place to consider spreading a sleeping blanket. Jungle camping is done with hammocks covered with fine mosquito netting, which also sheds the occasional snake or spider falling from the overhead branches.

The Amazon had all the bugs and creatures I had seen in the Costa Rican rain forest, and then some, but the biggest unknown were the Yanomamo Indians, the fierce ones. Just how "fierce" were these Indians? I read a report in the world atlas that described Venezuela's population distribution. These "rarely seen" Indians were spread over the one hundred and fifty by one hundred mile area of the Sierra de la Neblina.

I rationalized the problem; ten thousand Indians located in fifteen thousand square miles. Easy—I would find a way around them. I continued to read books and study the possible routes, when I came upon a staggering reference.

Written by Benedict Allen, *Who Goes Out In The Midday Sun?* is a first person adventure told by Allen of his trip through the Amazon. He started his journey in Venezuela. His trail took him through Santa Elena on the border with Brazil, the closest civilized settlement to my destination, only two hundred and fifty miles to the west. He described his trip to Santa Elena on a dirt road "hammered from the dust by Colonel Llabanera and his unit, the only road to have made it across the savannah. Finishing off at Santa Elena, he dismissed his men and set up house in a pleasant spot overlooking the shaded town plaza. Like so many people before him, he had remained here ever since. He had become an expert on flying saucers, which frequently appeared over the savannah."

I couldn't believe my eyes as the words jumped off the page. Allen was describing the first part of my dream; the "savannah" and the distant mountains. But when he casually mentioned "flying saucers, which frequently appeared over the savannah,"[1] I had a rush of emotion that made me light-headed.

Several pages later, Allen again mentioned UFOs when he said, "A miner with a blue parrot feather in his sombrero and a cutlass in his hand stopped me to sketch a flying saucer into my notebook." Was this all an amazing coincidence or was it, as I believed, documentation, supporting my quest to go to Tamacuari?

Will I ever go to Tamacuari? Maybe. As compulsive as it seems, I continue to plan for that possibility.

---

[1]Benedict Allen, *Who Goes Out In The Midday Sun?*, Viking Press, 1986.

APPENDIX 1

NATIONWIDE REPORTS OF THE GULF BREEZE–TYPE UFO

Eyewitnesses have reported seeing the Gulf Breeze–type UFO throughout the United States and around the world. The object has a unique look distinguished by the often brilliant and sometimes discrete "power ring" at its bottom (see photo 19). Completely silent in its operation, and with the ability to disappear suddenly, very often the eyewitnesses believe they have seen something unlike anything anybody has ever seen before.

On the last page of *The Gulf Breeze Sightings,* I gave my mailing address and wrote:

"The events that happened to me and my family during those five and a half months were both incredible and threatening. One of the threats was that of ridicule.

"Many witnesses, both from Gulf Breeze and elsewhere, have wrestled with the same question about telling what they have seen and what some have photographed.

"If you have had a sighting, been involved in an incident of 'missing time,' or taken photographs of a UFO and wish to share the event with me, I guarantee to withhold your identity, and I encourage you to write and send your photographs to me."

Publicly documented and openly reported, hundreds of people in the Gulf Breeze area have seen the UFO, but, as a result of my request, I have received an overwhelming number of letters reporting UFO sightings and encounters. In letter after letter, witnesses report their excitement and shock when they see the published photographs taken by others showing what they also saw. The following reports represent only a few of the scores of witnesses nationwide who have seen the same kind of UFO craft we have seen in Gulf Breeze.

The Photo 17 UFO

Over four years apart and thousands of miles from each other two of the four witnesses saw the UFO (photo 17) that I photographed on December 17, 1987. Linda Bird is a trained pilot and could not explain away what she saw. Mr. Henthorn wanted to explain what he saw as a hot air balloon, but at twenty feet over his car he saw swirling gases below the object and said, "... it was no balloon, it was metal and real."

Mr. Henthorn
Bay Pines, Fla.

I have read your book and was going to write to you before this. Photo #17 in your book is what I saw passing over my car one night in St. Petersburg in the year 1982. What I saw on that night over the car was the same object that you photographed.

I was driving down the road on 62nd Ave. near 28th Street. It was a very nice night, the temperature was mild. I had my door windows a little down and enjoyed the drive going east towards Tampa. For some reason I felt a ring in my head and felt something above me. I looked out the windshield above to the night sky. I saw what looked like a rim of a very, very large object just showing past the top of my windshield view. It was slowly floating 15 to 20 feet above my car. It was just clearing the street light lines and silently moving past my car. The object very slowly rotated and I saw silver streaks of metal or swirling gray smoke or gases in the center of the bottom. It was so low that I could not see the sides of the object.

At first I could not believe it and then I thought it was an air balloon. I rolled down my window and looked up to see and it was no balloon, it was metal and real.

Lissa Arrons
Ft. Myers, Fla.

You must be covered with mail and phone calls but I had to at least try. I am full of questions and very confused. I hope you can help me understand.

I was driving home from Wednesday night choir practice when I saw the UFO in your photo 17. It was over the road in front of me when I turned out of the church parking lot. This is all too crazy but suddenly I was driving up to a gas station about a mile from home. I was confused and trying to remember what I saw and when I went to pay for the gas, I saw the gas station neon clock. It said 11:00 pm! Choir practice was over at 9:00 pm and it's only a five minute drive to the gas station from church.

I hope you can help me with this. It's driving me crazy but there is more. When I walked back to my car, after seeing the clock, a man was standing there—leaning on the trunk. This is embarrassing but I must know what you think. He was gorgeous! Beautiful blue eyes! He spoke. I stopped and stared at him. He smiled. I stuttered and couldn't believe my mouth when I offered him a ride. I have never, ever done such a crazy thing before but he was different. Somehow I couldn't stop myself. I took him to my house. I live with my parents. I knew it was crazy but I couldn't stop. We walked in and past the kitchen. Mom spoke to us as we went straight to my bedroom.

I am twenty-three years old and considered attractive. I have been with two other men in my life but nothing—ever—ever—like this. If you know what I mean.

Crazy, I must be crazy, but later that night I felt him get up from the bed. The night-light in my bathroom was on and I could see him standing naked next to a full length mirror. This next second is frozen in my mind. His reflection in the mirror was unreal. What I saw was the image of a small dark creature with a big head and huge eyes. I sat up in bed. He moved into the bathroom and out of sight. When I finally looked in the bathroom, he was gone and there is no window in my bathroom.

I know this sounds crazy but please tell me what you think.

Linda J. Bird
Mesa, Az.

I earned a pilot's license in April 1978 and also have a Ground Instructor's Certificate. My husband, Loren, has been flying since the late 1960's and has a Certified Flight Instructor's Certificate. I know airplane lights when I see them. I know airplane types when I see them and I can sometimes tell what kind of airplane it is just by the sound of the engine.

This incident occurred as the sun was going down, on March 6, 1988. It was between 6:00 and 6:30 p.m. My husband and I had gone for a flight around the area near Falcon Field, Mesa, Arizona. We were back and were walking towards the car parked in the lot in front of the flight school. Suddenly in the north a glowing yellow object appeared in the sky. What it looked like most was photo 17 in your book. I just stayed there, I could barely talk but managed to say, 'Loren, do you see that?' I kept waiting for a noise. Just then the object moved to the left and—poof—it vanished.

Scott Taylor
Greenville, S.C.

When I saw the UFO in your book (photo 17) I almost screamed. The object in the photo was exactly what I saw! I was in the car at the time and didn't have a camera with me. It was about 9:30 PM. Like many people I didn't come forth with what I saw because I was afraid that if I said something to the police, my name would get out and everybody would think I was a total idiot.

Daytime Sightings of Gulf Breeze–Type UFOs

Daytime UFO sightings are less common than would generally be expected. UFOs seen in the daytime do not normally display the lighting associated with a UFO seen at night and, therefore, are less obvious. Here are two examples out of hundreds of witnesses and their letters reporting a Gulf Breeze–type UFO sighted during the daytime.

Kay Shone
Brandon, Fla.

I saw your UFO pictures and I could not believe my eyes. In the fall of 1987 I saw a flying object. Since that day I have watched programs on UFO sightings, hoping to see something that resembled the shiny object which I had seen. Until I saw your pictures, nothing ever came close.

Summer vacation had ended and my kids were back in school. It was almost 2:00 p.m. and I had set up two lawn chairs in my front yard for my girlfriend and myself. We were relaxing before our children arrived home from school. It was a beautiful day. The sky was a deep blue except for couple of small fluffy white clouds. I was reclined in my chaise lounge facing east. As I lay there staring up at the sky and talking with my girlfriend, a bright shiny object suddenly caught my eye. It was so unusual I couldn't take my eyes off of it. After a few seconds I jumped up from my chair and yelled at my friend. It appeared as though the object was falling. I stood there frozen as I watched, not knowing what to do. I soon realized it was not falling. The craft was stationary in the sky but the entire center of it seemed to be spinning around at a high rate of speed. The sun was reflecting off what appeared to be panels.

I was seeing this object in the broad daylight and I thought that there must be an explanation, others would be seeing it too. The craft hovered for a few minutes and then it moved slowly to the south. It stopped and hovered there for a minute or two and then slowly ascended. I watched in amazement as it disappeared into the blue sky.

I have never forgotten what I saw. I remember vividly, as though it were yesterday. Thanks for going public with your pictures.

Michelle Gross
Pembroke, Fla.

I saw your book! The photo on the front cover stopped me dead in my tracks. My whole body went chilly.

You see, I'm now 37 years old, and 25 years ago, in the Washington D.C. area, in 1965, my family was visited by a UFO like the one in your photos. It was July, 1965. I was out back alone getting some sun. I was on my back looking up into a very clear blue sky. It was about 3:00 in the afternoon, when out of nowhere I saw 'it.' Just as you explained, it just winked in. Right there over me, over our house in broad daylight!

I leapt up and ran screaming into the house calling for my dad and mom, and 2 brothers. Yelling, 'go out and see, Hurry, Hurry!' My parents were shocked at my excited state. We all ran out the front to see and to my relief it was still there. We all saw it, a rounded silvery looking craft with a dome on top.

We lived on a very busy street at the time, and people actually stopped on the street, got out of cars to see the thing. Finally, the object split into 5 separate ships (like it multiplied). They all hovered for about 2 minutes together, then all at the same moment they vanished. Gone! Nowhere to be seen and we never saw them again.

I knew the moment I saw your photos that my 25 years of silence was about to be broken. Thank you for sharing your story to help people like me know we were not alone in our thoughts and experiences.

Gulf Breeze Type–UFOs That Disappear

One of the most bizarre details of the Gulf Breeze–type UFO sightings is the way in which the UFO often arrives and departs. I video-recorded the UFO on December 28, 1987. Clearly visible, the UFO glided above the Gulf Breeze High School soccer practice field. Approximately four or five hundred feet away and less than one hundred feet off the ground, the UFO traveled slowly and sometimes smoothly retraced its own airspace. After one minute and thirty-eight seconds, and in clear view, the UFO suddenly disappeared. To the amazement of all the witnesses who have seen this happen, they have no explanation, but like myself, they realize that something "normal" could not perform such a feat. Some witnesses describe the disappearance with words like, "blinked out" or "winks out." Here are some examples of normal people seeing this abnormal event.

Sally Nash
Atlanta, Ga.

I also know for a fact that UFOs exist as I have seen one, too. It was 1974, but I remember it like it was yesterday. This was in my hometown of Gainesville, Ga. and some of the details of the sighting are similar to yours and what I saw looks like your photo 22. I saw it very close-up and was absolutely stunned and fascinated.

At the time of my sighting, I was too enthralled to be frightened and in fact I tried to get closer in my car. When I did this the craft took off and was gone in a blink of an eye. This occurred at about 10:00

p.m. and the sighting lasted for about 30 seconds as it hovered over a 4 story doctor's building. The craft was round and as one 'porthole' window would light up, the next one to it would go off, giving the appearance that the craft was rotating. It, at no time, made any noise. I know what I saw and I will never forget it. I felt very fortunate to be at the right place at the right time.

Vincent Hawkes
Fort Walton Bch, Fl.

I, too, saw the craft that you describe in your book. What I saw looked exactly like what you photographed. This may sound crazy (what doesn't when talking about UFOs) but consider the possibility that the UFO is some type of time travel object. This would help explain how the UFO winks in and just as suddenly winks out. As our science grows and we learn more about tackeyons and super conductors, who knows? One thing I know is that I saw a real object that did not look like anything that should be in our skies.

No Sound from the Gulf Breeze Type– UFO

One detail that is unanimous with the witnesses of the Gulf Breeze type–UFO is the lack of sound. This feature, when judged by our current scientific technology, makes powered flight impossible, yet the witnesses agree, there was no sound. Is there any wonder that a majority of scientists must disbelieve in UFOs. Unless he or she is a witness, soundless powered flight must be branded ridiculous. However, it is well-known that scientists through the ages have branded all that they cannot explain as impossible or ridiculous. Soundless flight? Yes, indeed. Notice how often the eyewitnesses exclaim, "there was absolutely no sound."

James C. Hirst, PhD
Spring City, Pa.

As a State Licensed (PS-00080L) Professional Psychologist, I do not take the UFO sighting that I and my family witnessed lightly. On a clear Sunday afternoon in June of 1983, we witnessed a soundless, metallic object. With no sign of rotation, the object was approximately 45 feet in diameter and had "windows" and a flangelike protrusion toward the bottom. This sighting took place at my residence which is on a 400 foot hill with a panoramic view 40 miles east to west and 20 miles north. What we saw looked like the UFO photographed by Ed Walters.

UFO—Same as Gulf Breeze Photos

These eyewitnesses, like all the rest, are confident as to what they saw. They often point to the photographs and proclaim, "That is what I saw."

On January 12, 1988, I photographed the UFO as it hovered about Soundside Drive (Highway 191-B) in Gulf Breeze. Only three to four feet off the blacktop surface, the UFO cast a bright glow on the road. Witness Judy Francour recalls a similar event thirty-eight years ago.

Judy Francour
Pensacola, Fl.

I saw a UFO. In the summer of 1952, my cousin and I were walking down Barrancas Avenue coming from a Girl Scout meeting. We looked up over to the north and saw a ship like the one in your book. It sure scared us because back then we just didn't know about UFOs. Well, we started to run and it kept up with us, we stopped and it stopped. At about that same time my grandfather and my mom saw the UFO early one morning before the Navy yard traffic got started down Barrancas Avenue. They both saw this orange glowing object going down Barrancus but neither one knew that the other had seen it. My grandfather came over early every morning (he lived next door) to see and have his first cup of coffee with my mom. He said, 'Paul (short for Pauline) I saw something this morning that I never saw before, going down Barrancas Avenue.' Mom said, you saw it, too. It flew about three feet off the road and it shot right up and out of sight before you could blink your eye.

A few years later my family and I went on a trip to Milwaukee, Wisconsin. We rented a cabin on one of the lakes up there. We were enjoying the cool summer breeze and up to the north was suddenly this flying object. Well, it came in close and it had a strong orange glow. (Guess what the officials said it was? . . . that's right, a weather balloon!) Well, I knew it then; it was not a weather balloon. What we saw was the same UFO that you photographed. I know what I saw and this is something that you don't forget.

Deborrah Langston
Duluth, Ga.

Last May I was dating a pilot, Bob "Esterson," and the subject turned to UFOs. He told an incredible story about seeing the same type of UFO that you photographed. It was over the mountains of Asheville, North Carolina. He said, '. . . the sight of it made the hair on my head stand out. It had the same dome lights and light under the bottom.' The control tower saw it and inquired as to what it was. He said he watched it wink-out. It was only there for a few minutes then gone. 'It was almost sitting still with only a slight wobble.'

Mike Cranfill
Naples, Fla.

On the night of June 10, 1990, my wife and I saw something glide through the sky that greatly resembled your Photo 18. We viewed them from our front porch. They were to our east and moving quickly to the south. Funny, but my first thought was, 'you sneaky bastards.' I have been camping on Santa Rosa island near Gulf Breeze before and have seen odd lights but what we saw on this night in Naples was clear.

Rita O'Connor
Vienna, Va.

When I read your book and saw the photos, I was just amazed. The left most object in photograph 20 is what followed me through the rural wilderness of North Carolina in the summer of 1969. My fiancé was being released from Camp Le Jeune at 6 a.m., so I was driving down to pick him up. Somewhere between Wilson and Jacksonville, N.C. The area was swampy and woodsy, without towns, farm houses, or lights of any kind.

I don't frighten easily, but fear started creeping through my body at this point. My next reaction is a little embarrassing. I started to talk out loud to it. This one-way conversation continued as we travelled through the countryside, for what seemed a long time. The object was always there, until suddenly it wasn't there anymore.

I got really excited over the size of the UFO that you saw most frequently. One thing that really threw me off about what I saw was my preconceived notion that a UFO is a huge craft. What I saw was close, about tree top level and I couldn't reconcile the size of the light with the idea of a UFO. I felt somehow relieved when I read your book.

I just know what happened, and nothing that anyone else thinks or believes can change what happened.

The letters I receive from witnesses who report seeing the Gulf Breeze–type UFO are very detailed and of obvious interest to those of us living in Gulf Breeze. Larry

O'Keefe from Burlington, Vermont, is a schoolteacher who works with a youth group called the Paradise Project. In the winter of 1987, Larry and eight students drove through Gulf Breeze and spent the night at the beach. His five-page letter describing the UFO was very specific. He said, "We were looking out over the Gulf when we saw the UFO. It hovered there for some time without moving. Then, suddenly, it zipped to the west so fast we hardly saw it moving! It stopped, hovered again, and then disappeared. A few minutes later it came back and immediately zipped over our heads toward the north."

These letters have been a learning experience for me. By calling the UFO that I have seen the "Gulf Breeze UFO," it is as if the UFO is a resident of Gulf Breeze. But letters from witnesses around the world who have seen this craft support the fact that its presence is clearly a worldwide phenomenon.

From Saudi Arabia, Abdur Rahman saw this distinctive craft and sent a drawing of what he saw (see drawing S) and a letter in which he pointed out that the word "zehaas" means beautiful in his language. During many of my earlier encounters I heard the word "zehaas" when the UFO was present. Another letter from a Spanish-speaking woman translated "zehaas" to be eyebrows so it is difficult to conclude what the definition of "zehaas" might be.

The UFO descriptions and drawings have a common bond. Consistently the nighttime sightings depict a "power light" at the bottom and the daytime descriptions and photos show a dark ring on the bottom of the UFO. The sightings are soundless and often the UFO disappears suddenly.

APPENDIX 2

DAYTIME UFO PHOTOGRAPHS

From across the nation and around the world, UFO eye-witnesses have responded to my request for them to share their sightings, encounters, and photographs. Daily, I received detailed letters from UFO witnesses describing what they saw and occasionally photographs taken during the sighting. Without exception it is up to each eyewitness to decide whether or not to go public. I have not and will not break my guarantee to withhold the identity of those sharing their sightings and encounters with me. All the names of UFO witnesses mentioned in this book have been used with their permission, while others have chosen to withhold their identity.

The thousands of letters I have received are compelling and my eyes have been opened to the massive worldwide scope of this phenomenon. Of particular interest are the frequent photographs being taken of unexplained lights and objects suddenly appearing in the sky. I do not present myself as a photographic expert and I fully realize that some of the photographs mailed to me may be of natural, explainable objects. For example, airplane landing lights that are directly approaching a witness can give the appearance of an object hovering in the sky. There are many normal lights in the night sky that can be mistaken for UFOs. Therefore, whenever possible, a detailed description from more than one person as to what the lights did can usually answer the question, UFO? or IFO (identified flying object)? But when the photograph is a nighttime shot showing structure, or a daytime shot of a detailed flying object, there is no mistake. There are only two options:

the photograph is fake or the photograph shows a real UFO.

Many of the photographs mailed to me, along with concise letters, are daytime shots of what appear to be unmistakable unidentified objects. But a few of the photographs that I have received are clearly fake and I assume mailed by pranksters or possibly debunkers in the hope that I would accept them as authentic. (A debunker is a person who will create false evidence in an effort to distort and discredit UFO sightings, especially UFO photo evidence.) One could imagine the joy that a prankster might get from having his or her fake UFO photograph published along with valid UFO photos. The same is true for a debunker motivated by an effort to discredit this book and the hundreds of exceptional UFO sightings from Gulf Breeze and around the world. Had I accepted a debunker's hoax UFO photo as valid, he certainly would rush to the media and proclaim all the UFO photos in this book to be fake by pointing out how he had tricked me into accepting his hoax. Unfortunately, motivated UFO debunkers go to a lot of trouble in their efforts to ridicule the UFO phenomenon. Discrediting real UFO photographs with their fake photographs is a common practice used by debunkers to influence negative stories in the media. This tactic was used against me and the Gulf Breeze UFO sightings during 1989, but fortunately the debunkers were exposed and their fake UFO photographs denounced.

Out of all the photographs I have received, I have chosen three examples that are extraordinary because the detail of the craft is obvious. These photographs, as with the Gulf Breeze photographs, leave no question that what we are looking at is not a conventional aircraft.

Here is a letter that accompanied two photographs (see photos L and N) from Barbara H. of Green Bay, Wisconsin.

Dear Mr. and Mrs. Walters,
　　Last night I began reading *The Gulf Breeze Sightings* and I stayed up all night reading. The alarm

clock went off and I went through the motions of breakfast and getting my children off to school.

I am stunned and excited because I know what you saw and felt. I saw and photographed "them" also.

On Dec. 5, 1989 (Monday) at about 2:00 pm the house shook so hard that I thought the windows were going to break. It was like thunder but with no sound so I looked out to check the weather. Blue sky and clouds are what I saw when the house shook again. Earthquake in Green Bay? I ran outside and stood by myself. My husband works in town and the nearest house is half mile away. After five minutes or so I felt pretty foolish. I started back inside when suddenly I saw a ball of light flash in the clouds followed by the rattle of the house windows.

"I could see a dark shape in the clouds but it was not moving like an airplane. It was very still but not a helicopter. There was no sound, only shaking of the house windows when the white light would flash (with smaller balls of light shooting out) and gradually fade. This happened four times as I stood there and watched (four or five minutes) before I ran to the phone. I dialed the operator but somehow got a tape saying the 'number you dialed is not in service in this area code.' Over and over the same tape. My heart was pounding and the house was shaking every minute or two so I went back outside but this time with my camera. The dark shape was gone from the west side of the house but then it reappeared in the clouds on the east side. I aimed the camera, the white light burst below and I took the shot. As the light faded I took another. The clouds moved across and I lost sight of it. As the clouds moved on, the object was gone.

I showed these pictures to my husband and friends. They don't seem to care and now they tease me about UFOs. I can share this and the pictures with you because I know that I saw a UFO.

You said, 'I guarantee to withhold your identity,' I trust that you will. Some of the kids around here call me the UFO lady and my son fights them. He is such a little-man but I don't want to hurt him by starting this up again. It doesn't matter what others think, I KNOW I SAW WHAT YOU SAW.

Barbara's photographs show a disk-shaped object with a bright center in the clouds. Also captured in her photograph, as Barbara described, are the "smaller balls of light shooting out." We do not know the height of the clouds surrounding and partly covering the UFO but they clearly establish that the object is many hundreds of feet away, which in turn supports her story.

A very important part of Barbara's sighting is the rattle of her house that she first thought was an earthquake and later identified by her to be somehow related to the repeated bright flashes beneath the UFO. This type of rattle, which I documented in a previous chapter, has happened often in the Gulf Breeze area and is known as a "sky quake."

All of what Barbara reports is classic UFO data and fits exactly with the UFO sightings that are so common in the Gulf Breeze area and around the world. Soundless and disk-shaped, the object hovered and displayed a bright light source from beneath.

If Barbara's photographs are really the work of a prankster or debunker, and I do not believe that they are, then it proves that someone has spared no expense in trying to distort and distract attention from the mounting evidence that UFOs are real.

To analyze Barbara's photo, a computer-aided study was performed that can detect the slightest hint of a suspension string or even a thread. The electronic filter that was used to enhance the photograph found no evidence of hoaxing. The scientific conclusion supported Barbara's sighting. There was a large object in the sky and the energy force beneath the object was large and powerful enough to block out part of the image of the UFO (see computer photo N-1).

I can not even begin to imagine how somebody could fake such a photograph of a flying disk in the clouds. Add to that the bright light and the smaller light balls shooting from the object and I conclude that there was a real object in the sky over her house in Green Bay.

The next example of the types of photographic evidence I have received is from Karen of South Bend, Indiana. The unidentified silver-colored disk that she photographed is very similar to that of Barbara's in Green Bay. Karen's photographs do not show the bright light beneath the UFO, but under close examination a dark ring can be seen beneath the silver disk (see photo Q).

Here is the letter from Karen D. of South Bend.

Dear Ed and Frances,

Your book is wonderful. I admire the courage of your family.

On November 6, 1989 my 9 year old daughter got home from school and we were taking pictures of her new puppy. Across the road I saw what I thought was a blimp but it was too small and was not moving. After I took a picture it moved out of sight behind the pine trees next door.

About 10 minutes went by and we were on the ground playing with the dog. My daughter looked up and yelled 'the blimp.' It was now closer and stayed there for a long time, about five minutes, until I yelled for the neighbor next door. Then it went back to the left again and before being blocked by the trees, it just disappeared. In plain sight it just winked out, just like you said.

My husband thinks it's a bad idea to talk about it but I had to write to you. He is worried that the people out to get you will go after him. He is an Officer in the Army and I think he knows more than he is telling me.

Keep the photographs, there is nothing I can do with them.

Karen has detailed a not so uncommon story in which she happened to have a camera and captured a strange object hovering in the sky. Like most of us, she would rather have explained it away, in this case as a blimp, but it was clearly not a blimp. As Karen said, ". . . it suddenly disappeared." and blimps don't suddenly disappear. Hundreds of letters from UFO eyewitnesses report the incredible detail of seeing the UFO "wink out." On December 28, 1987, I videotaped the Gulf Breeze UFO for one minute and thirty-eight seconds before it suddenly disappeared. (To receive a copy of the video see Appendix 3—Where To Write.)

The tape was analyzed by many experts with computer-aided controls. Mr. Oechsler, a former NASA systems specialist, said, "This is an astounding mystery. The UFO disappeared within one-thirtieth of a second." Many other witnesses have shared their videotapes with me and in almost every case the UFO suddenly disappears or sometimes it collapses into a very bright white ball of light and then disappears. All the scientists, and even nonscientists who have reviewed the tapes agree that no known aircraft has such an ability.

The cautious side of me demands that photographs like Karen's be studied closely. Could this be a hubcap tossed into the air by a prankster? Maybe, but it doesn't look like a hubcap. The possibility of a debunker's toy model suspended on string was ruled out by computer image analysis. Notice how the trees are lower than the UFO and are in sharper focus than the UFO. The size proportion of the tree branches is much larger than the UFO. A toy model or "hub cap" tossed into the air over those trees would not appear so distant and so small relative to the trees, but those arguments are not what convinced me. Four months after receiving Karen's letter I received a set of UFO photographs from Nathan J. of Rochester, New York, that closely matched those from Karen.

A complete skeptic might dismiss these photos because these witnesses are withholding their names and wish to stay out of the controversy, but I consider the chances very strong that these three UFO witnesses saw and photographed the same type UFO and maybe the exact same craft. Further supporting these photographs are the very similar UFO photographs involved with the "Gulf Breeze Six" (see photo A).

Here is the letter from Nathan J. of Rochester, New York.

Dear Ed Walters,

Enclosed are two of the photographs that I took on 89 07 15 at 1300. Camera direction NNW. Object came from the WSW, made a slow circle and shot away back to the WSW. All ten photographs from the pack of film have those big white patches (before and after the disk) but later the next pack of film looked fine so it was not the camera. (The film was old and had been in the camera for a long time.)

One of the strangest things, is that my youngest boy said he did not see what my older boy and I saw. I did not understand how this could be because we were all together and looking up at it so at first I thought that he was only scared but as we talked about what had just happened I stopped and saw it was almost dark. I don't know how but it was suddenly 1700.

My eleven year old son (who saw nothing) does not answer when I ask him about that day. It all sounds crazy and even my wife now does not want to talk about it but I feel like something else happened. I don't bring it up anymore so I give you my last 2 photographs and hope that you can put it all together.

Also I have enclosed a single photograph that I took the next day when I went back to the area to look it over. I was standing at about where the boys and I were standing when, Bingo, there it was again, a little more distant but the same disk. With a 110 camera I caught the shot.

That Saturday I showed some of my neighbors and then gave two of the 4 shots to my C.O. A week later I was told that it was a trick done with a frisbee, and told to drop it. That was it until my neighbor's wife told me about you from a *Woman's Day* article. Then last week I saw your name again in an old *Sentinel* newspaper about 35 witnesses.

THIS WAS NO FRISBEE! Please leave me out of this and don't give my name to others, I trust you so please don't let me down.

Nathan said, "This was no Frisbee!" I agree. What Nathan photographed (see photos O and P) doesn't look like a Frisbee. But it does look like what Barbara and Karen photographed and what hundreds of other eyewitnesses have reported. Notice the dark ring at the bottom of the UFO with a glint of sun reflecting from the curve of the silver disk and from the curve above the dark ring.

Of great significance within Nathan's sighting is the loss of time from 1300 to 1700. He indicates that he has no recall of those four hours from 1:00 P.M. to 5:00 P.M. As I learned from my own missing-time incident, the possibility of an alien encounter is almost a certainty.

Nathan's photographs are astounding and I believe them to be valid. The same dimensional ratio applies here as with Karen's photographs. The UFO is substantially more distant from the camera than the trees. Notice how the size of the leaves on the trees is relatively large when compared with the distant image of the UFO. Had this been a "Frisbee" or some type of model suspended between the camera and the trees, the image of the UFO would be proportionally much larger than that of the tree branches and leaves. In Nathan's third photo, the UFO is blurred and the trees are in reasonable focus. This supports my conclusion that the UFO was a large, distant, moving object but my confidence in Barbara's, Karen's, and Nathan's separate photographic sightings rests jointly on the evidence contained within all three.

I have often been asked the skeptical question as to why there are not more UFO photographs taken by witnesses if there are so many hundreds and thousands of sightings each year. The answer is simple. Maybe there are more witnesses like those I have presented here who believe they have too much to lose to get involved. Yet another answer to this question is based on our own life-styles. We could equate the odds of seeing a UFO to the possibility of seeing an automobile accident or some other news-making event and realizing that you don't have a camera with you. How often in your daily routine do you carry a camera with you? When you go out at night on an errand to the store, do you take a camera with you? When you drive your car home from work, I imagine that most of you pay attention to traffic, with little notice given to any strange lights in the sky above. And if you noticed an un-identified object, would you have a loaded camera in your car at your side? When you consider these drawbacks, I am impressed with the number of quality photographs that have been taken.

The one thing that I have learned to do to increase your odds of seeing a UFO is go outside and look. If you come home and remain inside, the chances are very low that you will have a sighting. Every night, weather permitting, Frances and I go outside for a four-mile walk. For more than an hour each night our chances are greatly increased of having a sighting. One night, halfway through our walk, we watched seven different aerial displays of a spiraling object hovering over Gulf Breeze. Children playing in their backyards yelled to one another to look. People on bicycles stopped to watch in amazement, yet no official re-ports were made of the UFO sightings on that night.

I am convinced that only a small percentage of UFO sightings are ever officially reported to the police or the media, so considering that there have been over three hun-dred recorded sightings in Gulf Breeze, the number of un-reported sightings could be in the thousands.

APPENDIX 3

WHERE TO WRITE

If you have experienced a UFO encounter or had a UFO sighting and wish to share your experience with me, I extend my welcome and encouragement for you to write to me with the details *and a drawing* of what you saw. If you took photographs, I would like to compare them to the many others I have received.

Please specify in your letter if you wish your name to be held in confidence. Otherwise, for the good of continued research, your eyewitness report will be added to the growing documentation of UFO sightings and encounters.

Copies of the December 28, 1987, UFO videotape ($17.00 plus $3.00 shipping) and professional color posters of photo 19, the "road shot" ($7.50 plus $2.50 shipping), are available.

Write to: Edward Walters
            P.O. Box 715
            Gulf Breeze, FL 32562
     (Please enclose a Self-Addressed Stamped Envelope.)

If you wish to learn more about the Mutual UFO Network, subscribe to their international magazine, or join their network of UFO field investigators:

Write to: Mutual UFO Network
          103 Oldtowne Road
          Seguin, TX 78155

If you are interested in receiving documentation compiled by leading scientists on UFO sightings or specific research on the Gulf Breeze UFO sightings, send for the current listing of reports available.

Write to: Fund For UFO Research
F.U.F.O.R
Box 277
Mt. Rainier, MD 20712